A Wizard of Their Age

A Wizard
of Their Age

CRITICAL ESSAYS FROM
THE HARRY POTTER GENERATION

Edited by
Cecilia Konchar Farr

with Contributing Editors
Kate Glassman, Jenny McDougal, Sarah Wente, Evan Gaydos,
Rachel Armstrong, Kalie Caetano, and Tréza Rosado

Foreword by
Giselle Liza Anatol

Cover image: © Vadmary / dreamstime.com

Published by State University of New York Press, Albany

For information, contact State University of New York Press, Albany, NY
www.sunypress.edu

Production, Diane Ganeles
Marketing, Kate Seburyamo

Library of Congress Cataloging-in-Publication Data

A wizard of their age : critical essays from the Harry Potter generation /
edited by Cecilia Konchar Farr ; foreword by Giselle Liza Anatol.
     pages   cm
 Includes bibliographical references and index.
 ISBN 978-1-4384-5447-4 (hardcover : alk. paper)
 ISBN 978-1-4384-5446-7 (pbk. : alk. paper)
 eISBN 978-1-4384-5448-1 (ebook) 1. Rowling, J. K.—Criticism and interpretation. 2. Potter, Harry (Fictitious character) I. Farr, Cecilia Konchar,
1958– editor.
 PR6068.O93Z955 2015
 823'.914—dc23
                                    2014007242

10 9 8 7 6 5 4 3 2 1

We dedicate this book to J. K. Rowling, who,
through her novels, taught us the magic
and wonder that comes with reading well.

Contents

Foreword

GISELLE LIZA ANATOL

A few months ago, Cecilia Konchar Farr approached me about contributing the foreword to a collection of undergraduate essays about the Harry Potter series.

I must confess: I was a bit hesitant. When I initially began teaching *Harry Potter and the Sorcerer's Stone* in the spring semester of 1998, only two or three of my thirty-five students had even heard of "the boy who lived," Voldemort, Quidditch, or Hogwarts. As years passed, that number grew; now, I typically have only two or three students who have *not* read the series, and they are fully cognizant of the whimsical names, central plot points, and some of the religious controversy surrounding the narratives. Most of them got started on the Potter books sometime around the third grade, and they grew and matured as the protagonist did: as each new installment was released, featuring a Harry Potter who was one year older, these students had similarly aged one year. They came to see the characters—and the books themselves—as sharing in an intense relationship built over a decade—much as Maria Ignacio expresses in "My Harry Potter Story" in the current volume. However, despite the eagerness with which most of my students awaited each new work; listened to the chapters read to them in classrooms, public libraries, or before bed each night; and repeatedly scrutinized the novels on their own, they usually had difficulty engaging with the stories *analytically.* They possessed incredible knowledge about the Potterverse and conveyed strong feelings for the characters and the situations in which Rowling wrote them but did not often take the steps to develop the details they had gleaned/memorized from the books into a sustained understanding of the themes and larger implications of the series.

Many were surprised, for example, when they learned that apparently nonsense names held symbolic meaning: Gringotts incorporates the word "ingot" (a gold bar); Professor McGonagall's first name, Minerva, is the same as the ancient Roman goddess of wisdom; Draco Malfoy's sidekicks' surnames echo the words "crab" and "gargoyle" and thus reflect their stony exteriors. Others were astonished to see the parallels between Harry's trajectory and Cinderella's. Some embraced the idea that Rowling challenges rules instituted for the comfort or authoritarian desires of adults rather than the safety of children but resisted readings of the text that were based on socioeconomic class and grounded in Marxist theory.

How amazed I was, then, when I took up the manuscript for *A Wizard of Their Age.* In addition to eating "Potter foods" like chocolate frogs and butterbeer, playing Quidditch, and replicating tea-leaf readings in a simulated Divination classroom, the student writers have engaged in rigorous and creative examinations of J. K. Rowling's novels—and revealed my initial concerns to be groundless. Those who served as editors as well as contributors have also gained valuable experiences: they put out calls for papers, read submissions for accuracy, learned to recognize innovative perspectives as well as sound arguments, and selected a balanced assortment of essays for the collection. Whether they decide to attend graduate school and embark on future careers as literature professors, or enter the world of editing and publishing, or simply gain a new appreciation of themselves as readers—not only of texts but of the world—they have demonstrated their capabilities exceptionally well.

Although Konchar Farr takes very little credit for the project, she has clearly motivated her students and skillfully trained them for the tasks at hand. The contributors read for pleasure *and* they research; they peruse the narratives with patience as well as passion; they approach the texts with careful thought as well as with critical theory. And hopefully this collection of essays will inspire others to read and think analytically, and to write, write, and write some more—whether in the journals of the academy, or on fanfiction websites, or in diaries and blogs.

It is an honor to be associated with this project and to be able to connect with this most recent generation of Potter scholars.

September 2013

Acknowledgments

All of us would like to thank St. Catherine University for being the kind of place where magic can happen in the classroom. We also thank Professor Lynda Szymanski and the Summer Scholars' Program, Professor Joanne Cavallaro and the English Department, and the Sr. Mona Riley Endowed Chair in the Humanities for the funding that made our project possible. Thanks to State University of New York Press and its outstanding editors, particularly James Peltz for believing in this unorthodox project. Thanks also to Glassman Indexing Services, for the nepotism that gave us our index work pro bono. Finally, we thank our contributors, who clearly love these books as much as we do and have the essays to prove it.

Cecilia Konchar Farr: I would like to thank the seven student editors for their creativity, energy, and insight and for approaching this project without hesitation, like my very own Dumbledore's Army! Thanks also to Tanner and Daley, without whom I might have stopped after *Sorcerer's Stone*. I am also grateful that my mom, Grace Konchar, read to me and with me and taught me to love what she loves. My dad deserves particular posthumous thanks for his inspirational parenting. Thanks to my dear friend (and temporary Floridian) Ken Bryk, who enthusiastically led me through Universal Orlando's Wizarding World. And, as always, thanks go to Cubs, who is my companion in all of life's adventures—even the nonmagical ones.

Kate Glassman: I want to heap mountains of shiny gold thanks onto my classmates and this fantastic editorial crew—bright and brilliant minds at the head of a long list of those I've met and loved because of Rowling's books. Thanks to Hardcastle for enduring my abrupt and insistent intrusion into her life, and for the endless opportunities she's given me, both as a critical thinker and as a human being. Most importantly, endless affection and gratitude to the parents who raised me right: my mother, who kept up a steady stream of peanut butter sandwiches the day I spent curled inside a large TV box reading *Goblet of Fire*; and my father, who taught me to do whatever the hell I loved best.

Jenny McDougal: I would like to thank my family, particularly my mother, Bayla McDougal, for reading to me and with me, and for humoring a soon-to-be sixteen-year-old and buying *Sorcerer's Stone* for my birthday all those years ago. I would also like to thank my fellow editors for their insight, smarts, and crazy-good discussions about all things HP; Cecilia for her mentorship, guidance, and passion; and the first Harry Potter class at St. Kate's for further defining my love for this series. And finally, a huge thank-you to my husband Evan for his love, humor, and unending support.

Sarah Wente: I would like to express the sincerest gratitude first to the wonderful people who comprise this editorial board: thank you for allowing my young self to join your ranks and for sharing your brilliance and friendship with me throughout the years. "Mischief managed." Particular thanks to CKFarr, for her intellectual prodding, valuable feedback, and enduring patience. You truly brought out the best in us. Many thanks to my family and friends, for their encouragement and support and for putting up with my random outbursts of scholarly excitement and Harry Potter rants. In a special way, I would like to thank my mother, who fostered my love of reading and gave me the first Harry Potter book, even when I was considered too young to read it. Finally, thanks to my brilliant high school teachers, Carol Ottoson and Elissa Meuwissen, for growing my love of English and teaching me how to write about the literary world in the first place.

Evan Gaydos: First, much love and thanks to my family and friends for all of their support. To my mother, for finally letting

Harry out of the closet under the stairs, allowing me to go on so many adventures; to my father, who eventually joined me on the journey for Hallows and Horcruxes while I narrated the pages. Continuous thanks to this fantastic editorial board, who all have wit beyond measure. I am truly grateful to be counted among you and call you my friends. Endless appreciation to Cecilia, for seeing something in two first-year college students and allowing us to help build a class teaching what we love, in addition to all the support and the occasional push to take chances over the years. To Rachel, for all the hours we have spent bringing Harry to the academic world and all the fun we've had doing that, thank you always. And finally, thanks to the class that spoke up and planted the idea for this book, and to all the classes after.

Kalie Caetano: I owe a deep well of thanks to my aunt, Linda, who first gifted the Harry Potter books to me and unwittingly sparked a lifelong obsession. I also want to thank Michael, whom I love even though he never finished *Half-Blood Prince*. Many more thanks are owed to my lovely classmates for a riveting months-long discussion about all things Harry Potter, and our fearless leader, Professor Cecilia Konchar Farr, who made this book possible.

Rachel Armstrong: I'll start by thanking my parents, through whom I first heard Hagrid's deep grumble and McGonagall's sharp tongue. To my friends and fellow explorers on the intrepid editorial board: your curiosity, brilliance, and unabashed love of learning will stay with me for years to come. To Evan, constant friend, editor, and fellow night owl. How did we manage this mischief? To Cecilia, who gave a timid first-year the opportunity to explore literature and theory through books I've loved so much. Thank you for your patience, curiosity, and listening ear. The only way you could possibly be a better professor is if you were a witch. Finally, thanks to every student who sat nervously under the sorting hat while two TAs and one professor dressed as witches sorted them into their houses. My undergraduate career would have been very different (and decidedly less interesting) without you.

Tréza Rosado: First, and most importantly, I would like to thank my mom for hearing about a "fun kids' series from Britain" and then gifting the first three books of that series to her ten-year-old daughter for Christmas. I know she's really proud that purchase ultimately fueled my life and career choices . . . I would also like to thank Cecilia Konchar Farr, professor/mentor/friend, who really introduced me to the idea that "middlebrow" is an unfortunate cultural construct and that Harry Potter can (and should!) sit comfortably beside my similarly well-worn copy of *Anna Karenina*. Finally, thank you to the women with whom I have spent several years arguing about the sketchy morality of Albus Dumbledore and the relative uselessness/brilliance of Ron Weasley—not a Muggle among you.

Note on Citations

All citations from the Harry Potter novels throughout this collection are taken from the first-edition Scholastic hardcovers as follows:

Rowling, J. K. *Harry Potter and the Sorcerer's Stone*. New York: Scholastic, 1997.

———. *Harry Potter and the Chamber of Secrets*. New York: Scholastic, 1999.

———. *Harry Potter and the Prisoner of Azkaban*. Scholastic: New York, 1999.

———. *Harry Potter and the Goblet of Fire*. Scholastic: New York, 2000.

———. *Harry Potter and the Order of the Phoenix*. Scholastic: New York, 2003.

———. *Harry Potter and the Half-Blood Prince*. Scholastic: New York, 2005.

———. *Harry Potter and the Deathly Hallows*. Scholastic: New York, 2007.

These abbreviated versions of the titles appear throughout: *Sorcerer's Stone*, *Chamber of Secrets*, *Prisoner of Azkaban*, *Goblet of Fire*, *Order of the Phoenix*, *Half-Blood Prince*, and *Deathly Hallows*.

Spoiler Alert: In order to examine the novels thoroughly and with the depth of analysis they deserve, we had to, in multiple places, give away the endings. Read at your own risk.

Introduction

Teaching Them to Love
What They Have Loved:
Harry Potter Goes to College

DALEY KONCHAR FARR AND
CECILIA KONCHAR FARR

What We Have Loved: Daley and Cecilia

Daley Konchar Farr, Augsburg College, junior English major: The summer I was nine years old, my mom, little brother, and I embarked on the long and familiar drive from our tidy neighborhood in St. Paul, Minnesota, to the grand, dusty Utah desert. We were going to drive part of the way with my grandparents, then visit old friends we had left behind in Provo five years earlier; the musty orange tent bouncing in the trunk signaled our plans to camp outside Moab while we were there. Throughout the trip, the three of us alternated reading aloud from a new book that my mom's friend had recommended for us—*Harry Potter and the Sorcerer's Stone*. My brother Tanner and I bickered over how long each of us got to read before the other's turn; he was only six years old and I was a recent third grade graduate, but we were both eager to practice our blossoming reading skills on the exciting story of a shy English boy and his motley crew of magical friends.

In Moab, we spent hours huddled together in the tiny tent, reading about Harry as a wild desert storm lashed the red dirt

1

outside. When we turned the last page in the car on the way home, we sped toward the next town to pick up the newly released *Harry Potter and the Chamber of Secrets* as quickly as our still-sandy vehicle would take us. Reading Harry Potter with my mom and brother was the first time I ever discussed a book with other people who loved it as much as I did; it was during that road trip that I discovered how much I delight in talking about literature (especially while camping out in southern Utah), something that feels as natural to me now as the red sand felt between my toes.

Cecilia Konchar Farr, St. Catherine University, parent and professor: That summer road trip was a milestone for me, too. I didn't know it, but it was the last time I would be with my dad before he succumbed permanently to the dementia that accompanied his advancing Parkinson's disease. When he insisted on taking his turn driving just outside of Chicago, he panicked on the freeway and had to pull off. Embarrassed and frustrated, my dad, the long-haul trucker, operator of heavy construction equipment, unflappable driving teacher to eight children, surrendered the wheel to my mom, who drove most of the way to my brother's house in Denver as I squeezed into the back of my Suzuki Sidekick with Daley and Tanner. As we took turns reading Harry Potter, I was attuned not just to our story but also to every subtle shift in behavior that marked the impending loss of the father I had known. When he grabbed Tanner's wrist too firmly in a McDonald's restaurant and Tanner cried, I cried, too, furtively. I had to protect my six-year-old son from my father—the man who taught me to play chess and rummy, to ride ponies and mini-bikes, to fish, swim, and skate. One winter he attached an old car hood to the back of his tractor like a sled and drove us around and around for hours in our snowy field. Soon the whole neighborhood was grabbing on and flying off, rolling through the snow choking with laughter alongside my brothers and sisters and me. That was the dad I remember, full of fun and playfulness, the kind of parent I wanted to be.

If that trip marked an end to his playful parenting, it was a beginning for mine. The Harry Potter books punctuate my memories of the years Daley and Tanner lived with me. Harry often got them out of bed an hour early so we could read over hot chocolate at neighborhood coffee shops before school. He got them back and forth through many more road trips to visit both sets of grandparents in Pittsburgh. I remember Daley carrying Harry to Girl Scout camp in her pillowcase and Tanner lounging intently with Harry on the front porch. When I get out the hammock each spring I remember cuddling together reading Harry on sticky Minnesota nights until it got too dark for us to see the pages. And that fierce desert storm is one of my most cherished memories, the amazing smells, sounds, and flashes of lightning (*"Lumos!"*) that amplified the magical world we were lost in inside that little tent. We are all readers now; Daley and I delight in our regular discussions of novels over coffee or on rollerblades, and Tanner's collection of fantasy novels and manga threatens to annex his room. Because I haven't driven a tractor in years, Harry served as well as a sled in the field for me and my kids.

When a group of St. Catherine University English majors requested a class on Harry Potter a few years ago, they didn't have much work to do convincing me it was a good idea. I had spent years loving these books (almost) as much as they do. And my kids never did take much to rummy or chess.

"I've been studying for this class since I was ten years old."

What Others Love: Cecilia

Inaugurated as the first woman president of the Modern Language Association in 1980, Harvard professor and literary scholar Helen Vendler delivered a now-famous speech entitled "What We Have Loved, Others Will Love." She referenced these lines from William Wordsworth's autobiographical poem, *The Prelude*: "What we have loved / Others will love, and we will teach them how." She concluded, in a passage often cited by literature teachers, that "We owe it to ourselves to show our students, when they meet us, what we are; we owe their dormant appetites, thwarted for so long in their previous schooling, that deep sustenance that will make them realize that they too, having been taught, love what we love" (40). What we love, in her essay, includes Keats, Yeats, and Dickinson, Milton, Dostoevsky, and Shakespeare, in addition to Wordsworth. It's a given in the text that these writers will meet with resistance from our college and university students. Our job, she suggests, is to educate them, to draw them in with our passion, to demonstrate irresistibly our love for this literature.

Check, check, and check. As is the case with many professors, more than half of my job is teaching students who aren't English majors, so my work has always been inspiring them to love what I love—Gatsby and Sula, Cather and Woolf. Sometimes it works. Often, despite my obdurate enthusiasm, it doesn't. I had one English major, Lennon Sundance—creative, sharp, valedictorian of her class—who could not see what people found so charming about Jane Austen. All that privileged aimlessness, the wandering from drawing room to drawing room, the pointless, dishonest politeness. But, seriously, I thought, what intelligent woman doesn't love Jane Austen, with her obvious preference for intelligent women? I knew Jane Austen would work for Lennon if she just read more of her. I was wrong; Lennon never took to Jane.

It took a few smart, perceptive, and resisting readers like Lennon to get me moving in a different direction with my teaching. Though I subscribed to radical *ideas* about teaching—pedagogies like Paulo Freire's that would have us see students as fully formed human beings in conversation with us rather than as empty vessels waiting to be filled with our wisdom—my practices, it seemed, had not caught up. I *did* know best.

Until I taught Harry Potter.

Freire writes about a teacher who "is no longer merely the-one-who-teaches, but one who is [her]self taught in dialogue with the students, who in turn while being taught also teach" (74). It takes about ten minutes of sharing a classroom space with Harry Potter readers to see the balance of power tip, to realize where knowledge resides. My traditional-age college students know Harry Potter—all seven volumes—the way my children do, the way I know *The Great Gatsby*, chapter by chapter, character by character, intimately and thoroughly—the knowledge of avid book lovers. They *know* these novels from years of reading and rereading them as they awaited the next book or movie release. They don't need my enthusiasm; they have their own.

This collection of essays springs from the experience of studying Harry Potter at St. Catherine University in Minnesota's Twin Cities. Two outstanding student leaders (Evan Gaydos and Rachel Armstrong) joined me in constructing our course, "Six Degrees of Harry Potter," and then served as my teaching assistants as we taught it three times (see the syllabus, appendix 1). Students from several schools in our consortium (Macalester and Augsburg colleges and Hamline and St. Thomas universities) joined the "Katies" in the class, as you will observe in the section About the Contributors. The course became a study in the power of these novels to affect deeply these American, mainly Midwestern readers—quite a distance physically and culturally from author J. K. Rowling's Anglo-British wizarding world.

Far from Vendler's "thwarted" students with "dormant appetites," the Harry Potter students were engaged, eager, and astute. When I offered them critical tools (six approaches to textual analysis, the "six degrees"), they knew exactly how to use them to deepen and expand their understanding of Rowling's stories. One group read Joseph Campbell's *Hero with a Thousand Faces*, for example, and with each novel traced Harry's hero journey. Another group was charged with examining the texts as children's literature and demonstrated to us (carefully and textually) not only how the characters mature but also how the issues deepen, the morality becomes more nuanced, and the language more complex as the series progresses. We took the issue of Harry being anti-Christian head on, as a third group, using Francis Bridger's *A Charmed Life: The Spirituality of Potterworld*, led us through a serious moral and theological examination of the novels and their place in contemporary culture. Groups also studied the texts as fantasy, as (capital-L) Literature, and as speculative science.

The classroom came alive with their projects, presentations, and papers—and their playfulness. Over those three semesters, we ate chocolate frogs and drank butterbeer, held a Quidditch tournament, and followed clues to the Chamber of Secrets in the basement of Whitby Hall; we watched a hilarious twenty-minute puppet show of all seven novels, attempted to read tea leaves in a heavily scented, simulated Divination classroom; competed at Harry Potter trivia, Scene-It, and *Jeopardy!*; and MacGyvered our Muggley way through the challenges of the wizarding world with only a cell phone. Though few of the students were English majors, they all knew what it meant to love novels and to draw "deep sustenance" from them. The things we learned together seemed significant enough to pass along.

In this collection, my two teaching assistants and I, along with five student editors, have gathered thoughtful academic essays written by students aged seventeen to twenty-seven from across the country, each examining the Harry Potter books from various perspectives—theological, mythological, psychological, postmodern, postcolonial, genetic, gendered, and literary. We even have a nursing care plan for Tom Riddle. The book has its roots in the course. The first semester we taught it, as we read scholarly essays on Rowling's work, the students were frustrated with the way the academic critics sometimes mixed up significant details and characters, conflating Professor Severus Snape with Lord Voldemort, for example, or confusing James Potter and Sirius Black. "We could do better than this," they said. And, in fact, they did. We called for more essays online, and, in several rousing editorial board meetings where the students argued with impressive insight and integrity over which essays to include, we completed our selection.

And as a gesture toward recognizing the diverse ways Harry has walked with them through adolescence and helped them become the people they are, we also decided to include a few vignettes, selections we're calling "My Harry Potter Story," where young people who grew up with these novels share narratives and memories.

Our book begins with a foreword by Professor Giselle Liza Anatol, editor of the two excellent scholarly collections of essays on Harry Potter that we found most useful in our studies, both for class and for this book—*Reading Harry Potter* and *Reading Harry Potter Again*. After that, this introduction, coauthored by me, the supervising editor, and my English-major daughter, is the last we hear of the over-thirty generation for the remainder of the collection.

The first part of the collection, "Muggle Studies," is devoted to how the wizarding world has affected our own. First, Kate Glassman reviews "The Harry Potter Phenomenon," a statistical tracking of the expansion of the Harry Potter franchise from its obscure beginning as a children's book in Britain to a worldwide marvel with over 500 million copies in print in English alone. She argues that, over the course of a decade, the rise of Harry Potter has had a profound and enduring effect on the publishing industry, blurring the line between children's and adult literature and changing the way in which the literate world conceptualizes a bestseller. Kate McManus follows with "Loading the Canon," an introduction to the prolific world of fanfiction that has burgeoned in response to the (gaps in the) Harry Potter series. McManus familiarizes readers with the genre and its history (which includes *Robin Hood* and *Wide Sargasso Sea*) as well as the language and trends of today's fanfiction writers, such as "canon" versus "fanon" writing, the tendency toward romantic themes, and the appearance of "Mary Sue" characters. Next, Kyle Bubb examines "The Simulated World of Harry Potter" with a theoretical venture into the postmodern hyperreality of Universal Orlando's Wizarding World. With similar mastery of contemporary theory, Hannah Lamb deploys postcolonial practices to examine class and race divisions in Harry's world in her essay, "The Wizard, the Muggle, and the Other," arguing that the novels, in the end, send decidedly mixed signals. Tréza Rosado closes out this part with her careful cultural examination of why this series, with its finely shaded views of right and wrong and good and evil, has been so meaningful to young people post 9/11.

The second part, "Defense Against the Dark Arts," tracks the villains and heroes of the series, beginning with three studies of Voldemort's villainy. Sarah Wente examines how Nazi ideology, leadership models, and methods of education are repeated by Voldemort and his followers in "The Making of a New World," and Kalie Caetano investigates "The Nuances of Mastering Death" and the acts of homicide and self-sacrifice in the series. Caetano pays particular attention to Voldemort's obsessive avoidance of death and deftly contrasts his choices with the complex compromises of Severus Snape. Sarah Sutor focuses on the state of Voldemort's soul, in all its broken pieces, in "The Wickedest of Magical Inventions," looking at the idea of a "separable soul" in medieval folklore and in Rowling's novels. Callie Knudslien then turns our attention to the novels' hero, with a theological examination of the Christian roots of Harry's morality in "WWHPD: What Would Harry Potter Do?" Considering the opposition to Rowling's portrayal of magic and witchcraft among some Christian communities, Knudslien argues that Harry Potter actually epitomizes Christ-centered values rather than contradicting them. Jenny McDougal concludes this part with a call for a more finely shaded understanding of one of the most beloved characters in the series, the Headmaster of Hogwarts, Albus Dumbledore. In "Doubting Dumbledore," McDougal argues that the headmaster is the epitome of Rowling's preference for moral complexity. She analyzes how Dumbledore molds Harry into the wizarding world's sacrificial lamb, releasing and withholding information as it suits his purposes, and builds a case that Dumbledore's utilitarian sense of right and wrong does not always work in Harry's favor.

The book's final part, "Transfiguration," places the Harry Potter novels in various academic contexts to yield unusual textual readings. Courtney Agar and Julia Terk imagine a "Wizard's Gene" in their genetic analysis of Potterworld. Using the family connections Rowling reveals in the novels, along with theories of population genetics, the authors posit that magical ability is a genetically inherited trait that follows the classic rules of Mendelian theory. As they demonstrate cleverly and creatively, these rules account for magical ability appearing in both Muggle-borns and half-bloods, such as Hermione Granger and Severus Snape, as well as how two magical parents can produce a Squib, such as Argus Filch. Kiah Bizal approaches Harry Potter and Tom Riddle with the tools of Freudian psychological analysis to understand how two boys from similar circumstances can turn out quite differently in "Give Nature a Wand and It Will Nurture Magic," while Kari Newell imagines a nurse's intervention into young Tom Riddle's burgeoning psychoses with "A Nursing Care Plan for Tom Riddle." Newell's delightful conclusion, speculating on the results of her intervention, is unlike anything a Muggle school nurse might confront in the course of a regular workday.

The concluding essays, by the student inventors of the Harry Potter course, employ literary approaches. Evan Gaydos takes a formalist look at "Literary Arithmancy" in her study of how the numbers three, four, and seven operate symbolically in the series and across cultures and time, and Rachel Armstrong engages queer theory to examine the "Sexual Geometry of the Golden Trio," using Eve Kosofsky Sedgwick's erotic triangle. Putting Hermione at the center of the gendered tensions between Harry and Ron but focusing on this central female character's refusal of the classic role of feminine foil or beard, Armstrong argues that the novels effectively challenge given gender stereotypes and open possibilities for young women readers.

The book's afterword retraces our path through Potter-world, as the seven student editors reflect on what it means to study the novels we love.

"I've never been so invested in a class before."[1]

And They Can Teach Us How: Daley and Cecilia

Daley: Not red dirt, not a red train, but a red bus bore me back to Hogwarts, and I learned of my acceptance through an e-mail rather than a letter in green ink. I was twenty-one—ten years late. I cringe a little to put it in those terms; having never quite taken to the Harry Potter movies, few things about being in Oxford annoy me quite so much as the breathless way fellow American students explain to me, "Christ Church's dining hall is the Great Hall in Harry Potter, did you know that? Did you know Magdalen's cloisters are where Malfoy got turned into a ferret?" As I write, I am halfway through my junior year abroad here, and in what little time I have, I prefer to enjoy Oxford as Oxford, my real school, with wonders and charms of its own and no need for fictional embellishment. But my eye rolls aren't entirely honest, either. I think it must feel strange for all of us who have loved Rowling's books to enter, as adults, something resembling the most cherished fantasy of our childhood. And even though I wouldn't say that my love for Harry Potter drove me to Oxford as a means of realizing my younger self's Ravenclaw aspirations, I do think that I got here because of what I learned from reading those books: falling in love with characters, examining my world through texts, finding the joy in wordplay, and hanging on for the long haul. Perhaps my frenzied reading and rereading of *Harry Potter and the Goblet of Fire* and *Harry Potter and the Order of the Phoenix*, my favorite books in the series as well as two of the longest, forecasted my more recent attachments to *Ulysses* and *Moby-Dick*.

No matter how many times I combed my program's website for some bit of information I may have missed, now it seems that I made all of my most significant preparations for my time here through reading novels. I received images and atmosphere from Harry Potter, culture from the occasional Buck Mulligan jest, and a little bit of geography from Philip Pullman's His Dark Materials series. I have had other English students here describe to me what they knew of Oxford before arriving in terms of *Brideshead Revisited* or *Alice's Adventures in Wonderland*. I know that something of my experience with Harry Potter is always bound up in my time in Oxford; through all of my worldly and literary travels, I carry with me the adventure, the intellectual thrill, and maybe even the magic I felt as I held my flashlight aloft and read those pages as if they contained a spell to keep us safe and dry in the storm ravaging our tent in Utah.

These days, my mom and I argue about the Blooms' as well as Snape's and Dumbledore's moral ambiguity, and coffee-and-book dates with her are one of the things I have missed most during my time away. But it's okay—for now, I have a different café, different texts to read, different people to discuss them with, and a different world to explore. Before I came here, Oxford was shrouded in mystery and a hopeful, hesitant expectation, just as Hogwarts once was. Now, just as it happened with Harry and his friends, I am starting to feel at home.

Cecilia: What Daley and I cherish about the Harry Potter novels, what my students cherish, is the way these novels speak to our imaginations as well as our intellects, to our passions and our minds. It's the way they draw us in and don't disappoint us on the second, third, or seventh reading. In this, the Harry Potter books fit comfortably in the democratic tradition of enthusiastic novel-reading in the United States. Literary historians have remarked on the similarities between the spirited midnight Harry Potter book release parties and the stories of throngs of impatient nineteenth-century Americans waiting dockside for the next installment of a Charles Dickens novel. Americans have, for more than two centuries now, learned from novels, been entertained by them, and used them for social and cultural connection. We dive in and get lost together in alternate worlds, returning better readers and sometimes better scholars and citizens. Most English professors want our students to experience this charmed interchange for the rest of their lives. As a parent, I certainly want that for my children.

Harry Potter reminds us that young people in this generation, like many generations before them, love what pre-internet children like me loved. Despite their more flexible thumbs and frequent sojourns in digital universes, today's college students read with pleasure and draw deep sustenance from long, absorbing novels—a fine fact to remember as we mark Charles Dickens's two hundredth birthday.

When I teach Harry Potter, I more easily bring what I know as a parent with me than I do in my other teaching. I arrive ready to find joy in our reading together, ready to respect my students' preferences, ready to play. But I also bring what I know as a professor. I suggest reading practices and paradigms, theories and critical approaches; I provide good questions and a careful plan for our study. In this situation, with the Harry Potter novels, I have found that Vendler's model of teaching students to love what we love misses the mark. It is too linear, too top-down. While I offer ways to examine more thoroughly and, thus, appreciate more deeply these novels my students love, from there, the transaction is more circular. I honor (and cannot match!) the depth and breadth of their knowledge of the Potterverse, their informed and passionate reading. It is apparent in the essays that follow that Harry Potter readers love, draw deep sustenance from, and are eager to understand these novels they grew up with. The real magic comes here—in letting them teach us how.

Notes

The featured quotes on pages 4 and 9 are taken with permission from the end-of-semester evaluation, spring 2010, of Kate McManus (see her essay on fanfiction, "Loading the Canon," chapter 2 in this volume).

Special thanks to Lennon Sundance—for letting me use her as an example here and for all she taught me while she was my student, and since.

Works Cited

Anatol, Giselle Liza, ed. *Reading Harry Potter*. Westport, CT: Praeger, 2003. Print.

———, ed. *Reading Harry Potter Again*. Westport, CT: Praeger, 2010. Print.

Bridger, Francis. *A Charmed Life: The Spirituality of Potterworld*. New York, NY: Image, 2002. Print.

Campbell, Joseph. *Hero with a Thousand Faces*. 3rd edition. Novato, CA: New World Library, 2008. Print.

Freire, Paulo. "The 'Banking' Concept of Education." In *Falling into Theory: Conflicting Views on Reading Literature*, 2nd edition, ed. David Richter and Gerald Graff. New York: Bedford, 1999. 68–78. Print.

Vendler, Helen. "What We Have Loved, Others Will Love." In *Falling Into Theory: Conflicting Views on Reading Literature*, 2nd edition, ed. David Richter and Gerald Graff. New York: Bedford, 1999. 31–40. Print.

My Harry Potter Story

PHILLIP AWAYAN AND MARIA IGNACIO

Phillip Awayan, twenty-one, Brentwood, California. Para educator, studying psychology at California State University, East Bay. Photo by Maria Ignacio.

Phillip Awayan: In the sixth grade, Harry Potter saved my life. Here's how it happened: I was gone from school for a few weeks, and I forgot that my quarterly book review was due when I got back. These book reviews were a big part of our grade, and I panicked because I hadn't read any books. The lunch period before it was due, I ended up writing a couple pages about Harry Potter as my book report—and I got an "A."

And that's how he saved my life.

But in all seriousness—I really like the series. That's my favorite thing about them: it's a continuation. The books grow throughout Harry's life and his journeys at Hogwarts. I was drawn in by the surprises in each book and the new twists that were in store. It was exciting to read and never got boring.

Growing up reading the entire Harry Potter series expanded my imagination. I started reading the books in the third grade, which was around the time that we had to write our own stories and essays in school. Referencing what I'd read in the Harry Potter books allowed me to think in ways I'd never thought before. At that age, I was imagining more than I normally would have, different worlds that could exist in our realm but were still all make-believe.

Being a fan of such an amazing series hasn't affected my personal life too much, though. It's not like I walk around pretending to wave a wand or speak with a British accent to people on the street. But reading and watching Harry Potter has allowed me to keep in touch with my inner child. The series of movies has definitely appealed to a bigger crowd of people, but the concept of the storyline reminds me what creativity can bring to this world.

I haven't picked up one of those books in a while, but I can assure you the events are still embedded in my mind.

Maria Ignacio, twenty-three, St. Paul, Minnesota. Photographer and web producer in marketing and communications at St. Catherine University. Photo by Rebecca Zenefski.

Maria Ignacio: My parents always told me that I needed to read every day for at least fifteen minutes. So, begrudgingly, I would pick up whatever book I got from the weekly trip to the library at school and would read. As I got older, the pictures from the "age-appropriate" books began to disappear, and the longer, chapter books proceeded to fill the shelves. It was around this time that my aunt suggested I read Harry Potter. I was eleven years old.

From the moment I met "the boy who lived," I was hooked. I can honestly say that Harry Potter was what really got me into reading. The intricacy of the plot, the characters, and the magic of the wizarding world drew me in. It was a book that I could not put down . . . I wanted to know what was next. So from then on, I waited for each book as it came out to go on adventures with Harry, Ron, and Hermione.

While the dynamic trio was having adventures, I was having adventures of my own. I was eleven when my family made the first move I can remember. Being a child in a military family, "home is where the army sends us," as they say. My family did a lot of moving, a lot of traveling, and I constantly had to start over, make new friends, and make a new life in each place.

It was with that first move that Harry Potter became my traveling buddy. I have lots of memories of traveling, whether it was having to stay at the airport the whole day, really long plane rides from overseas, or shorter two-hour flights, almost all of them include me with a J. K. Rowling book in hand, ready to open it whenever we stopped for a minute or two. Now, if I am ever in search of a book to take with me when I travel, I know exactly where to go. Harry Potter never lets me down. Each time I read, I'm still on the edge of my seat. Each time, I learn something new and notice something I didn't notice before. Harry Potter is more than just a book series; it's a relationship I've built over the years, constant throughout the ever-changing life around me.

PART I

Muggle Studies

One

The Harry Potter Phenomenon

Locating the Boy Wizard in the Tradition of the American Bestseller

KATE GLASSMAN

When *Harry Potter and the Philosopher's Stone* was first published in 1997, its first UK print run was a paltry five hundred copies, three hundred of which were distributed to libraries (Fraser). Taking on the new, more fantastical-sounding title *Harry Potter and the Sorcerer's Stone*, the boy wizard crossed the pond in 1998 to sell roughly 6 million copies over the next year in the United States (Bowker Annual 2000, 651,656). Ten years after children and adults alike picked up a book about a scrawny, bespectacled boy who discovered he could do magic, the final installment hit shelves at midnight on July 21, 2007, and *Deathly Hallows* sold 8.3 million copies in a single day. No other book in history has sold so well in so short a time (Stevenson 279). J. K. Rowling's seven-part series went from "good read" to global phenomenon in the span of a decade and in doing so had a profound and enduring effect on the publishing industry and the way in which the literate world conceptualizes a "bestseller."

It took Rowling five years to plan the series once the concept of Harry Potter and his magical world arose in 1991 (Fraser). Almost every fan knows the anecdote of how a down-on-her-luck Rowling had the idea come to her on a train to Manchester and knew right away that Harry's story would take him through seven books. Though *Philosopher's Stone* was published in 1997, it took several attempts before the Christopher Little Agency finally agreed to represent her and nearly a year and twelve dozen publishers before Bloomsbury Press took on the book for publication (MacDonald 40). Three days after her novel was published in the United Kingdom, "Scholastic Books bid a record-breaking $105,000 to publish the book in the United States" (MacDonald 41).

Though Harry Potter arrived quietly on the scene in 1997, it had just begun a relative groundswell when Scholastic released it in the United States a year after its UK debut. Once stateside, the inaugural book of the series—newly renamed *Sorcerer's Stone*—slipped by virtue of water-cooler gossip and word-of-mouth reviews onto the *New York Times* bestseller list. By July of the following year, *Sorcerer's Stone* had spent thirty weeks on the list—just fourteen weeks short of its entire time on the market (Maughan, "Halo"). The demand for the next installment was so immediately prevalent and emphatic that the 1998 UK edition of *Chamber of Secrets*—not due to arrive in US bookstores until September of 1999—was being bought off the Bloomsbury website and shipped to the United States in significant and therefore concerning numbers. Michael Jacobs, senior vice president of trade at Scholastic, announced in February of 1999 that despite the growing demand and cross-territorial consumerism, Scholastic had no plans to change its September publication date (Maughan, "Race"). Not a month and a half later, however, the publisher had to bow to the masses in order to staunch the potential hemorrhaging of sales and announced their modified plan to release *Chamber of Secrets* a full three months ahead of schedule (Maughan, "Potter's Publication"). By the time *Prisoner of Azkaban* was ready for publication, the release dates were only three months apart; however, the phenomenon that Harry Potter was to become found its catalyst in *Goblet of Fire*.

By the April before *Goblet of Fire*'s July release date—before its name had even been changed from the tentative title of *Harry Potter and the Doomspell Tournament*—the book had been in the number-one spot (or at least in the top five) on Amazon's bestseller list for months ("New Heights"). Though only a year stood between *Goblet of Fire* and its predecessor, the simultaneous US and UK release created a synergistic buzz of excitement the likes of which had never before been witnessed in the literary domain. As with any icon of popular culture, with success came controversy. The militant demands for the series to be banned in schools and public libraries, or to be burned rather than chosen for another print run, spread across the United States in tandem with the nation's increased fan base, which represented a correlating increase in the number of impressionable children in danger of Rowling's supposedly sinister promotion of witchcraft and anti-Christian morals. Parallel to the apparent moral crisis, *Goblet of Fire* brought with it the second real issue of publishing ethics for the series. Though it was by no means the last issue Harry Potter would face in that industry, the book represented the discernible turn in the series' popularity as well as the books' rising share of controversy, dispute, and forced reformation of publishing practices.

With *Goblet of Fire* set to debut July 8, 2000, Amazon announced that it would ship overnight to 250,000 customers for arrival on July 8 (Milliot and Maughan). The implications of this announcement—that Amazon would receive copies of the coveted fourth book before other booksellers, and that the aforementioned novel would be in transit for delivery a full twenty-four hours before it was to be available to the public at large—sent both booksellers and consumers into a frenzied tailspin. Surely there was some ethical publishing injustice in this. Scholastic's Michael Jacobs was prompted once again by public outcry to release a statement regarding Amazon's supposed distribution privileges: "When we found out from Bloomsbury that they were allowing non-walk-in, pre-sold copies of the book to be shipped on July 7th for delivery on July 8th, we decided we could allow our accounts the same opportunity," Jacobs announced (Milliot and Maughan). Yet not all accounts were created equal. Any booksellers who wished to ship books on July 7 were required to provide Scholastic with proof of a "secure plan" that included receipt of the shipment, organization of orders, employee confidentiality, and timed delivery (Milliot and Maughan).

This stringent control of security and protection against the preemptive leaking of the book's implied, and therefore highly coveted, secret contents became one of the tamer protection requirements bestowed upon the series by the time Harry Potter reached his final battle in 2007. As is often the case with anything from album release parties to Oscar winners, taking strict care not to divulge any information or details to the public at large is a surefire way to increase both the fanatic frenzy and the energy with which fans attempt to ferret out those details in spite of (or because of) the heightened security. However, the kerfuffle regarding Amazon's overnight shipping was nothing compared to the serious policy change that came out of the *New York Times* in response to the series' increasing popularity and domination of its weekly bestseller list in the *Book Review*.

By the year 2000, three of the Harry Potter books had already been published in the United States, and the series, by June 25, had been on the *New York Times'* bestseller list for seventy-nine weeks (Smith). A year and a half after *Sorcerer's Stone* made its unheralded appearance on the bottom of the list, "the top three places on the hardcover fiction list were held by Rowling titles" (Garner). With another book on the way—easily predicted to take up the fourth slot on the list—the *New York Times* announced it would begin printing a separate bestseller list for children's books starting on July 23 (Smith). While some publishers had spent months pushing for just such a change, others considered the change both a politically timed blow to the series and a detrimental limitation of books' classification on a grander scale.

Harry's move to the children's list implied that it was meant only for children, a sentiment confirmed by the *New York Times'* deferring to the books' publisher, Scholastic, to decide whether it was a series for adults or children (they indicated it was the latter). When examining the progression of the series as a whole, the irony of the move is even more frustrating. Just as the books began to take on an adolescent—even adult—tone, they were moved to a specialized children's list. Barbara Marcus, president of the Scholastic Children's Book Group, notes that 30 percent of the first three Harry Potter books were purchased by and for a reader thirty-five years or older: "It would seem to me that if we were tracking adult bestselling reading behavior, one would say that the book should be on both lists" (Bolonik).

Yet the sixty-eight-year-old national institution chose instead to debut its first new offshoot in sixteen years, all on account of a wizard who—though inspiring millions to read—was childishly keeping new adult titles off the bestseller list.

Though the initial debate was furious—the new children's list being called anything from a "lucrative niche" to a "ghetto" where cross-generational books like *Harry Potter* are shuffled off to in shame—representatives of the *New York Times* insisted that the children's list would remain a permanent fixture in the *Book Review*, a statement which up to this point has remained true. While there was no demonstrable fallout from the move, nor any significant decrease in adult consumerism as a result of the new categorization, Potter fans were dealt yet another blow in 2004 when, in the interim between books 5 and 6, a further offshoot of the bestseller list was instigated for children's "series" books, which "ignored the sale of individual titles and instead tracked each series as a whole" (Garner).

Given its extensive build-up, the *New York Times*' controversial plan to move Harry Potter from the adult bestseller list to one reserved for children's titles, and the alluringly off-limits connotation *Goblet of Fire* derived from its jump in security, it should have been unsurprising when 3 million copies of the book were sold over the release weekend, not including the 180,000 copies of the audio book shipped by Listening Library—the largest lay out ever for a children's audio title (Mutter and Milliot).

Then, at the peak of the public's rising awareness, fans were crushed when Rowling announced that Harry's quest to defeat the Dark Lord in *Order of the Phoenix* would not arrive in print for another three years. Fans were kept from spiraling into a complete depression only by the advent of the Harry Potter movie franchise, with the first cinema adaptation (of *Sorcerer's Stone*) opening in theaters November 14, 2001. With the first film came a merchandising blitzkrieg. Bookstores, toy stores, and shopping centers were filled with toy wands, vibrating broomsticks, plasticized action figures, trading cards, wizarding world candies, House scarves, coloring books, and Potter renditions of board game classics. Daniel Radcliffe's twelve-year-old face papered the sides of double-decker buses on Tottenham

Court Road and stretched across cardboard cutouts in the lobbies of US theaters. Voldemort might have risen again, but while it would take three years for readers to find out what his return meant for the safety of the wizarding world, Potter fans were adamant about celebrating the boy wizard's back catalog.

It was during this hiatus from the books that Harry Potter fans took it upon themselves to spread the love, so to speak. Three years was more than enough time for the fans to work themselves into a frenzy, recruiting more readers by the sheer force of their enthusiasm and zeal. Others were pulled onto the vastly overcrowded bandwagon by way of cinema—the movie debuts of both *Sorcerer's Stone* and *Chamber of Secrets* drew significant crowds of movie-lovers, many of whom then felt either obligated or encouraged to pick up the books. With the adaptations acting as something of a gateway drug into the Potterverse, the premiere dates of both movies correlated with an increase in sales for the earlier four novels as a second wave of fans succumbed to the intoxicating literary high that the first wave of die-hard Potter devotees had been riding for four years.

It became an issue of cultural standing, potentially the first literary status symbol, for children and young adults—kids the world over wanted to be in on the discussion, especially since "by May 2001, nearly three out of four kids ages 11–13 had read at least one *Harry Potter* volume," according to the NPD Group (Hallett). It wasn't enough to see the movies. If you didn't want to be the kid sitting alone in the classroom while everyone else debated House superiority, you had to get your hands on the books, and fast. At the turn of the millennium, Harry Potter had become a staple of the world's popular culture, and as sociologist Dustin Kidd writes in "Harry Potter and the Functions of Popular Culture," "popular culture, like crime, is a necessary and healthy element of modern society" (71).

In the interim between books 4 and 5, Rowling published two companion pieces to the Harry Potter series, *Quidditch Through the Ages* and *Fantastic Beasts and Where to Find Them*, under the pseudonyms Kennilworthy Whisp and Newt Scamander, respectively. Eva Mitnick of the *School Library Journal* noted at the time, "Harry Potter fans who pride themselves on knowing every minute bit of Hogwarts trivia will devour both books" ("J. K. Rowling"). The two books were quickly amalgamated into the Potter lexicon, and a new brand of micro-analysis took hold in a fan base with relatively no new material to distract them from doing otherwise. Fans created catalogues of Famous Witch or Wizard cards, league standings for favored Quidditch teams, and hundreds of theories on topics ranging from Professor Albus Dumbledore's true desire in the Mirror of Erised to Voldemort's plans for renewed dominion over the wizarding world post–*Goblet of Fire*. Fan forums and news sites began to spring up across the internet, including the inception of some of the greatest online Harry Potter resources to date; both *The Harry Potter Lexicon* (hp-lexicon.org) and *The Leaky Cauldron* (the-leaky-cauldron.org) appeared on servers in 2000 on the heels of *MuggleNet*'s (mugglenet.com) arrival in the fall of 1999 (Vander Ark; Anelli; Spartz). Though many started as a simple rolling newsfeed, over the following ten years they have become comprehensive and reliable databases of canonical information, spirited discussion, and entertaining journalism regarding all things Potter (see chapter 2 in this volume).

The growing internet presence (represented here by the three aforementioned sites) facilitated the exchange of ideas and theorized events-to-come in book 5. As new technological advancements hit the market and the internet became a part of the mainstream day-to-day, the Harry Potter phenomenon took full advantage of the world's newly emphasized connectivity, exploiting the channels of communication to spread the wizarding world from country to country, laptop to laptop.

Through data streams and megapixels, fans united across gaps of gender, age, race, and location to produce a total effect greater than the sum of the their individual elements of fanaticism, a synergism-fueled explosion of Pottermania that showed no signs of abating until months after the final chapter of the seven-part series was released. It was largely through the internet that events and promotions were arranged—for, and largely by, the fans. Harry Potter conventions were generated on discussion boards; Wizard Rock bands—their names and song content inspired by the books—were formed, releasing CDs and posting their amateur tunes on MySpace; midnight release parties were organized for the up-and-coming book, complete with resplendent costumes, caffeinated beverages, and carpooling parents.

Midnight parties hosted by bookstores like Barnes and Noble, Borders, and Waterstone, as well as superstores like Wal-Mart and K-Mart, were advertised weeks in advance of *Order of the Phoenix*'s arrival. Children in home-sewn wizard's robes, the seventeen-year-olds who had been eleven with Harry, and adult fans and chaperones packed store aisles and lined up on shop-front sidewalks hours before sunset. When registers opened at midnight across the world in 2003, the buying frenzy began. *Order of the Phoenix* sold an estimated 5 million copies on the first day of publication, setting sales records throughout the United States, Canada, and the United Kingdom ("Order").

These record-breaking sales were achieved regardless of the apparently stringent allocation system developed by Scholastic in order to avoid unsold books that would eventually be sent back to the publisher. While this is a problem often faced by supposed bestsellers and overly hyped sequels, it's hard to imagine that by 2003 Scholastic was not ecstatically aware of just how popular the series had grown to be, or that it was subsequently lacking any sort of confidence in ordering a correspondingly high print run. Stores, mainly smaller chains, either sold or received fewer copies than anticipated, insisting that the "problem stem[med] from Scholastic's reluctance to commit to a larger initial printing" than 6.8 million ("Order"). Two years later, when *Half-Blood Prince* was released, Scholastic redeemed themselves by ordering an initial print run of 10.8 million that was not only a record-breaking number but one of legitimate need and not just wishful thinking on the part of the publisher (Nelson). The demand was so great after the three-year waiting period that readers were willing to buy *Order of the Phoenix* at any cost and from wherever they could find it.

Earlier-released English editions of *Order of the Phoenix* became black market commodities in non-English-speaking countries. Personal translations were poorly but hastily done and then posted on the internet, some only a day after the book had been released. This trend would persist for the remaining two novels. With the amateurish convince-me-you-can-protect-it policy of *Goblet of Fire* firmly in the past, *Order of the*

Phoenix was treated to an excess of checks, balances, and anti-spoiler protocols in the weeks leading up to its release that even kept secret some of the plants in which the book was being manufactured. Once the books were released, however, Bloomsbury and the country-specific publishers for the series were ill-prepared to deal with the breadth and scope of black market trading, eBay flash auctions, and a general disregard for territorial publication rights. Piracy in the literary world became an issue in a way it never had before, making the Anglo-American quibble over *Chamber of Secrets* look like an argument over seating arrangements.

In China, at least five thousand English-language copies of *Order of the Phoenix* had already been sold not two weeks after the original release—a startling number given the country's low rates of English fluency—though China's own translation was not due until October. French citizens bought six times as many copies of the English edition, and those thirty thousand magical books made *Order of the Phoenix* the first bestseller in France not written in French. Similarly incapable of waiting for what was to be a November release, Potterphiles of Germany went through back channels to buy the Bloomsbury edition online. German publisher Carlsen actually sued Amazon.de for "having sold a reported 450,000 copies" of the UK edition to its German patrons in the first two weeks of its release (Zeitchik).

The concerns regarding piracy and the implied threat to territorial rights held by publishers in separate countries necessitated continuing countermeasures and sometimes excessive security policies for the subsequent two books in the series. Both *Half-Blood Prince* and *Deathly Hallows* were subject to heightened security, but with *Deathly Hallows* being the long-awaited conclusion to the series that had spanned over a decade, particular care was taken in guarding Rowling's would-be readers against spoilers. Locations at which the seventh book was being manufactured were kept closely guarded, though there were rumors circulating that the R. R. Donnelley plant in Crawfordsville, Indiana, was one such location. To detail the extent to which the book's contents were protected, the testimony of an anonymous Crawfordsville informant reveals that employees had lunch box searches at the end of each workday and a ban on all cell phones for the duration of the project. They also "wrap[ped] up the books in black cellophane and [kept] them in a secured storage area" (Kirch). Though seemingly excessive, these measures were implemented to protect the final installment and, at Rowling's request, to protect her readers from a ruined experience. The tearing of black cellophane and clear shrink-wrap from pallets of the 759-page (US) tome signaled an end to the decade-long sales frenzy and, finally given the chance to breathe, allowed the publishing industry to examine the Harry Potter series and encompassing phenomenon in its entirety.

Cumulatively, the series boasts approximately 500 million English copies in print, 118 million on US bookshelves. There are likely twice as many (~800 million) copies combined in the sixty-seven languages into which the Harry Potter series has been translated (Stevenson 290; Bowker Annual 2000-2011). In *USA Today*'s list of the 150 bestselling books of the last fifteen years (October 28, 1993–October 23, 2008), the series took seven of the top nine spots, only prevented from sweeping the list by *Dr. Atkins' New Diet Revolution* at number two and *The Da Vinci Code* at number three ("USA TODAY's"). The breadth of its physical distribution speaks to the continuing presence the Harry Potter series will have on the literary world as a whole and the legacy it will leave behind across numerous mediums.

The sheer numbers garnered by the seven-part series is impressive in the context of both a children's novel and a work of fiction. The total number of sales of each book, in both hardcover and paperback, were tracked each year by *The Bowker Annual*, a compilation of the highest-selling books of the year for the United States in both adult and children's literature categories (see figure 1.1). As evidenced in the following graph and "in all territories where Nielsen BookScan monitors book sales data . . . peak sales of Harry Potter titles consistently coincide with the launch of the new hardback editions and continue to break records" (Gyimesi). Similarly, the aforementioned spike in readership during the gap between *Goblet of Fire* and *Order of the Phoenix* is visually apparent in the jump of first-year sales from roughly 8 million copies sold to over 12 million.

With the by-year accounting of Harry Potter sales, it is possible to calculate the number of copies sold, by book, in the

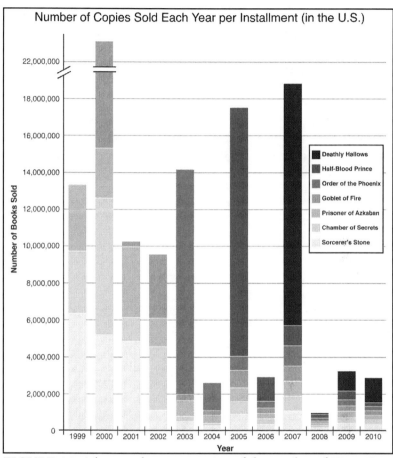

FIGURE 1.1. A bar graph representation of the number of Harry Potter copies sold each year in the United States, by book, from 1999–2010.

United States from 1999 to 2010 (see figure 1.2). Given that it has been on the market the longest, *Sorcerer's Stone* logically takes the top-number-printed spot with 21.4 million; however, the correlation between printings and the longest span of availability does not extend beyond the second book: *Chamber of Secrets* comes in second but is then followed by *Half-Blood Prince*—the sixth in the series.

Looking to other proclaimed literary "phenomena" allows for the sheer magnitude of these numbers to be put into

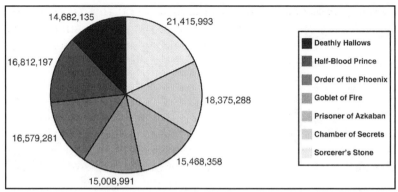

FIGURE 1.2. A pie graph representation of the total number of Harry
Potter books in print in the United States from 1999–2010, divided by
book.

perspective. At its relative height, the conclusion of Stephenie
Meyer's popular Twilight tetralogy, *Breaking Dawn*, was number one on the children's hardcover frontlist in 2008 with 6.1
million copies sold (Library and Book Trade Almanac 2009,
591). When the Potter conclusion, *Deathly Hallows*, occupied
that same spot just one year earlier, it sold more than double
that, with its unprecedented sale of 13.1 million. It is also significant to note that in 2008 a 128-page companion book of fairy
tales for the Harry Potter series, *The Tales of Beedle the Bard*,
was published; it sold 3.5 million copies and was the second
most highly sold children's hardcover in 2008, after *Breaking
Dawn* (Library and Book Trade Almanac 2009, 591).

A similarly popular young adult series, Suzanne Collins's
The Hunger Games trilogy, released its final installment in 2010.
Mockingjay, number four on the hardcover frontlist with 1.5
million copies, fell short of Harry Potter's own third book, *Prisoner of Azkaban*, which debuted at 3.6 million, and not even as
a conclusion to a series could it hold up to *Deathly Hallows'*
astounding numbers (Library and Book Trade Almanac 2011,
588).

What can be construed from these numbers is that, while
their fan bases and the subsequent film and media presence
may be significant, neither of these two series can be considered

literary phenomena on the same scale as the Harry Potter series; though, they perhaps come the closest. Only the coming-of-age adventures of a British boy wizard brought children and adults alike to reading in staggering and record-breaking numbers.

No matter how you break those numbers down, the inescapable fact remains that in just ten short years, Rowling created the literary basis for a global phenomenon that has forever changed the practices of the publishing industry and the field of bestselling novels. Even now, eight years after the final installment of the series was published, these widespread effects have yet to be repeated or surpassed by any other series. The Harry Potter phenomenon remains, to this day, just that.

Works Cited

Anelli, Melissa, ed. "A Brief (Believe It or Not) History of The Leaky Cauldron." *The Leaky Cauldron.* 6 Dec. 2007. Web. 6 May 2010. http://www.the-leaky-cauldron.org/info/siteinfo.

Bolonik, Kera. "A List of Their Own." *Salon.* 16 Aug. 2000. Web. 2 May 2010. http://www.salon.com/life/feature/2000/08/16/bestseller.

Bogart, Dave, ed. *The Bowker Annual 2000: Library and Book Trade Almanac,* 45th edition. New York, NY: R. R. Bowker, 2000. Print.

———, ed. *The Bowker Annual 2001: Library and Book Trade Almanac,* 46th edition. New York, NY: R. R. Bowker, 2001. Print.

———, ed. *The Bowker Annual 2002: Library and Book Trade Almanac,* 47th edition. New York, NY: R. R. Bowker, 2002. Print.

———, ed. *The Bowker Annual 2003: Library and Book Trade Almanac,* 48th edition. New York, NY: R. R. Bowker, 2003. Print.

———, ed. *The Bowker Annual 2004: Library and Book Trade Almanac,* 49th edition. New York, NY: R. R. Bowker, 2004. Print.

———, ed. *The Bowker Annual 2005: Library and Book Trade*

Almanac, 50th edition. New York, NY: R. R. Bowker, 2005. Print.

———, ed. *The Bowker Annual 2006: Library and Book Trade Almanac*, 51st edition. New York, NY: R. R. Bowker, 2006. Print.

———, ed. *The Bowker Annual 2007: Library and Book Trade Almanac*, 52nd edition. New York, NY: R. R. Bowker, 2007. Print.

———, ed. *Library and Book Trade Almanac*, 53rd edition. New York, NY: R. R. Bowker, 2008. Print.

———, ed. *Library and Book Trade Almanac*, 54th edition. New York, NY: R. R. Bowker, 2009. Print.

———, ed. *Library and Book Trade Almanac*, 55th edition. New York, NY: R. R. Bowker, 2010. Print.

———, ed. *Library and Book Trade Almanac*, 56th edition. New York, NY: R. R. Bowker, 2011. Print.

Fraser, Lindsey. *Conversations with J. K. Rowling*. New York, NY: Scholastic, 2001. Print.

Garner, Dwight. "Ten Years Later, Harry Potter Vanishes from the Best-Seller List." *New York Times*. 1 May 2008. Web. 2 May 2010. http://papercuts.blogs.nytimes.com/2008/05/01/ten-years-later-harry-potter-vanishes-from-the-best-seller-list/.

Gyimesi, Karen, dir. "Harry Potter Charms the Entertainment Industry." *Nielsen*. The Nielsen Company. 10 July 2007. Web. 25 Apr. 2010. http://en-us.nielsen.com/etc/medialib/nielsen_dotcom/en_us/documents/pdf/press_releases/2007/july.Par.82638.File.dat/pr_070710_download.pdf.

Hallett, Vicky. "The Power of Potter." *US News and World Report Online*. N.p. 25 July 2005. Web. 29 Apr. 2010. http://www.usnews.com/usnews/culture/articles/050725/25read.htm.

"J. K. Rowling." Contemporary Authors. Gale Group, 28 Aug. 2009. Web. 27 Apr. 2010.

Kidd, Dustin. "Harry Potter and the Functions of Popular Culture." *The Journal of Popular Culture* 40.1 (2007): 69–89. Web. 29 Apr. 2010. http://www.glendale.edu/library/instruction/LibWorkshops/documents/HarryPotterCitExamples.pdf.

Kirch, Claire. "Guarding the Potter Secrets in Crawfordsville." *Publishers Weekly*. 5 July 2007. Web. 1 May 2010. http://www.publishersweekly.com/article/406654-Guarding_the_Potter_Secrets_in_Crawfordsville.php.

MacDonald, Joan Vos. *J. K. Rowling: Banned, Challenged, and Censored*. Berkeley Heights, NJ: Enslow Publishers, 2008. Print.

Maughan, Shannon. "The Race for Harry Potter." *Publishers Weekly*. 15 Feb. 1999. Web. 1 May 2010. http://www.publishersweekly.com/article/425179-The_Race_for_Harry_Potter.php.

———. "Potter's U.S. Publication Pushed Up." *Publishers Weekly*. 5 Apr. 1999. Web. 1 May 2010. http://www.publishersweekly.com/article/415062-Potter_s_U_S_Publication_Pushed_Up.php.

———. "The Harry Potter Halo." *Publishers Weekly*. 19 July 1999. Web. 1 May 2010. http://www.publishersweekly.com/article/429256-The_Harry_Potter_Halo.php.

Milliot, Jim, and Shannon Maughan. "Harry Potter IV: 'Goblet of Fire' Sparks Controversy." *Publishers Weekly*. 3 July 2000. Web. 1 May 2010. http://www.publishersweekly.com/article/414601-PW_Harry_Potter_IV_Goblet_of_Fire_Sparks_Controversy.php.

Mutter, John, and Jim Milliot. "Harry Potter and the Weekend of Fiery Sales." *Publishers Weekly*. 17 July 2000. Web. 1 May 2010. http://www.publishersweekly.com/article/ 424209-PW_Harry_Potter_and_the_Weekend_of_Fiery_Sales.php.

Nelson, Sara. "We've Got Harry's Number." *Publishers Weekly*. 4 Apr. 2005. Web. 1 May 2010. http://www.publishersweekly.com/article/430947-We_ve_Got_Harry_s_Number.php.

"New Heights for Harry." *Publishers Weekly*. 17 Apr. 2000. Web. 1 May 2010. http://www.publishersweekly.com/article/428292-PW_New_Heights_For_Harry.php.

"Order of the Phoenix Debut Smashes Records." *Publishers Weekly*. 30 June 2003. Web. 1 May 2010. http://www.publishersweekly.com/article/417841-Order_of_the_Phoenix_Debut_Smashes_Records.php.

Smith, Dinitia. "The *Times* Plans a Children's Best-Seller

List." *New York Times*. 24 June 2000. Web. 28 Apr. 2010. the-times-plans-a-children-s-best-seller-list.

Spartz, Emerson, ed. "About Us." *MuggleNet*. 2010. Web. 6 May 2010. http://mugglenet.com/aboutus.shtml.

Stevenson, Iain. "Harry Potter, Riding the Bullet and the Future of Books: Key Issues in the Anglophone Book Business." *Publishing Research Quarterly* 24.4 (2008): 277–284. *SpringerLink*. Web. 5 May 2010. http://www.springerlink.com/content/6mj42586348jt3h3/.

"USA TODAY's Best-Selling Books of Last 15 Years." *USA Today*. 30 Oct. 2008. Web. 1 May 2010. http://www.usatoday.com/life/books/news/2008-10-29-top-150-books_N.htm.

Vander Ark, Steve, ed. "History of The Harry Potter Lexicon." *The Harry Potter Lexicon*. 7 Aug. 2009. Web. 6 May 2010. http://hp-lexicon.org/help/lexicon.html.

Zeitchik, Steven. "Potter Around the World: English-Language Lessons, Piracy Fears and Juhannus." *Publishers Weekly*. 2 July 2003. Web. 1 May 2010. http://www.publishersweekly.com/article/432711-Potter_Around_the_World_English_Language_Lessons_Piracy_Fears_and_Juhannus.php.

Two

Loading the Canon

Harry Potter and Fanfiction

KATE MCMANUS

J. K. Rowling often receives credit for getting kids to read, but perhaps she should also be credited with getting kids to write. Have you ever wondered how Lily Evans and James Potter got together; the story behind Daphne Greengrass or Su Li, students in Harry Potter's class; or what the members of the Order of the Phoenix were up to during the first wizard war? All of these questions have fan-generated answers in the form of fanfiction on websites like fanfiction.net, mugglenet.com, and livejournal.com. Harry Potter fanfiction, original stories written by fans of Rowling's series, is an immensely popular phenomenon. Using familiar characters, settings, and plot devices, fanfiction authors write their own storylines, participating in the creation of Harry's world. The internet allows communities like fanfiction.net to flourish, with thousands of authors, stories, and readers generating conversation around fanfiction. Acting as a new form of dialogue between readers and texts, fanfiction is a place of speculation and imagination. Authors and readers are able to question and create possible futures in the wizarding world or construct what happened in the past. But perhaps most importantly, fanfiction creates a space in which readers and writers can analyze a text and place it firmly in the context of their own world. The vast world of fanfiction is often an overwhelming place for beginners, but as an experienced reader (and sometimes

writer) of fanfiction, I hope to guide you through, to introduce
the history and importance of fanfiction, and show how it often
enriches readers' experiences in the world that Rowling so deftly
created. This analysis is based on data and content from one of
the largest Harry Potter fanfiction archives, fanfiction.net, home
to many communities, not just Harry Potter. *Star Trek* and
Star Wars boast thriving communities, along with *Glee*, *Avatar*, and *Merlin*. While fanfiction communities began as small,
insular writing groups, the trend has steadily grown over the
past decade. Now there are over 645,000 Harry Potter stories
archived on fanfiction.net alone, and, due to fanfiction's anonymous nature, it is nearly impossible to say how many people are
writing or reading fanfiction.

While fanfiction seems like a relatively new phenomenon,
people have been rewriting and retelling stories throughout
history. According to Erica Christine Haugtvedt's 2009 thesis, "*Harry Potter* and Fanfiction: Filling in the Gaps," Virgil's
Aeneid is a rewrite of the Iliad and Odyssey stories by Homer.
The *Aeneid* parallels the *Iliad* and the *Odyssey* but follows the
Greek heroes as they flee Troy and find Rome (Haugtvedt 5).
This is an ancient example of fanfiction, for though the *Aeneid*
mirrors the Greek epic, it serves a different purpose, written for the glorification of Rome. Likewise, stories change in
the retelling. An excellent example is the seemingly traditional
Robin Hood legend. As Stephen Knight argues in his book,
Robin Hood: A Mythic Biography, what began as a story about
a medieval yeoman who robbed from the rich and gave to the
poor changed and evolved for an increasingly romantic audience. Robin became a Saxon man defying Norman invaders,
then a wronged nobleman who lost his lands to the evil sheriff
and took to the forest to exact revenge. In later legends, he goes
on crusades with King Richard. Maid Marian, Little John, and
Friar Tuck, characters we see as central to the legend of the Lincoln Green, were all later additions to the tales (Knight). There
are more examples, of course, most recently, E. L. James's *Fifty
Shades of Grey*. This trilogy began as a lengthy Twilight fanfiction that the author later rewrote as an original story. Other
examples include *Wide Sargasso Sea*, by Jean Rhys, which tells
the story of Bertha Rochester, Mr. Rochester's first wife in *Jane*

Eyre. Another retelling of *Jane Eyre* is the 1938 novel *Rebecca* by Daphne du Maurier. *Rebecca* follows the story of the second Mrs. de Winter. She marries Maxim de Winter without knowing quite what she is getting into and returns with him to Manderley. In that sinister house, she is confronted with the past, echoing the scenario Charlotte Brontë leads us into in *Jane Eyre.* More recently, Seth Grahame-Smith's *Pride and Prejudice and Zombies*, which places zombies in the beloved tale of romantic misunderstanding, drew from Jane Austen's classic text and added horror elements. Before you shout, "Are the shades of Pemberley to be thus polluted?" I would urge you to consider the novel's purpose. Perhaps Grahame-Smith wants to introduce this classic novel to an audience more interested in cult classics, which *Pride and Prejudice and Zombies* has become. It's fanfiction—published fanfiction. These examples illustrate the historically ubiquitous act of taking a story and rewriting it on different terms to serve a different purpose.

Even with this historical precedent, however, recent fanfiction has raised questions regarding copyright law. Fans fear lawyers like they fear Death Eaters, hoping they will not swoop in and take away everything writers have worked to create. However, as Rachel Vaughn points out in her essay, "Harry Potter and Experimental Use of Copyrighted Material: A Proposed Exception for Fan Works," "lawyers believe that fandom activity is not a big concern in the realm of copyright law" (28). Indeed, most fanfiction falls under "fair use" laws. In her 2011 law review, Stacey M. Lantagne argues that fair use is judged by a four-factor test defined by the US Supreme Court. While flexible enough to protect the original copyright without stifling creativity, the four factors require 1) an examination of whether or not the work in question is for educational purposes, 2) an understanding of the exact nature of the copyrighted work, 3) an analysis of the amount of the original work used in the parody or fan-based work, and 4) an assessment of whether or not the fan-based work decreases the value of the copyrighted material. Lantagne also argues for attention to be paid to the moral and immoral elements of the law (Lantagne 3). While copyright infringement is certainly punishable, it is not usually seen as immoral. To complicate matters further, there "has been no true

case evaluating [fanfiction] under a fair use analysis" (Lantagne
4). She argues that there can be no blanket statement made to
cover all fanfiction. Lantagne briefly outlines a history of copyright laws in the United States, pointing out,

> while the more immediate and obvious beneficiary of
> copyright law is the copyright holder who collects roy-
> alties for his or her work, the copyright holder is not
> supposed to be—and was never intended to be—the pri-
> mary beneficiary of the law. Rather, the primary bene-
> ficiary was meant to be the general public, who would
> benefit from the rich creative society expected to result
> from the encouragement of artists. (Lantagne 2)

I would argue that those creating fanfiction (who make no
money from their efforts) are only adding to this "rich creative
society."

Although fanfiction is new material based on an old text, it is
often seen as transformative and therefore does not always interfere with published works. Rachel L. Stroude argues in her law
commentary, "Complimentary Creation: Protecting Fan Fiction
as Fair Use," that fanfiction is participatory: readers comment
on the original stories using their own fiction, and their work
should, therefore, be judged as parody. Fanfiction meets a need
that the original work creates. Effectively, fanfiction does the
same work as a parody, in that both genres comment on and
criticize the original text while simultaneously mimicking it.
Writers can create elaborate backstories to set up what happens
in the original work, also referred to as the "canon" in the fanfiction universe. There are many stories that conjure the founding of Hogwarts or a romantic relationship between Professor
Albus Dumbledore and Gellert Grindelwald, for example. If
there is a hint of something in the canon, chances are a fan has
identified it and elaborated on it. When posting a story to a website like fanfiction.net, many fanfiction writers leave a disclaimer
stating that they do not own the characters; they are not making any profit off their story and therefore shouldn't be sued.
However, there is a difference between this participatory work
and reference works, like that of *The Harry Potter Lexicon*. *The
Harry Potter Lexicon* (*HP Lexicon*) is an unofficial, fan-made

website that provides a point of reference for characters, spells, atlases, magical creatures, and anything else you could wish to know about Harry's world. While the *HP Lexicon* is the ultimate internet guide for any fan, the authors got themselves into legal trouble by attempting to publish the website in the form of a book, even after Rowling announced her intention to publish her own definitive encyclopedia. Warner Brothers acted quickly, blocking publication of the *Lexicon*.

Attempting to take legal action against fanfiction authors who make no attempt to monetize their work is difficult, and not just because of the sheer number of stories published. Discouraging fan activity would be like cutting off one's nose to spite one's face. Since Rowling has said that she does not plan to continue the series past *Deathly Hallows*, it seems unlikely that she would be upset that fan communities are maintaining the hype in the absence of a new installment, keeping the community excited and engaged about the boy wizard and the world in which he lives.

Rowling herself acknowledges the existence of the fan communities she has inadvertently spawned. In an online chat in 2000, she told a fan, "I have read some [fan stories] and I've been very flattered to see how absorbed people are in the world" (Barnes and Noble). In a 2005 interview, she went on to say, "I think people will continue to theorize about the characters even at the end of Book Seven because some people are very interested in certain characters whose past lives are not germane to the plot, they're not central to the story, so there is big leeway there still for fanfiction" (*Leaky Cauldron* interview). Though Rowling could not possibly have gone into such detail in seven books, she can allow her fans to do so. That is not to say she completely sanctions all fanfiction. A spokesperson for the Christopher Little Literary Agency (the agency through which Rowling is published) said that Rowling hopes "that the stories were not obscene and were credited to the author and not to J. K. Rowling" (Waters). Given the fact that most authors leave ratings and warnings about the content of their stories, Rowling's concern, while valid, is somewhat mitigated by this practice.

Rowling has even gotten in on the fun of canon expansion herself. Just type "J. K. Rowling Prequel" into your search engine and it appears, like magic: in 2008, Rowling auctioned off a story for charity and then allowed the British bookstore chain Waterstone to publish it on their website. Though it is no longer posted there, the intrepid fan can unearth it fairly easily. It is an eight-hundred-word misadventure, told through the eyes of a Muggle policeman who has apprehended two young men, James Potter and Sirius Black. After a brief and cheeky discussion, the two wizards (unbeknownst to the police constables) see something at the end of the alley: "James and Sirius had shouted something incomprehensible, and the beams from the headlights had moved. . . . The policemen wheeled around, then staggered backwards. Three men were flying—actually FLYING—up the alley on broomsticks—and at the same moment, the police car was rearing up on its back wheels" ("Prequel"). The two wizards escape, as do the policemen. It's a funny tale, and audiences will treasure it for years to come. Rowling also says that she plans to publish an encyclopedia in the future, which will hold all of the backstories and facts that the reader cannot glean from the seven published books. Almost certainly, this will inspire more fanfiction, as fans put even more pieces of the giant puzzle together and strive to fill in even more gaps.

The world of fandom does not restrict itself to fanfiction either. Over the years, we have seen Wizard Rock bands (Wrock), puppet shows (The Potter Puppet Pals), three full-blown Harry Potter musicals (by theater company/friends Starkid Potter), and countless examples of fanart. Recently, Rowling also added to this community with another gem, Pottermore.com. *Pottermore* is a way for fans to relive the books again, chapter by chapter, finding the magic, learning spells, brewing potions, competing for House points, and learning backstory to what exists in the novels. It's part role playing, part wish fulfillment.

Fanfiction provides a creative place for speculation and conversation, not only between the readers/writers and the text but also between the writers of fanfiction and the readers of their stories. Fanfiction authors crave feedback, and many ask readers to point out mistakes or to give constructive criticism. Most have "beta readers," informal editors, to help catch everything from plot holes to spelling and grammatical errors. It is a safe community for experimentations with style, characters, and plot. Excellent examples of this type of canonical speculation are all the stories about Professor Severus Snape. Throughout the first six books of the series, Rowling never makes it clear to Harry (or to the reader) where Snape's loyalties lie. Thus, when Snape kills Dumbledore at the end of *Half-Blood Prince*, theories about the potions master spread like wildfire. Was he evil, good, or just desperate to stay alive? Many fanfiction authors explored possible motives and outcomes to justify Snape's actions, for better or for worse. There are even stories predating the publication of *Deathly Hallows* that place Lily and Snape in the same circle of friends. This was an exciting time to read fanfiction to some degree independent of the text. Writing fanfiction before the "canon law" of the text was complete gave authors time to explore storylines that had not been closed yet, and Snape, brave or cowardly, good or bad, was just one example.

Another excellent example of this exploration surrounds Dumbledore. In October of 2007, a few months after *Deathly Hallows* was released, Rowling confirmed at a conference that Dumbledore was homosexual and had an intellectual and romantic relationship with the wizard Grindelwald (a wizard Dumbledore later defeated in an epic battle that the seven Harry Potter books reference but do not describe). In their article, "Writing Harry's World: Children Co-Authoring Hogwarts," Ernest L. Bond and Nancy L. Michelson note that fanfiction writers immediately began constructing stories about the two men. Fans had a gut reaction to the news of their beloved headmaster's sexuality, and many responded by writing fiction, either ignoring the announcement or by going back and creating a relationship between Dumbledore and Grindelwald. Perhaps reading or writing these stories helped some authors understand the relationship that Rowling said was present, between lines she had already written. Rowling may never actually spell out the details of the relationship beyond saying it was romantic, but fans can certainly theorize about the progression from friends to lovers.

Authors also sometimes write original characters (known as OCs). While these characters can be interesting and dynamic, they often fall under the category of "Mary Sue" (or "Gary Stu") characters. Mary Sues turn up when authors more or less write themselves into the wizarding world as prominent characters. A

Mary Sue is usually brilliant but clumsy, pretty without knowing it, and she typically falls in love with a major character.
Because they have become cliché, stories centering on Mary Sues
are often dismissed and have very few reviews or hits. Yet Mary
Sues can be indicative of a trend in fanfiction. If fanfiction is a
desire to rewrite a beloved story, Mary Sues are a literal version
of this wish, and nearly everyone in the community has a different view of the trend. Fanfiction author orange_crushed, who
writes Remus Lupin and Sirius Black stories primarily on live-
journal.com, argues:

> Aside from the pure wish fulfillment or ego-driven
> aspect of the Mary Sues, there's a deeper phenomenon—
> in that these are primarily young women writing them-
> selves into texts in a very specific way. They're inserting
> themselves into the story as powerful individuals: physi-
> cally beautiful or stunningly intelligent, tough, cool, a
> role model, the love of someone's life. The story revolves
> around them. And for a lot of these texts that are so pop-
> ular for fanfiction, they're inserting a major female (self)
> character into a story that revolves around male protag-
> onists (Harry Potter, Star Trek, Lord of the Rings, etc.).

She goes on to argue that the Mary Sue phenomenon developed
not from a lack of strong female characters in the Harry Potter series specifically but rather because the genre of fantasy/sci-
ence fiction suffers more generally from a lack of strong female
characters. For these young authors, inserting themselves into a
story comes from a need to see an identifiable character. Author
Mrs. Tater, who writes mainly Remus Lupin and Nymphadora
Tonks stories, posted to both fanfiction.net and livejournal.com:

> It's similar to why people role-play, they like to lose and
> improve themselves in a fictional world they love in a
> more concrete way than just daydreaming. Something
> about writing a fantasy makes it more real. But that's not
> totally it, because Mary Sues aren't necessarily self-insert
> characters; sometimes they're just an example of inex-
> perienced writers not knowing how to create strong but
> believable female lead characters! They want to write

about powerful characters that are worthy of the original book's hero, so they give them all sorts of skills and abilities, when really that's not what good characterization is about at all.

Although the official Harry Potter series is complete, Rowling left plenty of room for fans to work in their own interpretations and ideas. In some areas, what is "canon" is debatable. Many people feel that only what is in the novel can be considered canon. Yet Rowling has extensive notes on characters that she wanted to elaborate on but, due to space or pacing, ultimately could not. (This is especially true in the first three books, which are heavily edited in comparison to the final four.) When interviewed by the BBC in 2001, Rowling gave readers a glimpse at the vast amount of knowledge she held about her fictional world:

> It's just stuff I need to know for my own pleasure—partly for my own pleasure and partly because, I like reading a book where I have the sense that the author knows everything. They might not be telling me everything, but you have that confidence that the author really knows everything . . . the name of everyone in Harry's year and all these little symbols mean what house they're in, how magical they are, what their parentage is, because I needed this later for the Death Eaters and so on, and the various allegiances that will be set up within the school. ("Harry Potter and Me")

Have you ever heard of Su Li? She's a Ravenclaw in Harry's class. Daphne Greengrass (who is mentioned once in *Order of the Phoenix*) is a Slytherin in Harry's year, but her younger sister, Astoria, eventually marries Draco Malfoy. Audrey, whose last name we do not know, marries Percy Weasley. Luna Lovegood marries Rolf Scamander (whose grandfather, Newt Scamander, is the fictional author of *Fantastic Beasts and Where to Find Them*, which Rowling published for Comic Relief in 2001). Characters such as these create a complicated conversation surrounding what is "canon," because Su, Astoria, Audrey, and Rolf do not appear in the books, but they are discussed by

Rowling in interviews and depicted on family trees and the class list she released in 2001. Though these characters do not have nearly as many fan-generated stories as Harry does on fanfiction.net (Su has 28; Astoria, 1,681; Audrey, 261, and Rolf, 163, compared to Harry's 176,698 as of June 2013), authors are still investing time and effort creating backstories for characters who have no bearing upon the plot of the books. Canon or not, these characters' presence in fan-generated stories is illustrative of the level of engagement fanfiction authors experience with Rowling's world.

Not every fan-generated story, however, is written according to Rowling's imagination. "Alternate Universe" or "AU" fanfiction is a marker indicating the author is taking the characters and either radically changing their world or placing them in a different universe—on the Starship Enterprise or in the tenements of Dickensian London, for example. This is the forum to explore the "what-ifs" that readers constantly ask of the text—what if Hermione Granger had married Harry? What if Cedric Diggory had survived the graveyard and lived to tell the tale? "AU" could also indicate a radically different relationship pairing. One popular relationship or "ship" of this variety is of Draco Malfoy and Hermione. Draco and Hermione definitely do not see eye to eye in the books. (He insults her Muggle parentage in *Harry Potter and the Chamber of Secrets* by calling her a Mudblood and later makes fun of Rubeus Hagrid, causing Hermione to slap him in the face). It would seem that this would never be conducive to a healthy relationship. Yet fans find or create situations that result in romance for the pair. The same thing happens with Sirius Black and Remus Lupin. While Lupin has a canon love interest in the pink-haired Nymphadora Tonks, many authors choose to pair Lupin with his childhood friend Sirius (incidentally, Tonks's cousin). Bond and Michelson argue that these homosexual pairings, colloquially referred to as "slash," are not necessarily gratuitous sex (though some of them are) but more an exploration of same-gender relationships. (Another famous example of a same-gender, non-canon ship with a large following is Draco and Harry.) Apart from Dumbledore, who does not overtly display or discuss his sexuality, there are no examples of homosexual characters in the Harry Potter books. Bond and

Michelson argue that writing slash is a way "of seeing self and the world co-constructed, as people insert themselves and others into various storylines" (324). If fans do not see a character or a situation that reflects their reality, they will simply change the circumstances until they do.

In the nineteen-year gap between the final chapter in *Deathly Hallows* and the much-discussed epilogue, fanfiction writers like to speculate about exactly how Ginny and Ron Weasley, Harry, and Hermione made their return to King's Cross station to load their children onto the Hogwarts Express. Rowling herself cleared up a few things in a live, online chat in 2007, just a few days after the seventh book was released:

> Hermione began her post-Hogwarts career at the Department for the Regulation and Control of Magical Creatures where she was instrumental in greatly improving life for house-elves and their ilk. She then moved (despite her jibe to Scrimgeour) to the Department of Magical Law Enforcement where she was a progressive voice who ensured the eradication of oppressive, pro-pureblood laws. (Bloomsbury Webchat 2007)

Rowling also briefly outlined Harry's career as the head of the Auror Office, Ron's at "Weasley's Wizard Wheezes," and Ginny's as a professional Quidditch player for the Holyhead Harpies, ending with a position as senior Quidditch correspondent for the *Daily Prophet*. Some fan-generated stories during this period offer insight into Hermione's recovery of her parents from Australia, glimpses of how the Weasley family copes with the loss of Fred, and, of course, the rebuilding of the wizarding world after the second war and the Battle of Hogwarts. With so much time and so many characters to play with, it would be more remarkable if fanfiction did not exist. Rowling has only given us a glimpse into this world she has created. There is a sense of realistic continuity, and when Rowling makes an announcement about her characters (Dumbledore is gay, the professional future of the Golden Trio, etc.) her fans take note. So much of the wizarding world takes place offstage, in Rowling's mind, and it is this offstage realm that fanfiction attempts to develop.

This conversation allows the reader to respond and express opinions they would not be able to do, adding their own layers to the text (Schaffner 616). People who do not read fanfiction are sometimes quick to judge it as self-indulgent and merely a copy of something more popular. I believe they are missing the point. Fanfiction, at its heart, takes what the text says and transforms it, bringing forward subtext and pushing the boundaries of textuality. It is about writers playing with a fictional universe, changing it to reflect their own views, and inventing something new. Fanfiction requires an in-depth knowledge of the characters involved. It is a great enhancement to the text, there to satisfy the curious. Best of all, the fanfiction world is a place to obsess over the boy who lived (and the characters who surround him) with a community of fans asking some of the same questions—and speculating together about the answers in fictions of our own. Fanfiction is hardly a new phenomenon, but with the advent of the internet, it has expanded and become an interesting topic for debate. Between the lines of the copyright laws, the lightheartedness and creativity that this community of fans constructs can ultimately add new contours to texts we thought were completed.

Note

I would like the thank www.fanfiction.net for their dedication to fans, www.hp-lexicon.com for the extensive amount of information available, and www.Accio-Quote.org for their collection of interviews and webchats.

Works Cited

Bond, Ernest L., and Nancy L. Michelson. "Writing Harry's World: Children Co-Authoring Hogwarts." In *Critical Perspectives on Harry Potter*, ed. Elizabeth E. Heilman. New York: Routledge, 2009. 309–327. Print.

Deahl, Rachel. "E. L. James and the Case of Fan Fiction." *Publishers Weekly*. 13 Jan. 2012. Web. 29 July 2012. http://www.

publishersweekly.com/pw/by-topic/book-news/page-to-screen/article/50188-e-l-james-and-the-case-of-fan-fiction.html.

Haugtvedt, Erica Christine. "*Harry Potter* and Fanfiction: Filling in the Gaps." Thesis. U of Ohio, 2009. Print.

Knight, Stephen. *Robin Hood: A Mythic Biography.* Ithaca: Cornell UP, 2003. Print.

Lantagne, Stacey M. "The Better Angels of Our Fanfiction: The Need for True and Logical Precedent." *Hastings Communications and Entertainment Law Journal* 33 (2011): 159. Print.

Rowling, J. K. "Barnes and Noble & Yahoo Chat." Webchat transcript. 20 October 2000. Web. 6 May 2010. http://www.accio-quote.org/articles/2000/1000-livechat-barnesnoble.html.

Rowling, J. K. "Harry Potter and Me." BBC interview. 28 Dec. 2001. Web. 6 May 2010. http://www.accio-quote.org/articles/2001/1201-bbc-hpandme.htm.

———. "The Leaky Cauldron and MuggleNet interview Joanne Kathleen Rowling: Part One." *The Leaky Cauldron.* 16 July 2005. Web. 6 May 2010. http://www.accio-quote.org/articles/2005/0705-tlc_mugglenet-anelli-1.htm.

———. Interview. Webchat transcript via Bloomsbury Books, London. 30 July 2007. Web. 6 May 2010. http://www.bloomsbury.com/harrypotter/default.aspx?sec=3.

———. "Prequel." April 2008. Web. 1 May 2010. http://crushable.com/entertainment/the-harry-potter-prequel-read-it-here/.

Schaffner, Becca. "In Defense of Fanfiction." *Horn Book* 85 (2009): 613–618. Print.

Stroude, Rachel L. "Complimentary Creation: Protecting Fan Fiction as Fair Use." *Marquette Intellectual Property Law Review* (2010): 14. Print.

Vaughn, Rachel. "Harry Potter and Experimental Use of Copyrighted Material: A Proposed Exception for Fan Works." 2008. Web. 30 April 2010. http://works.bepress.com/cgi/viewcontent.cgi?article=1001&context=sensibleip.

Waters, Darren. "Rowling Backs Potter Fan Fiction." *BBC News.* 27 May 2004. Web. 28 April 2008. http://news.bbc.co.uk/2/hi/entertainment/3753001.stm.

Three

The Simulated World of Harry Potter

KYLE BUBB

After J. K. Rowling published *Harry Potter and the Philoso-pher's Stone* in the United Kingdom in June 1997, the popularity of Harry Potter spread throughout the UK and the United States like wildfire, spawning six sequels, eight film adaptations, and, on June 18, 2010, The Wizarding World of Harry Potter, a theme park in Universal Parks and Resorts in Orlando, Florida, that recreates significant aspects and locales of Rowling's fictional Harry Potter universe. Though the theme park undoubtedly exists primarily as a tourist attraction, it also serves as a simulacrum, a simulated re-creation of Rowling's novels, and as a virtual reality that blurs the distinction between the real and the unreal for fans of the Harry Potter series.

Universal Orlando Resort is large, with two full-sized theme parks inside: Universal's Islands of Adventure and Universal Studios: Florida. Within these two parks are numerous themed areas, or subtheme parks. Among the subtheme parks in Universal's Islands of Adventure are Jurassic Park, The Lost Continent, Seuss Landing, and The Wizarding World of Harry Potter. The Wizarding World contains three main attractions and two minor attractions for visiting tourists. "Harry Potter and the Forbidden Journey" allows guests to "make [their] way through the classrooms and corridors of Hogwarts [School of Witchcraft and Wizardry]. Then soar above the castle grounds on a groundbreaking new ride that lets [guests] join Harry Potter and his friends on an unforgettably thrilling adventure." Meanwhile,

"Flight of the Hippogriff" teaches "the proper way to approach a Hippogriff before [taking] off on a family-friendly coaster that spirals and dives around the pumpkin patch, and swoops past Hagrid's hut." Finally, there is the "Dragon Challenge," on which riders will "need the courage of a Triwizard Tournament champion as [they] climb aboard one of two ferocious dragons that twist, loop and nearly collide in a high-speed, intertwining roller coaster chase across the sky" (Universal Orlando). The Wizarding World also includes the Hogwarts "Frog Choir" and a "Spirit Rally" for the Triwizard Tournament.

For fans of the Harry Potter series, the attractions literally bring the novels, and even the film adaptations, to life. Rather than imagining what the inside of Hogwarts looks like, visitors to Wizarding World can experience firsthand the magic of Hogwarts and many of the other fictional venues in the Harry Potter series. Fans no longer have to rely on descriptions provided by the novel or the artistic visuals provided by the films. They can actually step into the fantastic world that was once merely a fiction.

This Wizarding World of Harry Potter can be described as what postmodern theorist Jean Baudrillard terms a "simulacrum." As a simulacrum, the theme park has become an entity that is "hyperreal." In their book *Postmodern Theory: Critical Interrogations*, authors Steven Best and Douglas Kellner explain Baudrillard's concept of simulacra. They write, "We are now . . . in a new era of simulation in which computerization, information processing, media, cybernetic control systems, and the organization of society according to simulation codes and models replace production as the organizing principle of society" (118). Baudrillard argues that this new era has brought about technology that simulates what once was material. Best and Kellner explain, "the postmodern era of simulations by contrast is an era of information and signs governed by models, codes, and cybernetics" (118). In other words, in today's society, *models* of the real, from sources like books, films, or the internet, replace the "real."

Furthermore, Baudrillard explains, "models and codes become the primary determinants of social experience. In a society of simulations, the models or codes structure experience and erode distinctions between the model and the real" (119). Baudrillard claims that once these simulations or models of the real are established, they replace the real versions of what they originally represented. Simply put, they become the new real. But Baudrillard has a term for this new real. This process of replacing the real with a simulation is called "hyperreality," or, as Best and Kellner explain, "the blurring of distinctions between the real and unreal in which the prefix 'hyper' signifies more real than real. . . . When the real is no longer simply given . . . but is artificially (re)produced as 'real,' it becomes not unreal, or surreal, but realer-than-real" (119). The hyperreal is the model that replaces the real. Society then uses this simulation of the real, rather than the original source that it represents, as a source of information.

The Wizarding World of Harry Potter, this simulation of a fictional universe, is a tangible example of Baudrillard's theory of simulacrum and hyperreality, and the attraction "Harry Potter and the Forbidden Journey" exemplifies this. When guests begin the "Forbidden Journey," projections of characters from the Harry Potter series refer to the tourists as Muggles. Using this term transforms the participants into an element of the series, instead of keeping them distanced from it as fans might be while merely reading the books or watching the films. In The Wizarding World, it is as if the guests' presence actually contributes to the whole that is Harry Potter. Thus, while they are guests there, the theme park becomes a simulation of the reality that is the Harry Potter universe, making the guests themselves participants in this once-fictional universe. They drink butterbeer on the streets of Hogsmeade, wander past the Hogwarts Express, and let their wands choose them in Ollivander's shop— all significant components of the series.

The Wizarding World extracts the fictional aspect of Harry Potter, making it a lived reality for guests. In "Harry Potter and the Forbidden Journey," guests make their way through the classrooms and corridors of Hogwarts. Among the most memorable details of the school are the moving and talking portraits, the Sorting Hat, Professor Albus Dumbledore's office, and the Quidditch pitch, all of which are present and interactive. The sensory, visual, and auditory interactions with these parts of the attraction allow visitors to physically become part of this world—they are embedded in the reality it creates. Guests overhear a conversation between Hermione Granger, Ron Weasley, and Harry; watch the sorting into Houses; and, while strapped into roller coaster seats, fly their brooms around the school grounds. Since The Wizarding World momentarily *replaces* the fictional universe of Harry Potter, guests of the park experience something more real than fiction, because the park incorporates the reality of their lives with the fictional world of Harry Potter. This creates an experience that is more than real—it is hyperreal.

Interestingly, that which makes The Wizarding World of Harry Potter hyperreal is also what makes it not quite hyperreal—not quite a conventional simulacrum. Common examples of simulacra are paintings, portraits, and photographs. Each of these things is a simulation, a re-creation of a tangible, physical thing; a painting often re-creates a place or an object, a portrait re-creates a person, and photographs do the same through a different medium. There are also cases of further simulation, for example, of a photograph taken of a painting. In this case, there are two existing simulacra: the painting of the original object or location and the photograph of the painting. The key, however, is that each simulacrum is a replacement of something tangible (i.e., a place, an object, a painting).

The difference between these examples of simulacra and the simulacrum of The Wizarding World is that the theme park is simulating something that was never real to begin with: a series of novels. Yes, it is true that the Harry Potter books are obviously tangible objects: they are books—they are part of our reality. However, the simulacrum of a book would likely be another edition of that book, or, more simply, the mass production or replication of that book. In these cases, the various editions of a book or the mass production of it are the simulacra, because they are representing the original version of it. This is not the case with Wizarding World. Instead, it simulates the ideas within the book—the fiction of the book—an immaterial reality that cannot be touched. Harry, Ron, and Hermione are fictional characters. The entire sport of Quidditch is fictional. Dumbledore's office is not a real place. They are created in Rowling's mind, and while these ideas may become real to readers when they envision the descriptions from the page in their minds, the fact remains that these are concepts, constructs that are not tangibly real. Therefore, the attractions in The Wizarding World that simulate specific aspects of the novels do not fit the typical definition of the simulacrum. They are not quite hyperreal, because they are not *more real* than *real*; they are actually *more real* than the *unreal* or a deliberate attempt to make the unreal, the imaginary, into something tangibly real. By doing this, The Wizarding World of Harry Potter has effectively blurred the distinction between reality and fiction, bringing Harry Potter to life in a physical way that had not been possible prior to the creation of the theme park.

The Wizarding World isn't the first theme park to blur the distinction between the real and the unreal. In "Disneyworld Company," Baudrillard describes Disney in a similar way:

> [The] Disney enterprise goes beyond the imaginary. Disney, the precursor, the grand initiator of the imaginary as virtual reality, is now in the process of capturing all the real world to integrate it into its synthetic universe, in the form of a vast "reality show" where reality itself becomes a spectacle . . . where the real becomes a theme park. The transfusion of the real is like a blood transfusion, except that here it is a transfusion of real blood into the exsanguine universe of virtuality. After the prostitution of the imaginary, here is now the hallucination of the real in its ideal and simplified version.

Here, Baudrillard argues that by creating theme parks like Disneyland and Disney World, the Disney enterprise captured the imagined world of its fictional stories and literally blended that imaginary world into the reality of the world we live in. No longer were people distinctly separated by media like books and films from Disney's fantasy worlds; instead, with the creation of these interactive theme parks, visitors to the parks would become a part of those fantasies through the parks' attractions.

The processes of The Wizarding World seem to closely mirror Baudrillard's theories about the Disney enterprise. For example, like the Disney enterprise, The Wizarding World attempts to "capture the real world." In other words, it attempts to capture fans of the Harry Potter series and then integrate them into

its "synthetic universe," the simulated models and physical re-
creations of the series throughout the theme park. Furthermore,
The Wizarding World becomes Baudrillard's "vast 'reality show'
where reality itself becomes a spectacle." The attractions in the
park, then, are more than "a sight to see"; they become, instead,
a *reason* to see, a means to participate in the unreal reality created by The Wizarding World of Harry Potter.

Like Baudrillard's analogy of the Disney enterprise as a
blood transfusion, the simulated reality of The Wizarding World
is created by making something that never was real into something real. (Hence the analogy of transferring real blood into
something that is bloodless.) By creating a real-life simulacrum
from aspects of a fictional series, The Wizarding World reaches
what Baudrillard describes as "virtuality." It simulates something that isn't real itself, but, by simulating that which isn't
real, The Wizarding World *appears* real. This apparent reality is,
really, what it all comes down to—why we spend thousands of
dollars and travel thousands of miles just to spend a few hours
in this virtual reality. It is to reify: to make the fantastic into the
tangible, to make the fictional into the material, and to make the
unreal into the real. Through this reification, the human imagination thrives. It allows the heart of creativity—storytelling,
imagining, believing, wondering, and proposing—to survive, to
live in previously unimaginable ways, ways that our postmodern world makes possible.

In doing this, The Wizarding World effectively serves as a
simulacrum, a physical simulation, of the fictional Harry Potter universe. It isn't quite the hyperreality proposed by Baudrillard in his theories, but it is, in fact, something more, something
beyond the hyperreal. It is virtuality. Similar to the way Baudrillard describes the Disney enterprise, The Wizarding World
serves as a simulation of the unreal, of that which doesn't tangibly exist, leaving tourists caught between reality and fantasy—
believing the unbelievable, even if it is only until the ride is over.

Works Cited

Baudrillard, Jean. "Disneyworld Company." *Liberation. The
European Graduate School*. 1996. Web. 23 Nov. 2010.

Best, Steven, and Douglas Kellner. "Baudrillard en Route to Postmodernity." *Postmodern Theory: Critical Interrogations*. New York, NY: Guilford, 1991. 111–145. Print.

Universal Orlando. *2-Park Map: Universal Orlando Resort.* Orlando: Universal Orlando, 2010. Print.

Four

The Wizard, the Muggle, and the Other

Postcolonialism in Harry Potter

HANNAH LAMB

J. K. Rowling's Harry Potter novels have become an international cultural phenomenon. She has "500 million English copies in print . . . [and] there are likely twice as many copies combined in . . . sixty-seven languages" (see chapter 1 in this volume). Each installment of the series became even more popular than the last, with the final novel selling more than 8.3 million copies in the United States within the first twenty-four hours of availability (chapter 1 in this volume). Her publishing and cinematic successes have made Rowling the richest woman in the United Kingdom, trumping even the queen (Bryfonski 20). In a postcolonial, increasingly globalized world, a distinctly British cultural product pervading, indeed dominating, global literary markets leads to the question of the politics within the children's books.

The books, set in Britain and written by a British author, offer a political allegory, even according to Rowling herself, who described the series as a "'political metaphor'. . .there are 'quite consciously overtones of Nazi Germany, there are also associations with other situations. . . . I wanted Harry to leave our world and find exactly the same problems in the wizarding world. So you have the intent to impose a hierarchy, you have bigotry, and this notion of purity'" (Bryfonski 12). While Rowling envisions

the magical world of her creation as analogous to a rejection of
fascist and racist ideologies, another opposing interpretation
also arises. All of the wizards of Harry Potter, even those whom
Rowling does not brand distinctly evil, participate in a collective
nostalgia for a past British colonial identity, one lost in a postcolonial world. The British wizards' relations with wizards of
other nationalities display their discomfort with entities outside
of British identity. Further, without providing a strict parallel,
Rowling's varied wizards' relations with the Muggle, or nonwizarding, world resonate with the imperial British attitudes
toward their colonial subjects. The magical characters of the
series represent a broad colonial spectrum, all harkening back to
an age with a distinctly British-fixed identity.

Although many wizards maintain problematic relations with
the Other, in the form of Muggles or nonhuman magical creatures, Rowling does offer an overt critique of racism. A con-
ception of wizarding blood maps onto race within the novels.
Pure-blood means, "a witch or wizard of 'pure' wizarding ancestry, without any Muggle ancestors. . . .Pure-blood families are
extremely rare, and thus are interrelated; given the limited selection of potential pure-blood spouses, purebloods are getting
rarer as their members either become more liberal and marry
out" (*Harry Potter Lexicon*). There are half-blood wizards, with
at least one wizarding parent and one Muggle parent or grand-
parent, such as Harry Potter himself, and Muggle-born wizards,
such as Hermione Granger, one of Harry's best friends, with no
wizarding ancestry (*Harry Potter Lexicon*). Blood-traitors, such
as Harry Potter's godfather Sirius Black, belong to pure-blood
families but do not believe in distinctions between wizards
(*Harry Potter Lexicon*). Some pure-blood wizards use terms
like Mudblood, implying dirty bloodlines, to refer to Muggle-
born wizards and assert their own superiority. On several occasions, Draco Malfoy calls Hermione a Mudblood, to the shock
of everybody present, for they "knew that 'Mudblood' was a
very offensive term for a witch or wizard of Muggle parentage"
(*Goblet of Fire* 122).

In the complexity of characters and their complicated histo-
ries woven throughout the increasingly lengthy series, Rowling
draws stark moral divisions between good and evil. She treats

as immoral those characters who believe in and act according to such bloodlines. The pure-blood families, continually represented by the Malfoys, who "prided themselves on being purebloods; in other words, they considered anyone of Muggle descent, like Hermione, second-class," are Harry's enemies throughout the novels (*Goblet of Fire* 102). The leader of the pure-blood movement, Lord Voldemort, reigned over the wizarding world, killing Muggles, Muggle-born wizards, and the wizards who support them, until his killing curse mysteriously backfired in an attempt to murder an infant Harry Potter. Through the character of Draco Malfoy, the reader learns about the other side of the wizarding world. In the fourth novel, the reader becomes aware of other wizarding schools, such as Durmstrang, described by Draco to Harry, Hermione, and Ron Weasley:

> Father actually considered sending me to Durmstrang rather than Hogwarts, you know. He knows the headmaster, you see. Well, you know his opinion of Dumbledore—the man's such a Mudblood lover—and Durmstrang doesn't admit that sort of riffraff. . . . Father says Durmstrang takes a far more sensible line than Hogwarts about the Dark Arts. Durmstrang students actually *learn* them, not just the defense rubbish we do. (*Goblet of Fire* 165)

Hogwarts only offers classes on the defense against the Dark Arts, not how to practice them, largely because the Dark Arts encompass the "unforgivable" curses, such as torture, mind control, or murder, that a wizard could commit (*Harry Potter Lexicon*). Draco acts as a mouthpiece for his parents' pure-blood views, rationalizing his racist ideology and his ambition to learn the Dark Arts as "sensible." Although Draco himself comes to represent a more complex version of evil, conflicted in the last novels in his duty to his pure-blood family, he and those on his side remain Harry's, and the reader's, enemies (Goldstein 75). The reader learns more of Voldemort's history with each installment, as each time he chooses evil and places himself firmly against the morality of Harry and his friends. Each novel but the third culminates in a battle between Harry and Voldemort; it is often good versus evil on a blatant level. Thus, the reader identifies, and most often sees, the wizarding world from the perspective of wizards such as Harry, enemy of Voldemort; Hermione, a Muggle-born witch; and the Weasleys, a wizarding family actively working against racist politics.

Although the central, continuing battle over the question of blood and purity offers an overt condemnation of racism, primarily through the depiction of Harry's enemies, the question of how far this tolerance extends arises. Harry and his cohorts respect and love Hermione; they never question her relation to them in terms of blood. And various critics such as Andrew Blake argue that "Hogwarts stands for a functioning multicultural society"; indeed, in their romantic relationships, all three main characters (Harry, Hermione, and Ron) pursue partners outside of their own nationality, as they "[live] in a multicultural community in which what the real world calls 'mixed-race relationships' are common" (83). Yet the novels' attempts at multiculturalism appear as superficial gestures when compared with the consistently racist treatment of Muggles, nonhuman magical creatures, and international wizards. The British wizards' treatment of international wizards displays their colonial attitudes toward unfamiliar, or "foreign," phenomena.

Goblet of Fire broadens the scope of the novels, allowing readers their first glimpse into the wizarding world outside of Britain and Hogwarts. Although, significantly, no character leaves Britain throughout the narrative (except as retold when they are back home), two major international wizarding events occur, bringing magical people from all over the globe to Britain. The single setting of Britain begins to emphasize the Anglocentric viewpoint of the novels. The Quidditch World Cup, the final match in the most popular wizarding sport, brings the question of international wizarding relations to the forefront. Ireland and Bulgaria are the two teams involved, establishing the apparent domination of Europe in the world of wizarding sports. Harry, traveling with his best friend's family, the Weasleys, overhears a conversation between two British government officials running the Cup:

"The Bulgarians are insisting we add another twelve seats to the Top Box."

"Oh is *that* what they're after?" said Bagman. "I thought the chap was asking to borrow a pair of tweezers. Bit of a strong accent." (90)

Before the reader ever meets a Bulgarian wizard, Ludo Bagman, the master of ceremonies at the Quidditch World Cup, emphasizes the thick accents of the Bulgarians, establishing their distance from the well-spoken English of the British. Bagman, portrayed as a brash former athlete past his prime yet still clinging to former Quidditch glory, connotes the vestiges of a Britisher's adherence to a linguistic superiority in a globalized world.

The mascots of the opposing teams further underlie the othering of non-British wizards. Arthur Weasley explains to Harry, "National teams bring creatures from their native land, you know, to put on a bit of a show" (*Goblet of Fire* 99). Harry becomes mesmerized as

a hundred veela were now gliding out onto the field. . . . Veela were women . . . the most beautiful women Harry had ever seen . . . except they weren't—they couldn't be—human. This puzzled Harry for a moment while he tried to guess what exactly they could be; what could make the skin shine moon-bright like that, or their white-gold hair fan out behind them without wind . . . but then the music started, and Harry stopped worrying about them not being human—in fact he stopped worrying about anything at all. The veela had started to dance, and Harry's mind had gone completely and blissfully blank. . . .And as the veela danced faster and faster, wild, half-formed thoughts started chasing through Harry's dazed mind . . .

"Harry what are you doing?" said Hermione's voice from a long way off. (103)

The veela glaringly represent an Orientalist representation of an Eastern woman, gyrating and captivating her British male audience. Harry's description of an unnumbered mass of women, "creatures" from a "native land," resonates with an imperial, imagined representation of the Eastern female: sexualized, foreign, and faceless. Harry emphasizes the physicality of the vela—specifically their skin tone and their nonhuman qualities—attempts to classify them in his knowledge of the world's creatures, fails, and becomes transfixed under their spell. Able to control men through their dancing and music, the veela cannot affect women, so it is Hermione, one of the only female members of Harry's party, who brings the title character back to reality. Here, Hermione resonates with the feminine wife of the British imperial officer, attempting to reclaim her British man from "a long way off," out of the exotic temptresses' hands. The national origin of the veela, Bulgaria, highlights the othering of even fellow European countries, harkening back to a British identity that faced a monolithic Eastern geography.

The British wizards' relations with the Other present in their country, the Muggles, demonstrate further the nostalgia for a British imperial identity. The most salient parallel resides in the question of blood purity, wherein wizarding families of pure-blood ancestry seek to intermarry and perpetuate their self-proclaimed superiority. More often than not, these characters belong to a wealthier class than those without pure-blood claims, and thus the similarities between the racist wizards and the aristocratic bluebloods emerges. Yet all of the wizards have relations with Others, specifically Muggles, that hark back to a lost British identity. First, Rowling capitalizes "Muggle" throughout the novels while "wizard" remains lowercase. The identity of the nonwizarding citizens of Britain appears to be a completely separate identity from the more naturalized moniker of wizard. A perhaps benign typographical choice illustrates the degree to which innocuous gestures can allow colonial attitudes to resurface and dominate. Each Muggle, defined only through their lack of magical abilities, represents the ultimate Other in the wizarding world of Harry Potter. And it is this biological characteristic, essential to the identity of each wizard, that sets them above the Muggles. The Weasleys, a clearly "good" family in the often morally stark novels, perpetuate the remnants of a British colonial benevolent, condescending attitude toward the Muggle Other.

Mr. Weasley's job primarily betrays his Orientalist behavior. He works in the Misuse of Muggle Artifacts Office at the Ministry of Magic and, by the end of the series, is promoted to the position of Head of the Office for the Detection and Confiscation of Counterfeit Defensive Spells Protective Objects. Maintaining a deep interest in the foreign world of Muggles, Mr. Weasley dedicates his life to the study and protection of the nonwizarding Other. Many scenes throughout the series depict Mr. Weasley as the bewildered British intellectual explorer, both infinitely curious and confused as to the workings of the Muggle world. His specific interest lies in the technology Muggles have developed for which wizards have no need; for instance, his dearest ambition is to "find out how airplanes stay up" (*Half-Blood Prince* 86). When the Weasleys descend upon the Dursley household, the distance between the Muggle and wizarding worlds becomes clear. Wizards travel by fireplace, stepping into one fire and coming out of another, possibly thousands of miles distant. The Weasleys become trapped in the Dursleys' fireplace, for, as Harry says to Mr. Weasley:

> ". . . the fireplace has been blocked up. You won't be able to get through there."
> "Damn!" said Mr. Weasley's voice. "What on earth did they want to block up the fireplace for?"
> "They've got an electric fire," Harry explained.
> "Really?" said Mr. Weasley's voice excitedly. "Eclectic, you say? With a *plug*? Gracious, I must see that."
> . . . Mr. Weasley was looking around. He loved everything to do with Muggles. Harry could see him itching to go and examine the television and video recorder.
> "They run off eckeltricity, do they?" he said knowledgeably. "Ah yes, I can see the plugs. I collect plugs," he added to Uncle Vernon. "And batteries. Got a very large collection of batteries. My wife thinks I'm mad, but there you are." (*Goblet of Fire* 43, 46)

Mr. Weasley has an avid interest in, yet extremely limited knowledge of, Muggle technological language, continually mispronouncing the key word to the nonwizarding technology: electricity. The discrepancy between the obvious explanation of the Muggle phenomena and Mr. Weasley's baffled attitude toward them offer a hilarious tone while defamiliarizing the reader, making simple technology appear foreign. In his conversation with Vernon Dursley, Mr. Weasley attempts to appear amiable, bragging about his collection of plugs and batteries. Yet, in his attempt to connect to the Muggle Other, Mr. Weasley only increases the distance between the two worlds, for Mr. Dursley, and the majority of Muggles, do not view items such as batteries as collectibles but rather materially useful and ubiquitous objects. Mr. Weasley, in fetishizing Muggle objects, harks back to an Orientalist colonial attitude, wherein the British imperial officer traveled the world collecting objects for the British archives to hold and categorize for objective study. As a former British colonizer may have studied the so-called primitive objects of a native culture, so, too, do wizards see Muggle technology as primitive. Wizards have progressed beyond the need for such products. Mr. Weasley's interest in the Muggle world solidifies his condescending, colonialist attitude toward the nonmagical Other.

Mr. Weasley's interest in Muggles, like the British Orientalist's interest in the colonized Other, serves to dominate the Muggles through the power of knowledge. The primary goal of his employer, the Ministry of Magic, "is to keep the Muggles from finding out about an entire culture of magical folk" (*Harry Potter Lexicon*). The Muggles are "*disabled*; by their lack [of magic ability] to rely on technology, while hopelessly unaware of the parallel world around them" (Blake 80). The wizard's superior abilities and intellect combined with the ineptitude and ignorance of the Muggles support the success of the ministry's mission. For example, the Weasleys and Harry travel to the Quidditch World Cup using a Portkey, an enchanted object that transports anyone who touches it to a predetermined destination. Mr. Weasley explains to Harry that the Portkey "can be anything. . . .Unobtrusive things, obviously, so Muggles don't go picking them up and playing with them . . . stuff they'll just think is litter" (*Goblet of Fire* 70). The Portkey illustrates both the wizard's cunning ability to turn a common object into an incredibly efficient, indeed effortless, mode of travel and Muggles' ignorance of the magical potential in their environment.

The Portkey works because of the coexistence of the clever wizard and ignorant Muggle.

An illegal practice called "Muggle-baiting," where wizards bewitch Muggle items, further highlights the ignorance of Muggles and Mr. Weasley's attitude toward them. Mr. Weasley describes an example where a wizard "[s]ell[s] [Muggles] a key that keeps shrinking to nothing so they can never find it when they need it. . . . Of course, it's very hard to convict anyone because no Muggle would admit their key keeps shrinking—they'll insist they just keep losing it. Bless them, they'll go to any lengths to ignore magic, even if it's staring them in the face" (*Chamber of Secrets* 38). Mr. Weasley's patronizing tone toward the Muggles becomes apparent in his "bless[ing]" of them along with his job to protect them from unknown dangers in the form of clever wizards. They remain separate from the wizarding world not simply because of their ignorance but also their stubborn refusal to alter their narrow perspective and knowledge base. Magic, the superior defining quality of wizards such as Mr. Weasley, remains fully external to the mindset of the primitive Muggle. Although Mr. Weasley has good humor and benevolent intentions in his treatment of the Muggles, unlike others who play tricks on the poor Muggles (and Mr. Weasley punishes them), he still reinforces the inferiority of the Muggle race.

Various minor characters, in their encounters with Harry, also establish the ubiquity of this superior attitude of wizards in relation to Muggles. For example, the character of Stan Shunpike, the conductor of the Knight Bus, "emergency transport for the stranded witch or wizard," holds the opinion that Muggles choose to remain ignorant (*Prisoner of Azkaban* 33). Stan says contemptuously, "Them! . . . Don' listen properly, do they? Don' look properly either. Never notice nuffink, they don'" (36). With his cockney accent and employment as a bus driver, Stan perhaps represents a lower socioeconomic class of wizard than the majority of the characters, except perhaps the Weasleys. Stan's answer to Harry's query of how Muggles do not notice the Knight Bus, which squeezes itself through foot-wide gaps in traffic and has a full-size bed for every rider, illustrates the superiority of the wizard identity in all classes of wizards. Again, the Muggles' inability, or unwillingness, to truly comprehend the reality of their environment becomes the key element in their inferiority to wizards. Stan's commentary suggests that if a Muggle were to try hard enough, to "look properly," then perhaps the gap between the two worlds could be lessened. The absence of the capacity for magic then represents not simply a cultural difference to the wizarding world but a pitiable, almost pathetic lack of knowledge about the reality of Britain stemming from a biological inferiority.

The superior abilities of the wizards, unimaginable to the Muggle world, manifest themselves in extremely varied relationships between wizards and Muggle. A metaphor of a colonial spectrum becomes apt in describing the variations within the wizarding world, with Mr. Weasley's behavior resonating with the project of the benevolent British colonialist of old. He views his duty toward Muggles as one of magnanimous protector. When his irascibly mischievous sons practice their practical jokes on a Muggle, Mr. Weasley shouts, "It *isn't funny*! . . . That sort of behavior seriously undermines wizard-Muggle relations! I spend half my life campaigning against the mistreatment of Muggles" (*Goblet of Fire* 53). Mr. Weasley retains the good intentions of the British Orientalist, maintaining a benign intellectual interest in Muggles while feeling the necessity of protecting them, due to their inferiority. Although Mr. Weasley perhaps moves beyond a strict identification with a British colonialist in his active support of better treatment of Muggles, the condescending attitude behind his good intentions remains rooted in a past colonial identity. He believes in the peaceful coexistence of the two worlds and seeks to learn more about the Muggle world yet never works for their integration, maintaining a rigid distinction between wizard and Muggle identities.

The distinction between wizards and their inferior Others extends back into the wizarding world, with the interrelations between wizards and nonhuman magical creatures. Magical creatures, a wizarding category for all beings not human, encompass a huge portion of the magical world, denoting everything from ghosts to giants, centaurs to three-headed dogs named Fluffy. Although all fall under the moniker "creature" in the wizarding taxonomy, an extremely vast range of cognitive and magical ability exists within this category. Creatures such as giants and

centaurs teach at Hogwarts, while other creatures cannot communicate at all with wizards and have seemingly no magical or
advanced cognitive ability, such as garden gnomes. Throughout
the series, the line between human and nonhuman continually
blurs, particularly in the case of Rubeus Hagrid, the Hogwarts
groundskeeper, professor, and close friend of Harry's. Some wizards, such as the Malfoys, view Professor Albus Dumbledore's
promotion of Hagrid to a professor as insulting to purebloods,
due to Hagrid's half-human, half-giant status. The Department
for the Regulation and Control of Magical Creatures attempts to
sort out these thorny questions: "They handle complaints about
magical creatures, including goblins and ghosts, they regulate
and monitor breeding of new magical creatures" (*Harry Potter
Lexicon*). The connotation of "regulation" and "control" reinforce the wizard's domination over those they deem inferior,
whether it be Muggles, whose relations also have a ministerial
cabinet, or nonhuman creatures. Creating governing bodies specifically to control and regulate the behavior, including breeding
habits, of the Other resonate deeply with the past British impe-
rialist project. The distinction between human and nonhuman
deepens with "clause three of the Code of Wand Use. . . . *No
non-human creature is permitted to carry or use a wand*" (*Goblet of Fire* 132; emphasis in original). Wizards attempt to regulate
their use of magic by making certain spells illegal (such as murder, torture, or mind-control) and placing age limits on the use
of magic, yet "non-human creatures" cannot even possess or use
a wand at all. Hence, the wizards, in one of many governmen-
tal regulations (that is only "clause three"), draw a distinct line
between themselves and their nonhuman counterparts. In not
permitting the creatures to use the defining superior characteristic of the wizards, the wizarding world controls and oppresses
nonhuman magical creatures.

A rich example of the emergence of a British colonial attitude in relation to the "control" of nonhuman magical creatures
emerges in the figure of the house-elf. First introduced to the
series in *Chamber of Secrets*, is the character of Dobby, the Malfoys' house-elf who tries to save Harry. The house-elf serves as
a type of indentured servant to a wizarding family (*Harry Potter
Lexicon*). If the master wizard offers the house-elf an article of

clothing, he or she frees the house-elf, as Harry frees Dobby in this manner at the end of the second novel. Later in the series, when a fellow house-elf and friend of Dobby's named Winky comes into the narrative, the question of the house-elf's freedom and rights arises. Winky discusses Dobby's current situation to Harry, saying:

> ". . . ah sir, meaning no disrespect, sir, but I is not sure you did Dobby a favor, sir, when you is setting him free."
>
> "Why?" said Harry, taken aback. "What's wrong with him?"
>
> Winky lowered her voice by a half-octave and whispered, "*He is wanting paying for his work, sir.*"
>
> "Paying?" said Harry blankly. "Well—why shouldn't he be paid?"
>
> Winky looked quite horrified at the idea and closed her fingers slightly so that her face was half-hidden again.
>
> "House-elves is not paid, sir!" she said in a muffled squeak. "No, no, no. I says to Dobby, I says, go find yourself a nice family and settle down, Dobby. He is getting up to all sorts of high jinks, sir, what is unbecoming to a house-elf. You goes racketing around like this, Dobby, I says, and next thing I hear you's up in front of the Department for the Regulation and Control of Magical Creatures, like some common goblin. . . . House-elves is not supposed to have fun, Harry Potter. . . . House-elves does what they is told . . ."
>
> "So that's a house-elf?" Ron muttered [to Harry]. "Weird things, aren't they?"
>
> "Dobby was weirder," said Harry fervently. (*Goblet of Fire* 98–99)

The house-elves' use of the English language serves immediately to set them apart as Other to their wizard masters; they speak a technically less standard English. Winky uses the address of "sir" six times in her short conversation with Harry, emphasizing her subordinate place to him within the wizarding world's power structure. In her technically incorrect speech patterns, she uses the verb "is" in almost all sentence formations, placing her statements in a uniform passive voice, linguistically mimicking her social position in the hierarchy of the wizarding world. Yet she places herself above other magical creatures, alluding to "some common goblin" who upset the wizard's place at the top of the magical hierarchy. Ron, whose family does not own a house-elf, describes them with the blanket, otherizing adjective of "weird," to which Harry responds that the nonwizard creatures only are "weirder" in the form of Dobby. Continuing the generalizing description of the house-elves, Winky attempts to speak for all house-elves, placing the multiplicity of creatures into a homogenous category for the wizard. Within the British colonial system metaphor, Winky comes to symbolize the appreciative slave, the good colonized subject who remains grateful for the colonist intervention throughout her oppression.

Winky also exposes a rift within the house-elf community over the question of pay. Certain revolutionary house-elves, such as Dobby, believe in a fair wage; whereas, other traditional house-elves, such as Winky, cannot fathom payment for their life's work of servitude. Within these two characters lie opposing views, with parallels in the colonial world of Britain and its empire. Two potential views of the enslaved and/or colonized subjects coexist: either they soundly reject slavery or appreciate the benefits of the system of "good" slavery. Yet, even in his rejection of wizard oppression, Dobby does not want to work for himself; rather, he seeks not as much payment or vacation time as he could, for according to Dobby: "Dobby likes freedom, miss, but he isn't wanting too much, miss, he likes work better" (*Goblet of Fire* 379; Goldstein 75). Hermione becomes outraged at the status of house-elves, balking that "we are all colluding in the oppression of a hundred slaves!" (*Goblet of Fire* 238). The injustice leads her to begin a group to fight for house-elves' rights, but her fellow wizards tell her that the house-elves are "happy" being servants/slaves (125, 239). All of the wizards show apathy in the face of slavery: "Some people, like Neville, had paid up just to stop Hermione from glowering at them. A few seemed mildly interested in what she had to say, but were reluctant to take a more active role in campaigning. Many regarded the whole thing as a joke" (239). The wizards, like their British colonial counterparts, confront their role in the slavery or oppression of the colonized others through justification (i.e., the slaves are grateful) or simply with apathy.

The British wizards' relations with the Other, whether in the form of international wizards or their ultimate Other, the Muggle, resonate with essentialist and racist views connected to an older, colonial British identity. The past Britishness and Anglocentrism the wizards embody comes in a multiplicity of forms, from the violently fascist Lord Voldemort to the benign Orientalist intellectual Mr. Weasley. These interpretations become even more troubling when the didactic purposes of the novels come into play. Many argue that the novels can serve a pedagogic purpose, making children aware of issues such as genocide, racism, and terrorism within the safety of a neutral magical fantasy world (Strimel, Dempsey). Yet, Rowling launches these critiques from a decidedly British perspective, which often serves to undermine her project. For a novel by a British author about British characters and British identity in Britain perhaps should not be the central text teachers and parents turn to in order to teach children about racism. Readers, children and adults, should not look to the Harry Potter series for a destabilization of a self-constituted superior British identity. Thus, while the books do offer wonderfully written stories while attempting to offer an overt critique of racism, the British identity pervasive within the wizarding world negates the progressive politics of Harry Potter.

Works Cited

Blake, Andrew. "The Harry Potter Books Take a Complex View of Race." *Political Issues in J. K. Rowling's Harry Potter Series*, ed. Dedria Bryfonski. Detroit: Greenhaven, 2009. 78–84. Print.

Bryfonski, Dedria. *Political Issues in J. K. Rowling's Harry Potter Series*. Detroit: Greenhaven, 2009. Print.

Dempsey, Rachel. "Human Rights Are at the Core of Harry Potter." In *Political Issues in J. K. Rowling's Harry Potter Series*, ed. Dedria Bryfonski. Detroit: Greenhaven, 2009. 124–126. Print.

Goldstein, Dana. "The Politics of Harry Potter Are Not Progressive." In *Political Issues in J. K. Rowling's Harry Potter Series*, ed. Dedria Bryfonski. Detroit: Greenhaven, 2009. 73–77. Print.

The Harry Potter Lexicon. Entries on: "Arthur Weasley," "Bestiary: The Creatures of the Wizarding World," "Blood Status," "Department for the Regulation and Control of Magical Creatures," "Dobby the House-Elf," "Encyclopedia of Spells: Unforgivable Curses," "Exploring the Muggle World," "Harry Potter and the Chamber of Secrets Chapter 18 Synopsis," "Ministry of Magic," "Stan Shunpike" (via Wizards, Witches Beings, A to Z). Web. 3 Dec. 2009 to 17 Dec. 2009. http://www.hp-lexicon.org/index-2.html.

Strimel, Courtney B. "The Politics of Terror: Rereading *Harry Potter*." *Children's Literature in Education* 35.1 (2004): 35–52. Print.

Five

The Generation(s) of Harry Potter

The Boy Wizard and His Young Readers

TRÉZA ROSADO

From the moment *Sorcerer's Stone* arrived on bookshelves across the United States, children were wild about the boy wizard. As endless research and statistics have supported, the Harry Potter series is the best-selling series of our time, possibly of all time (see chapter 1 in this volume). Scores of critics and academics have attempted to dissect the books' tremendous success; many more have set out to write or find the next great saga. However, the books possess a particular set of characteristics that are unique to the talents of J. K. Rowling and, thus, are unlikely to be replicated in the near future. Namely, Rowling trusts her readers, empowers them, matures with them, and capitalizes on universal themes of childhood longing and fantasy in order to enthrall them. The success of the series can be defined by "the manner in which the stories evoke intense reader involvement and somehow connect deeply with the imaginative and unconscious worlds of children" (Noctor 581). This potent mixture of psychology and good old-fashioned storytelling has assured the Harry Potter series a hallowed position within the canon of celebrated children's and adolescent literature.

Perhaps the most appealing aspect of the Potter books is Rowling's obvious respect for her reading audience, regardless of (or in spite of) their age. Harry Potter is a decidedly postmodern take on the classic genre of modern children's literature.

In place of passive protagonists manipulated by their social, political, and historical contexts, Rowling gives Harry Potter and his peers, and by extension, the readers, agency. She provides them with what education theorist Dr. Henry A. Giroux defines as "the ability to imagine the world differently and then to act differently" (qtd. in Chappell 282). Drew Chappell, working from this definition, argues that "Rowling's novels imagine a culture in which such child agency is possible, where young people become builders of context, awakening to the network of relationships and institutions that frame their lives" (281). Rowling's world takes the familiar powerlessness of children and adolescents and resituates these social and political nonentities into positions of independence, self-sufficiency, and heroism. If the adults of their world are paralyzed by their allegiances to, and indoctrination into, the institutions oppressing them, Harry and his friends—as outsiders to such institutions—can imagine new ways to construct the world they live in. Child and adolescent readers of the series can then see their own agency by proxy; Harry Potter plants for them an invaluable seed of agency and self-reliance to counter an overdependence on the structures designed to repress youth power.

Protagonists of modernist children's literature function more or less in an idealist state of unambiguous right and wrong. If we think of the heroes of C. S. Lewis's *Chronicles of Narnia*, we are called back to Peter Pevensie, the High King, and his unwavering integrity, courage, and moral compass. Similarly, the road for Frodo Baggins and his stalwart companion, Samwise Gamgee, is one of uncompromising self-sacrifice and total submission to a higher authority and purpose. In fact, each of the characters in J. R. R. Tolkien's Lord of the Rings trilogy exist in an impossible vacuum with a clear hierarchy of good and evil, embodied by the godlike wizard Gandalf and the literal Evil Eye of Sauron. Margery Hourihan writes,

> None of the characters in [the *Lord of the Rings*] has to struggle to understand what he should do. Those who do evil do it knowingly. They are not faced with situations where there seem to be no clearly good options available. The simplistic oppositions of the text deny the

possibility of doubt or confusion about ethical issues. The moral difficulties, the indeterminacies and uncertainties . . . which are intrinsic to the human condition, are absent in Tolkien and denied absolutely by the closure. (53)

Conversely, Rowling's Harry Potter series allows for the shades of gray that permeate our modern existence and have *always* colored the world. By eliminating a perfectly binary system, Rowling alleviates the anxiety children generally feel upon encountering such a system. Colman Noctor, writing in "Putting Harry Potter on the Couch," explains, "Children are relieved to encounter dark characters because they know that they themselves are not all good and find difficulties in the portrayal of all people as inherently good" (581). Thus, children require the nuances of characters like those that populate Rowling's books; they require the moral ambivalence of Rowling's villains to provide a reflection of (and answer to) their own moral uncertainties. The issue comes down to trust—and Rowling consistently trusts her audience to understand the difference between good and evil, even when the two are presented as less than mutually exclusive. This postmodern fantasy suits its postmodern readers: children, adolescents, and adults who are situated in a world constantly in moral flux. Terrorism is at once foreign and homegrown; world leaders are at once trusted and despised. Yet, enemies are "either with us or against us"—leaving no room for dissension, no room for ambiguity or ambivalence.

While those in positions of power and authority attempt to simplify the multiple discourses that make up our social and political landscape, Rowling has managed to elevate our collective discourse on morality with a supposedly "infantile" tale of a boy wizard and his quest to save the wizarding world: "As Harry and his friends age, they discover that where they had expected clear divisions and certain answers, they instead find subtleties and uncertainty" (Chappell 283). Thus, Harry's revered headmaster and blameless guardian is eventually revealed to be a flawed genius, potentially more interested in the greater good than the means necessary to achieving it (see chapter 10 in this volume). Harry's mortal enemy, Professor Severus

Snape, is eventually redeemed as a wizard capable of greater self-lessness and heroism than any other character besides Harry himself. Even Lord Voldemort, a supposedly straightforward villain of traditional children's literature, exists within a greater context of abandonment, sociopathy, and indulgent systems of racial hierarchy.

This exploration of morally ambiguous characters and institutions gives Rowling space to empower her young protagonists via resistance, a plot device that aims to embolden her child and adolescent readers. Issues of control and resistance are recurring, powerful reminders of the relative powerlessness of children in an adult world. Political institutions, the media, professors, and dark wizards are in a constant struggle for control over the minds and bodies of the young wards of Hogwarts. The corrupt Ministry of Magic at turns condemns, censors, and exploits Harry; the *Daily Prophet* works in conjunction with the Ministry to discredit Harry when it is convenient and to celebrate him when it is advantageous.

Although the students are largely independent at boarding school—away from parental authorities—they are still limited in their magical instruction, its application, and outside interactions. Furthermore, their curriculum is rigidly controlled and reflects the bias of the present headmaster: "For all their freedom, students are also confined, restricted from areas on the Hogwarts grounds, curfewed, and banned from using magic outside school" (Chappell 287). However, the students regularly transgress these restrictions and limitations, oftentimes doing so out of a sense of "greater good" but also out of typical adolescent rebellion, curiosity, and yearning to trespass established boundaries.

Additionally, the number of spells and curses that bind, freeze, or otherwise violate students' self-control over their bodies and minds increases with each installment. The moral value of these curses is debatable—both "good" and "evil" wizards use the spells to their respective advantages—but the overall tone of Rowling's narration suggests that this kind of literal and figurative body/mind invasion is largely despicable. The control of bodies and the control of minds combine in the Imperius Curse and in the horrific Cruciatus Curse, which causes insufferable pain and agony in the victim; thus, pain and violation of one's body are inextricably linked and condemned.

Our Post-9/11 World

The Harry Potter series arrived in our Muggle world at a unique juncture in our sociohistorical context. The first three books were published prior to the dawn of the new millennium—a period marked by anxiety and paranoia over the coming of a new era and the consequences of our modern world. Situated at the close of a century, the books located an entire generation of readers within something exotic and strange but familiar enough to be comforting and reassuring. The magical world of Harry Potter allowed readers to glimpse an occasionally dark and mysterious alternative dimension from the relative safety of their own homes and surroundings. While the world waited on the precipice of the new millennium, it waited in a state of hesitant anticipation; the Harry Potter series allowed its readers to process their disorientation with the unfamiliar through the comfortable distance of fantasy literature.

In contrast to the conflicting feelings of anxiety and optimism epitomized by the pre-millennial period, the post-9/11 world has been uniformly characterized by fear—particularly a near-crippling fear of the unknown. *Goblet of Fire*, the fourth installment in the series, arrived at a critical psychological juncture for readers and nonreaders of the series alike. Rowling, ever the astute judge of her audience, paralleled the terror of our world with physical and psychological terror in the world of Harry Potter. In fact, Courtney Strimel argues in her essay on "The Politics of Terror" that "the overriding theme of the *Harry Potter* series is coping with terrorism" (37).

The issue of terrorism is at the root of the first major scene in *Goblet of Fire*, when a group of former Death Eaters assaults a Muggle family. In the book's previous scene, Ireland triumphed over Bulgaria in an ecstatic Quidditch World Cup, and Harry and his comrades had an elated conversation about the match well into the evening. However, the interruption of the Death Eaters is a violent and abrupt intrusion upon the relative contentment and tranquility of a much-anticipated sporting match. Strimel suggests that this sudden onslaught of chaos mirrors our own experiences and responses to terrorism, writing, "Real terrorist attacks are commonly unexpected by victims; therefore, the lack of foreshadowing in this scene evinces a sense of startling, realistic fear" (38).

Additionally, terrorism is embodied in both the physical and psychological sense, a reality aptly captured by Rowling in her depiction of the attack at the Quidditch World Cup. The terror introduced by the Death Eaters is not limited to an assault on life and property. Arthur Weasley articulates the psychological terror wrought by the return of these decade-gone villains as he explains the situation to Hermione Granger, Ron Weasley, and Harry. Included in Mr. Weasley's analysis of the attack is his explanation of the fearsome Dark Mark conjured by an unknown wizard. This mark requires no physical assault in order to traumatize the mass of wizards who witness it; the mark itself is enough to induce psychological terror in any adult wizard or witch old enough to understand its context and the implication of its return. Furthermore, the scene evokes realistic responses from the book's characters: a combination of confusion, terror, panic, and decisive action. Strimel writes,

> The fantasy qualities of the HP world allow kids to experience the terrorist attack from a distance but still gain perspective on how to deal with periods of crisis . . . they may also witness the actions of characters working to stop the attack and using magic to bring safety and order back to the campground. Readers, then, are afforded the ability to learn that fear is an inevitable byproduct of terrorism, but that reason, teamwork, and calmness must override chaos in order to deal with terror. (38)

The adults immediately seize control of the situation. Mr. Weasley rouses the children and sends them to safety before joining other Ministry officials in attempting to save the Muggle family and disband the Death Eaters before more destruction can take place. Meanwhile, Harry, Ron, and Hermione wrestle with the complex and disturbing roots of the terrorist act. Although not altogether impervious to the fear that has invaded their surroundings, the three children reflect the primary responses of many American children to the events of 9/11—a surprising level of curiosity that outweighed the more primal response of fear and anxiety. Here, Rowling displays her comprehensive understanding of the child psyche, that what is "most frightening to children is to dream their own figures of fear and find no analog in anything they hear about or read. Children need to see their feelings, particularly the darkest ones, reflected in their stories" (Natov 135). These scenes allow children and adolescents to experience terror from a manageable distance, permitting young readers to digest the horror of the attacks and, more importantly, ideal reactions.

Beyond helpfully providing a context for terror, Rowling also provides a useful resolution to the situation by offering no immediate resolution whatsoever. The attack and its implications are not resolved neatly by the end of the chapter or even the book, which allows children to understand good and evil and the reality of their intersection. From this point on in the series, Rowling allows that intersection between good and evil to be dramatically blurred; she also delays simplistic resolution to the book's major conflicts.

To draw further examples from the pivotal fourth installment, we can analyze Rowling's treatment of the first major death in the series. The death of Harry's peer and friendly adversary, Cedric Diggory, frames the protagonist's response to deaths throughout the rest of the increasingly casualty-heavy series. Harry, with a mixture of grief, guilt, and disbelief, clings to Cedric's body until his professor literally pries his fingers from it. Harry, a fourteen-year-old boy, has just witnessed his first death, a murder committed out of cold-blooded apathy and complete disregard for human life. The trauma of this moment marks both Harry and the reader, instilling a sense of the permanence of death and the merciless nature of evil—something several shades beyond "bad":

> The evil callousness with which Voldemort carries out his execution of Cedric is frightening, but it is realistic because the victims of terrorism are often innocent.

> This scenario allows children to formulate the important question of why a good character was killed. . . . The answer children are directed to formulate is that senseless, malicious acts do happen and that Cedric did nothing to warrant his death. (Strimel 43)

From this scene and the scenes that follow, readers are introduced to the disturbing idea that acts of terrorism do not take into consideration the relative virtue of victims, their age, nor any other personal qualities; evil is inscrutable and its consequences are often incomprehensible. However, again, the traumatic implications of this scene (and many more to come) are diffused through the inclusion of magic and the lens of fantasy literature. Readers are thus initiated into the grief and feelings of helplessness that often accompany death but are also protected from the full depth of the tragedy. By the seventh book, Rowling has proven time and again the finality of death and the fullness of its consequences for those nearest to it. Readers situated in a context of endless war, terrorism, and senseless violence can relate to the chaos of the wizarding world while also extrapolating valuable lessons on processing grief and managing fear.

The moral ambiguity of characters (and, thus, of humanity) is another primary focal point for the series and for its author. A triumvirate of supposedly binary characters embodies this ambiguity by the end of the series: Snape, Voldemort, and Albus Dumbledore himself. Rowling cleverly manipulates her readers into making assumptions about characters based solely on behavioral patterns and their resultant expectations. The characters of Snape and Dumbledore are presumed completely evil and completely good by virtue of their deeds throughout the series; however, both are eventually revealed as completely human—flawed and morally questionable, although, in the case of these two wizards, ultimately "good."

Strimel argues that "the lesson of greatest import regarding children's understandings of terror issues is that of separating people from behavior. To have this ability allows children to refrain from stereotyping groups of people, and it complicates the labeling of people as wholly good or wholly evil in the wake of a terrifying event" (46). Particularly in the wake of 9/11, it has become increasingly important to illustrate for children the nuances of right and wrong, good and evil. We do these issues a disservice by limiting the discourse to black and white conceptions of the world. Rowling understands this and uses her position as a children's author to educate in a subtle and powerful way.

Works Cited

Chappell, Drew. "Sneaking Out After Dark: Resistance, Agency, and the Postmodern Child in J. K. Rowling's *Harry Potter* Series." *Children's Literature in Education* 39 (2008): 281–293. Web. 29 Apr. 2010. http://www.springerlink.com/content/30k858n772742587/.

Hourihan, Margery. *Deconstructing the Hero: Literary Theory and Children's Literature*. New York, NY: Routledge, 1997. Print.

Natov, Roni. "Harry Potter and the Extraordinariness of the Ordinary." In *The Ivory Tower and Harry Potter*, ed. Lana A. Whited. Columbia, MO: U of Missouri P, 2002. 125–139. Print.

Noctor, Colman. "Putting Harry Potter on the Couch." *Clinical Child Psychology and Psychiatry* 11.4 (2006): 579–589. Web. 29 Apr. 2010. http://ccp.sagepub.com/cgi/content/short/11/4/579.

Strimel, Courtney B. "The Politics of Terror: Rereading *Harry Potter*." *Children's Literature in Education* 35.1 (2004): 35–52. Web. 5 May 2010. http://www.springerlink.com/content/n415124h335761u3/.

My Harry Potter Story

LYDIA FASTELAND AND RICHELLE ILANGA

Lydia Fasteland, twenty-three, St. Paul, Minnesota. Graduate student in library and information science, St. Catherine University. Photo courtesy of the author.

Lydia Fasteland: I began reading the Harry Potter books when I was nine years old, just entering fourth grade. The only reason I picked up *Harry Potter and the Sorcerer's Stone* was because a friend of mine had said it was a good book, so I thought I would try it. That was when I discovered I have selective hearing, because I would become so entranced by the book during reading time that my teacher would have to come and touch my shoulder lightly to get my attention and tell me that reading time was over. Once I finished the book, I had to have more. So I kept reading until I finished all four of the books published at the time. Then I had to wait, which I detested. I was seventeen years old when I finished the series, the same age Harry was when he defeated Voldemort.

The Harry Potter books appealed to me because they were an escape. I was a quiet kid with glasses who studied and read a lot. Then I met Hermione, and I was blown away. Here was a character just like me. She strived to get perfect grades, read outside of the required reading for classes, was not considered the most beautiful girl, and so on. I could relate to her so well that whenever I would have a rough day at school, I would come home and read parts of the books where Hermione overcame her problems. The relatable characters were the most appealing thing about the books for me because these characters were going through the same things I was—the first crush, meeting new friends, taking exams, and writing papers. They made me love the books, and they became part of my life.

Before the Potter books, I was an avid reader, but I mainly read historical fiction like the Dear America series, The Baby-sitters Club books, or whimsical fairy tales. Harry Potter, however, was the gateway into the world of science fiction and fantasy. It is now my favorite genre.

Recommending the books to friends and family has been very important to me. However, the best moment was when my ten-year-old cousins, who do not like reading, told me that they started reading the books because I had recommended them. They loved them. That moment showed me that my passion for the books has passed to others, which makes me proud to be a Potter fan.

Richelle Ilanga, twenty-two, Sugarland, Texas. Nursing student at Texas Women's University, Houston. Photo courtesy of the author.

Richelle Ilanga: In the fourth grade, my older brother got the Harry Potter books, and I used to steal them from him and read to catch up to where he was. My brother got so annoyed with me, and we always fought about it until my mom finally bought me my own copy. From then on, every time I was in a bookstore, I would beg my mom to get me the books. She would eventually get them for me because she knew how much they meant to me and how much I liked reading them. The characters and I have so much in common. Luna Lovegood is sort of weird and different, and I can relate to that because sometimes I'm quirky and different, too. My personality also fits with the trio—Harry is brave, Hermione is responsible, and Ron is goofy. In that respect I can identify with all three of them; they all carry a piece of me. I get lost in their world. I would go to the bookstore right next to Mervyn's department store, sit in the corner next to *Captain Underpants* and *Amelia's Notebook* and keep reading and reading until my mom was done shopping. She always knew where to find me; I was in that same corner every time.

It wasn't until the fifth book that the series really "got" me. Harry was learning about the Order and Aurors and felt pulled to that line of work. This was around the same time that I was learning more about what it meant to be a full-time missionary. Everything Harry was learning, I was also learning. The Aurors went through set training, dropping school and careers to fight the Death Eaters. This is similar to missionary work because it's a service for something greater than yourself. There's something admirable about being an Auror, about dropping everything, fighting evil, protecting Harry Potter, and fighting the good fight for a greater cause. In the wizarding world, I wanted to be an Auror. In real life, I want to be a missionary.

Harry Potter played a bigger role in my life than I realized. The other day, I was reminiscing with my friends, and I realized just how much I've kept up with Harry Potter. He allowed me to dream. That may be corny or lame, but it made me see that anything was possible. I really appreciate the fact that this all started with J. K. Rowling sitting in a coffee shop writing. I go to coffee shops all the time to study, and when I'm there I can't help but think, "Man, this is where it all started." This has helped me to think outside of the box more. She created this whole new world, and that's really cool.

PART II

Defense Against the Dark Arts

Six

The Making of a New World

Nazi Ideology and Its Influence on Harry Potter

SARAH WENTE

In *Sorcerer's Stone*, the wandmaker Ollivander tells Harry Potter, "He-Who-Must-Not-Be-Named did great things—terrible, yes, but great" (85). There is a curious duality in those words. The line, descriptive of the series' primary villain, Lord Voldemort, is equally applicable to German leader Adolf Hitler. Hitler's Nazi movement in 1930s Europe, characterized by power and panic, required considerable leadership proficiency to undertake and achieve its goals, a talent Hitler ably supplied. Under his guidance, the German people unified and mobilized themselves, taking the necessary actions that freed their nation from the crippling conditions of the Treaty of Versailles. Regrettably, Hitler's agenda soon turned to genocide as he used this national support to cleanse Europe of "undesirables," causing the deaths of millions of innocent people. Overwhelmingly scarred by horror, yet responsible for the comeback of Germany following World War I, Hitler and the Nazi regime were nothing if not great and terrible.

As the Harry Potter series progresses, the connection between the two evils of the fictional Voldemort and the all-too-real Hitler grows, and it becomes apparent that Harry Potter, though shrouded in a fictional cloak of magic, is steeped in Nazi ideology. Elements of Nazism appear in many aspects of Harry's world, components revealed through the actions and characteristics of the books' antagonists. The connections between Nazism and Harry Potter are so numerous that attending to them all would require more time and space than I have here. Therefore, this discussion of Nazism in Harry Potter will be restricted primarily to an analysis of racism based on blood purity, of the Hitler-inspired characters, and of Nazi beliefs regarding education reflected at Hogwarts.

Though this analysis links the Nazi regime and Voldemort's amassing of power in the seven Harry Potter novels, I would not imply that they are comparable on every level. While certain beliefs and actions align, there are also considerable differences between the two, one of which is the magnitude of the respective empires—one actual and terribly destructive, and one fictional. Further, as author Nancy Reagin observes, "Voldemort and his supporters ruled over a tiny population, and the number of Muggle-borns persecuted by the Death Eaters is miniscule when we think of how many people fell victim to the Nazis" (149). While there are interesting similarities, they are not the same.

The Promotion of Racial Purity

A fundamental connection between Harry Potter and Nazism is the blood-purity racism in both worlds. Though racist ideas are not unique to the Nazi Party, the fact that they chose blood status as the distinguishing factor between people differentiates them from racist movements that discriminate by other means, such as skin color or national origin. Nazi ideology is defined by this particular brand of racism, mirrored in the wizarding world.

Initially, the racism of the Harry Potter series is difficult to perceive, as Harry himself refuses to take note of it. The world of wizards is seen primarily through Harry Potter's eyes, and while this point of view emphasizes his motives and actions, it masks the parts of the world he ignores. However, if readers can extend themselves beyond Harry's vision and read between the lines, the racism within the novels becomes apparent as early as the first book.

Not surprisingly, Draco Malfoy provides this initial encounter with wizarding racism. Harry's rival from the moment the two meet in Madam Malkin's robe shop, Draco is well aware of the racism in his society and constantly reminds others of its existence. In his very first meeting with Harry, Draco asks about Harry's parents and his surname in order to determine his lineage and, consequently, where he falls in the wizarding hierarchy (*Sorcerer's Stone* 78). On the way to Hogwarts, Draco tells Harry that "some wizarding families are much better than others" (108). He then illustrates what he means, calling Rubeus Hagrid and the Weasley family "riffraff" and warning Harry that if he hangs around them too much, their inferiority will "rub off" on him (109). He later calls Hermione Granger a Mudblood, which Ron Weasley explains is "about the most insulting thing he could think of . . . . Mudblood's a really foul name for someone who is Muggle-born—you know, non-magic parents" (*Chamber of Secrets* 115). Even when Harry does not see it, Draco, with his snide remarks and overwhelming sense of superiority, is a perpetual reminder of the racial stratification in the wizarding world.

Draco is not, however, the sole reminder of racism, though he is often the most prominent. Other students at Hogwarts express it as well, although usually in subtler, less antagonistic ways. Their discussions of bloodlines are tucked into casual conversation, such as the one that occurs during Harry's first start-of-term banquet. Amid the food-filled festivities, the talk at Gryffindor table turns to families, allowing readers to discover that Seamus Finnigan is half-and-half while Neville Longbottom descends from a family of wizards (*Sorcerer's Stone* 125). The students do not consider the implications of what they are discussing; they chat about it as a way of getting to know one another. Pedigree is one of the first things mentioned when Harry meets both Ron and Hermione as well (99, 105). And while there is little judgment attached to these delineations early in the series, the appearance of this sort of conversation reveals that the racism expressed by Draco is embedded in the larger wizarding culture. The students' discussion of what makes them different from one another, even if it is only out of curiosity, perpetuates the labeling of these differences and paves the way for discrimination based upon them.

The discussion of blood status in the first novel is vague when compared to the rest of the series, as the specific terminology used to identify these differences is not revealed until the second book, when Harry is ready to recognize the role racism plays in his new world. Reagin acknowledges the underlying importance of these terms when she writes, "A consciousness of ancestry—and of categorizing people by the amount of magical ancestry that they possess—must be very common in Harry's world, because almost all of the witches and the wizards we see use most of the terms listed previously ['pure-blood' or 'half-blood'] quite unself-consciously, with the exception of the insulting 'Mudblood'" (130). As Harry's journey continues, those terms become important markers of identity, a concrete acknowledgment of one's lineage and where one falls in the order of wizards.

Draco's constant reminders of this social order make him a mouthpiece for the story's racism, giving voice to implicit prejudices and making them more real both to readers and to Harry. Though Draco is rightly condemned for his attitudes, he nonetheless conveys a message that Harry must learn. Voldemort, like Draco, uses blood status as a basis for judgment, so it becomes imperative that Harry understand such prejudices in order to understand his enemy. Voldemort's ultimate goal is to establish a pure-blood ruling class and subject Muggles to hard labor, and by manipulating the racism present in wizarding society, he rallies supporters and propagates actions that will create the social order he envisions.

Hitler had similar ideas for Germany and worked to create an Aryan society free from those he considered unworthy (such as Jews, homosexuals, the disabled, or the mentally ill). In both the wizarding world and Nazi Germany, racism existed prior to the actions of Voldemort and Hitler, yet both men managed to mobilize racial prejudice, creating a menacing vehicle that cataclysmically affected their respective worlds. It is not only the existence of racism but also how it is used that connects Harry Potter to Nazism.

The racism of Hitler and the Nazis targeted a variety of people, most notably the Jews, who were blamed for Germany's loss in World War I (Altman 35). Hitler built his empire on the idea that "Jews . . . could not be judged as other men. They were creatures of alien and dangerous blood, doomed to corrupt everything they touched" (Altman 40). Consequently, Hitler believed that their destruction was required to make Germany great again and to ensure his power over the nation. The Nazi Party agreed. As historian Henry Friedlander observes, "Both Nazi ideologues and race scientists believed that German blood had been polluted, and that it was the nation's primary task to purge the German gene pool" (qtd. in Rhodes 95).

This idea began years of mass killings and the horrific vendetta of the Holocaust. Once Hitler appointed himself the Supreme Leader of Germany in 1934, he began "cleansing" the nation with surprising efficiency (Bartoletti 32). Sociologist Michael Mann writes, "The Nazi regime was the most genocidal the world has ever seen. . . . During its short twelve years (overwhelmingly its last four) it killed approximately twenty million unarmed persons" (qtd. in Rhodes 156). Concentration camps sprang up all over the eastern countries of Europe, places where Jews and other dissenters were subject to hard labor and abuse, then killed and cremated in giant furnaces. Though often remembered as a chief component of the Holocaust, these camps were not the Nazis' primary mode of execution. As author Richard Rhodes notes, more opponents of Nazism were executed by firing squads, as "shooting began earlier, [and] continued throughout the war" (156). Often, large numbers of people were shot and packed into mass graves, the largest of which holds approximately thirty-four thousand men, women, and children (Rhodes xi, 179). To the Nazis, these actions were not crimes against humanity; rather, they were a great step forward as they worked to make Europe "clean."

While the Nazis were condemning and killing "undesirables," they also strove to fortify those they felt exemplified the perfect race: Aryans. Defined as "Nordic or Caucasian people with no mixture of Jewish ancestry . . . [the Nazis] claimed that blond hair and blue eyes distinguished the 'purest' Aryans"

(Bartoletti 25). Eugenics, the "science of the improvement of the human race by better breeding," gained massive popularity as the Nazis worked to identify undesirable traits and eliminate their transmission (qtd. in Altman 71). However, cleansing the German gene pool required not only keeping out the perceived pollutant but also keeping in "clean" genes. Therefore, the Nazis took deliberate measures to ensure that there would be plenty of Aryan children to populate the new *Reich*. In 1933, abortions were made illegal for Aryan women, leading to the creation of *Lebensborn* ("Source of Life") houses in which Aryan women could give birth to unwanted progeny (Hammer). These offspring, as well as kidnapped Polish children with Aryan traits, were raised in foster families for the purpose of securing Aryanism in future generations (Hammer).

Aryanism makes an appearance in the Harry Potter series through Draco and the Malfoy family. The Malfoys not only represent the antithesis of Harry's beliefs and values, but they also exemplify Hitler's idea of Aryan perfection. Harry describes Draco as a "pale boy with a pointed face and white-blond hair" and identifies Draco's parents, Lucius and Narcissa, with this description, commenting, "Draco greatly resembled his father. His mother was blonde too; tall and slim" (*Goblet of Fire* 100–101). The physical appearance of the Malfoy family—blonde and presumably pale-eyed—makes them the embodiment of Hitler's Aryan profile. Additionally, the Malfoys are extraordinarily wealthy, a status evidenced beyond Draco's bragging by their various forms of conspicuous consumption: their presence in the Top Box at the Quidditch World Cup because of a "*very* generous contribution to St. Mungo's Hospital"; their buying the Slytherin Quidditch team a set of new brooms to get Draco on the lineup; and the massively ornate Malfoy Manor described in *Deathly Hallows* (*Goblet of Fire* 101; *Chamber of Secrets* 112). This wealth affords them a lot of power and influence in the wizarding world, as can be seen when Lucius, a member of the Hogwarts Board of Governors, uses his status to coerce the other governors to remove Hagrid and Professor Albus Dumbledore from Hogwarts in *Chamber of Secrets*. In this way, Lucius and the Malfoys can be seen preserving both

themselves and their ideas, engaging in actions that Hitler would
have supported in the name of Aryanism.

Similar racist actions mark Voldemort's empire, making them
a major component Harry must contend against. The annoyance
of Draco's harassment transforms first into the attempted murder of Muggle-borns and half-bloods by Tom Riddle in the second novel, then to the open hunting of them in the final book.
Though we are given to understand that such racism began in
the wizarding world long before Voldemort's time, as the primary villain of the series, he shoulders much of the blame for
perpetuating the idea.

The fictional Voldemort, much like the historical Hitler,
has strong views regarding race that develop at a young age.
His mission, as he tells his followers, the Death Eaters, is for
them to "cut away the canker that infects us until only those
of the true blood remain" (*Deathly Hallows* 11). In that statement, Voldemort includes himself among the infected, a classification perhaps gleaned from his heritage and the mixed blood
within his own familial line. An orphan when he arrived at Hogwarts, Voldemort was "obsessed with his parentage" (*Half-
Blood Prince* 362). He used his name to search extensively for
his family, a process that culminated in the discovery that his
father was a Muggle and his mother was a pure-blood witch.
After gaining this knowledge, he proceeded to kill his father and
paternal grandparents, thus "obliterating the last of the unworthy Riddle line and revenging himself upon the father who never
wanted him" (367). The elimination of his father's family frees
Voldemort from his Muggle roots and allows him to cling to
the pure-blood line of his mother. When professing his plans
for Hogwarts during the final battle, he reveals his pride in his
pure-blood ancestry, stating, "The emblem, shield, and colors
of my noble ancestor, Salazar Slytherin, will suffice for everyone" (*Deathly Hallows* 732). This desire for purity, formed from
his investigations into his parentage, comes to define his entire
worldview.

Ultimately, Voldemort's ambition leads to murder, just as it
did in Hitler's Germany. After killing his father, whom he blames
for the death of his pure-blood mother and the contamination

of his wizarding blood, Voldemort brings his vendetta to Hog-warts, opening Slytherin's Chamber of Secrets and attacking the Muggle-borns within the school, eventually killing one. Once he leaves Hogwarts, he disappears after murdering Hepzibah Smith, only to return ten years later and commit increasingly more violent acts. Anyone who is not a pure-blood or anyone who is a blood traitor opposes his idea of a master race of wiz-ards and therefore deserves to be destroyed.

Though Voldemort is discreet with his murders, he nonethe-less manages them with frequency and ease. Hagrid, when first describing Voldemort to Harry, comments immediately on his murderous streak, saying, "some stood up to him—an' he killed 'em," and that "[n]o one ever lived after he decided ter kill 'em" (*Sorcerer's Stone* 55). Other characters in the novel recognize Voldemort's predominant trait as well and pass this information on to Harry. Dumbledore explains that "[t]he years of Volde-mort's ascent to power . . . were marked with disappearances," and Sirius Black states, "Imagine that Voldemort's powerful now. . . . Every week, news comes of more deaths, more disap-pearances, more torturing" (*Goblet of Fire* 601, 526–527). Most crimes involving Voldemort are simply marked off as "disap-pearances," but people in the novels understand that those who disappear rarely (if ever) come back. The seventh novel begins with an example of what happens to those who "disappear" and tells of the murder of Charity Burbage, the Muggle Studies professor at Hogwarts. Voldemort explains how her teachings encourage wizards to accept that Muggles are not that differ-ent from wizards and that the decline of pure-blood ancestry is "a most desirable circumstance" (*Deathly Hallows* 12). These are both ideas that Voldemort finds deplorable, so he kills Bur-bage to keep her from spreading them to the youth at Hogwarts. The torture and execution of Burbage is the first time a disap-pearance is revealed in its entirety, giving readers a taste of what Voldemort does to his numerous victims.

Voldemort, like the Nazis, also attempts to preserve those who fit his pure-blood ideal so that they can perpetuate the line in the future. This is best revealed in his treatment of Neville Longbottom in the final novel. Though aware that Neville has been working against him, Voldemort offers to spare his life based on his pure-blood status. He tells him, "You show spirit and bravery, and you come of noble stock. You will make a very valuable Death Eater. We need your kind, Neville Longbottom" (*Deathly Hallows* 731). Just as the Nazis sought to protect Aryan blood, Voldemort seeks to preserve any pure-blood wizard. However, Voldemort prizes obedience over all else; so when Neville refuses to join his ranks, he reverts to his "original plan": murder (732).

By focusing his murderous efforts on a specific population of wizards and elevating the racism already present in society, Voldemort invites a correlation with the Nazis that only deepens as his influence spreads and is further described. With racism at the helm of their empires, both Voldemort and Hitler sowed seeds of conflict that would grow into movements of death and terror.

Harry Potter Hitler Figures

Though Voldemort is the primary antagonist of the series and the chief perpetrator of the story's racism, he is not the only figure whose leadership advances this cause. As the plot thickens and knowledge about wizarding history becomes known, the series reveals several characters who consolidate racist ideas and incite racist actions, individuals who embody traits akin to Hitler. A charismatic man with many ideas, Hitler was responsible for turning Germany's National Socialist Party from a small group of people meeting in a bar into the major political voice of the nation (Altman 38). Using the party as his platform, Hitler advocated for anti-Semitism, national reform, and territorial advancement. In 1934, he became the *Führer*—the Supreme Leader of Germany—and changed the nation beyond recognition. The character of this man resounds throughout the Harry Potter novels. No single person in any of the books is purely representative of Hitler. Rather, several individuals exemplify attributes of Hitler's nature. Just as Hitler's influence and ideas gained popularity as he grew in power, so do the ideas of racial purity in the wizarding world develop from one person to another.

Salazar Slytherin is the first Hitler character revealed in Harry's world, one of the earliest adult figures to suggest a hierarchy among wizards with respect to lineage. Though readers have seen blood purity ideas spouted by Draco and Voldemort prior to Slytherin's introduction in the second novel, in terms of the historical timeline of the series, Slytherin came before either one of them. This lends itself to the conclusion that the pure-blood views advocated by Harry's antagonists originated from Slytherin as opposed to Voldemort—or as Ron remarks, Slytherin was the one who "started all this pure-blood stuff" (*Chamber of Secrets* 152).

Of the four school founders, Slytherin "wished to be more *selective* about the students admitted to Hogwarts. He believed that magical learning should be kept within all-magic families. He disliked taking students of Muggle parentage, believing them to be untrustworthy" (*Chamber of Secrets* 150; emphasis in original). Due to conflict generated between the founders over these views, Slytherin left the school but not before building the legendary Chamber of Secrets. As the story goes, his heir would be able to open the chamber after he was gone and "purge the school of all who were unworthy to study magic" (151). Anyone with any sort of Muggle lineage would be subject to the beast locked inside, leaving alive only the pure-blood wizards Slytherin wanted at Hogwarts.

This action against certain wizards, though not realized until Voldemort's years at Hogwarts, marks the first step on the road toward pure-blood superiority. By developing personal ideas about racial purity and passing them on to his students through his House restrictions, Slytherin draws the wizarding world into a conversation about bloodlines. But that's as far as Slytherin goes with his beliefs. His development of the Chamber of Secrets is the only action he takes against those he finds unworthy; otherwise, he leaves behind the school and those who disagree with him without further disruption.

This pattern echoes the early years of Hitler's life, where he himself was trying to understand his ideas about bloodlines and his role in "purifying" them. A close friend of Hitler's remarks that he was a "pronounced anti-Semite" by the age of fifteen, an idea that only grew during the years he lived in Vienna (qtd. in Rhodes 30). Of his time there, Hitler himself writes in *Mein Kampf*, "my eyes were opened to two menaces of which I had previously scarcely known the names, and whose terrible importance for the existence of the German people I certainly did not understand: Marxism and Jewry" (21).

Yet just as Slytherin could not express his pure-blood preference within Hogwarts, Hitler had few outlets for his anti-Semitism. Alone and barely making a living in Vienna, he lacked the power to act upon his prejudices. In both cases, one man alone was not enough to change society as they desired. However, though neither of them knew it at the time, they were the beginning of something much bigger than themselves. In the wizarding world, Slytherin's pure-blood morality paved the way for Voldemort's rise to power, while Hitler's views marked his change in occupation and his ascent to authority.

Continuing on the historical timeline of the wizarding world, the next person to pick up Slytherin's ideas is Gellert Grindelwald. Grindelwald is not mentioned until the final novel of the series, but chronologically, he comes second. Though he plays a subdued role, elements of Hitler are reflected in his actions as well, mirroring Hitler's early adult life and involvement in Nazism. Grindelwald had been a student at Durmstrang, a wizarding school similar to Hogwarts but "famous even then for its unfortunate tolerance of the Dark Arts" (*Deathly Hallows* 356). Though he was an exceptional student, he was expelled after performing "twisted experiments," described as "near-fatal attacks upon fellow students" (356, 359). Though it is never made clear which students were on the receiving end of these experiments, in later conversations with Dumbledore, Grindelwald alludes to wizard dominance, lending support to the idea that his victims were those who went against this design. Muggle-borns and other Muggle advocates are likely targets. The fact that Grindelwald advocates wizarding dominance while a student at Durmstrang shows that ideas of racial purity had long spread beyond the confines of Hogwarts. No longer contained within that school's walls, Slytherin's views had found followers across the continent. Grindelwald picked them up with surprising alacrity.

Grindelwald's reign is never fully explored, as it took place far from the British world of magic familiar to readers. However, it took shape in Britain, where Grindelwald became friends with Dumbledore. The plans he formulated with Dumbledore revolved around obtaining the wizard dominance he had sought in his school years, which Dumbledore later describes as, "Muggles forced into subservience. We wizards triumphant. Grindelwald and I, the glorious young leaders of the revolution" (*Deathly Hallows* 716). Despite their efforts, however, Dumbledore abandoned these plans after the death of his sister, leaving Grindelwald to act alone, which he did with great success.

In the years following the dissolution of his friendship with Dumbledore, Grindelwald raised an army to fulfill his plans "for seizing power, and his schemes for Muggle torture" (*Deathly Hallows* 717). Grindelwald sought dominance for five years of "turmoil, fatalities, and disappearances" before his campaign was ended by his legendary duel with Dumbledore (359). In a twist of irony, the rest of Grindelwald's life would be spent behind the walls of Nurmengard, the prison he built "to hold his opponents" (360).

Nurmengard is a curious place, as in both name and function it mirrors Nazi elements. The fact that Nurmengard was first used to contain Grindelwald's opponents creates a strong connection to a Nazi concentration camp, as the sole purpose of the Nazi camps was the detainment and eventual death of those who opposed the government Hitler was building. For Hitler and Grindelwald, the simplest way to silence the opposition was to remove them altogether, as evidenced by their respective penitentiaries. The name Nurmengard also echoes the site of the annual Nazi Party rally: Nuremberg. A weeklong event with parades and speeches from Hitler himself, the rally bolstered support for both Germany and its leader (Bartoletti 76–77). Following the war and the decline of Nazism, Nuremberg became the site for the trials against Nazi officials, an ironic switch from its earlier uses (Bartoletti 147). It transitioned from a place of Nazi pride to one of penalty, just as Nurmengard did for Grindelwald.

Grindelwald's actions parallel the early adult years of Hitler, a time when he, too, enjoyed a short-lived bid for power that landed him in prison. When World War I began, Hitler petitioned to be a soldier of the German empire and was accepted, the first steady job he would hold in years (Altman 37). But when the war ended with the Treaty of Versailles, Hitler found himself out of a job in a country marked by increasing unemployment and a slew of postwar problems: "In his fury, he blamed 'Reds' (Communists), cowards, traitors, and Jews for what had happened to Germany. Something had to be done, he believed; and he was the man to do it" (Altman 38). Hitler recognized a serious problem and found his calling to become a politician.

He joined the German Workers' Party in 1919, when it was a "tiny group of social misfits, who gathered in beer halls" (Altman 38). Described as militaristic and anti-Semitic, the small group flourished with the addition of Hitler to its ranks. He worked hard to promote the party and increase its membership, and eventually changed its name to the National Socialist German Workers' Party, from which the term "Nazi" is drawn (Altman 38, 40). In the party, Hitler found the perfect platform from which to propose his ideas to the world, and he used this opportunity to press them further than they had gone before. In 1923, he attempted a revolution in Bavaria by holding three Bavarian leaders hostage in a Munich beer hall until they agreed to a Nazi government (Altman 41–44). However, this plan backfired and Hitler was arrested, forced to put his plans on hold as he spent the next sixteen months in prison.

For the wizarding world, Grindelwald's campaign marks a solid transition from thought to action. His endeavors, with the aim of establishing wizarding superiority, mobilize racist violence in ways not seen before. But although Grindelwald starts strong, Dumbledore ends his career swiftly and with finality. Hitler also marks a turning point from thought to action. Following the end of World War I, he began his ascent to power and moved toward his ultimate goal of racial purity. His failed rebellion, though temporarily ending his career in politics, brought about greater resolve when he returned to this arena.

Finally, there is Voldemort, the character most similar to Hitler, who embodies comparable characteristics and acts in a parallel fashion to Hitler in his glory days. Though the racism inherent in Slytherin, Grindelwald, and Voldemort stems from the same vein of thought, Voldemort uses it to start a revolution

that brings these ideas to public attention in a bold way. By starting small and working his way up, he amasses a huge following
and infiltrates the highest offices of wizarding government. Like
Hitler, he rules by fear and violence, believes in the immortality of both himself and his ideas, and works incessantly toward
their fruition.

Voldemort's racism is fed by his desire for power and his
tendency toward violence. These traits shape his form of racist
expression and cause him to see murder and dominance as an
effective solution for establishing pure-blood rule. As a child,
Voldemort experiments with cruelty, terror, and power over others, honing these techniques as he grows up. While living at the
orphanage, Voldemort bullies the other children, causing Dumbledore to remark that he used his magical abilities "against other
people, to frighten, to punish, to control" (*Half-Blood Prince*
276). Two incidents, involving a rabbit and a trip to the caves,
illustrate Voldemort's controlling and violent demeanor. These
characteristics transfer to his school life, where he surrounds
himself with those who share his opinions, not only about race
but also about violence. Dumbledore reports that he "gathered
about him a group of dedicated friends . . . the forerunners of
the Death Eaters" (361–362). Voldemort was their leader, one
"who could show them more refined forms of cruelty" (362).
Just as in the orphanage, "a number of nasty incidents" marked
Voldemort's school years, "the most serious of which was, of
course, the opening of the Chamber of Secrets, which resulted in
the death of a girl" (362). During this time, he also murdered his
father and grandparents, revealing an escalation from his former
bullying.

After he leaves Hogwarts, Voldemort seeks a position as a
teacher there, a reason Dumbledore attributes to it being a "useful recruiting ground, and a place where he might begin to build
himself an army," just as Grindelwald did many years before
him (*Half-Blood Prince* 432). Voldemort recognizes the power
inherent in a teaching position, the influence he could have over
others, and seeks to claim it for his own. However, both Head-
masters Armando Dippet and Dumbledore deny this post to
him. Following this incident, he disappears, only to resurface
years later as the Voldemort Harry knows.

THE MAKING OF A NEW WORLD

By the time he reappears, Voldemort has gained proficiency in both amassing power and inciting violence. He commands his Death Eaters completely; their submission leads Dumbledore to remark that they are "in the order of servants" rather than friends (*Half-Blood Prince* 444). Indeed, some Death Eaters go to prison rather than renounce Voldemort, revealing their utmost dedication to him as their master. Voldemort rises to power in the wizarding world and kills those who get in his way. Ironically, one of his most malicious actions causes his downfall. His attempted murder of Harry, at the time a defenseless child, temporarily breaks his power. However, nothing changes after Voldemort's rebirth; instead, he begins his rebellion anew, with more murders and more widespread grabs for power. Sirius states Voldemort's mission most plainly, its goals being "the purification of the Wizarding race, getting rid of Muggle-borns and having purebloods in charge" (*Order of the Phoenix* 112).

Oddly enough, a significant link between Voldemort and Hitler was that they both perpetrated ideas of a master race that did not include them. Hitler was born an Austrian, "in the town of Braunau near the German-Austrian border," and he was not a pure Aryan, as he had light blue eyes and dark hair (Altman 35). Yet despite this, Hitler advocated for Aryans, specifically of German origin. Voldemort is the same way. A half-blood, he advocates for pure-blood superiority though he does not fit this categorization himself.

Voldemort believes his rule, once actualized, will be eternal. He longs for immortality, as revealed by his obsession with Horcruxes, and takes extensive precautions to ascertain his dominion over mortality, intent on gaining a power that lasts as long as he does. His death finally frees the wizarding world of his tyranny.

In many ways, Voldemort corresponds to the adult years of Hitler, during which he controlled Germany and contorted it to suit his own vision. Hitler, like Voldemort, believed strongly in the powers of dominance and violence and worked incessantly to gain personal control over the affairs of Germany. After being released from prison, Hitler returned to the broken Nazi organization, seeking to elevate the party to a position of prominence. When the Great Depression hit Germany in 1929, leading to mass unemployment and levels of poverty, the Nazis saw an opportunity to insert themselves into the formal government (Altman 50). As a result of their efforts, Hitler was appointed chancellor of Germany.

From this position, Hitler continued to increase Nazi influence in the government. Driven by ambition, Hitler wrote of his ideal government in his manifesto, *Mein Kampf:* "There must be no majority decisions, but only responsible persons, and the word 'council' must be restored to its original meaning. Surely every man will have advisers by his side, but *the decision will be made by one man*" (449; emphasis in original). Hitler saw himself as this *"one man,"* the holder of supreme authority. On his way to achieving this, he appointed several Nazi officials to positions of power, created organizations such as the *Geheime-Staatspolizei* ("Secret State Police," also known as the Gestapo) to seek out enemies of his rule, and banned Jews from government employment (Altman 64). In this way, he created a solid foundation to stand on when he finally made himself the *Führer* of Germany in 1934.

This appointment began the cleansing of "undesirables" in Germany and the instigation of World War II. Hitler built up the German military "to conquer Europe for the German master race," a process that led to massive territorial expansion across Europe and brought Hitler's racism to a wider population, with many nations now subject to his "cleansing" agenda (Altman 56). Mass killings, in concentration camps or by euthanasia programs and firing squads, quickly exterminated anyone who did not fit Hitler's Aryan profile. Killing became streamlined and frighteningly common, and only Hitler's death could break the power of the Nazi war machine.

Hitler, like Voldemort, believed in the immortality of his ideas, and, until their failure became inevitable, he believed that Nazi rule would be eternal. As defeat drew closer to Germany, Hitler, unable to accept the crumbling of his empire, shot himself on April 30, 1945, in his bunker outside of Berlin (Bartoletti 142–143). He had dreamed of a "Thousand Year *Reich*," with Aryans dominating Europe for centuries, and at one rally, he told the German children, "You, my youth, never forget that one day you will rule the world!" (qtd. in Bartoletti 77). But Hitler's rule did not succeed, let alone last a thousand years.

Linked by their desire for power, their racism, and overwhelming violence, Hitler and Voldemort share many similar characteristics. Voldemort's movement in the wizarding world reflects the definitive action taken by Hitler in the adult years of his life. Additionally, both men gain the power they crave, and, ultimately, this power destroys them. Immortality fails them and shatters the hold they have over their respective nations. In many respects, Voldemort is the Hitler of the wizarding world, the greatest menace they have ever seen and will never see again. This link between leaders continues the connection between Harry Potter and the Nazis. The characters of Slytherin, Grindelwald, and Voldemort, though each unique in their own right, possess remarkable similarities with Hitler, a fact that strongly associates them with his image. Elements of Hitler live on in their words and actions.

The Hitler Youth and the Education System

The primary setting of the Harry Potter series is the wizarding establishment of Hogwarts School of Witchcraft and Wizardry. As such, the emphasis on education is substantial, and readers can easily see how the wizarding students learn. Having no technological access of any kind, students at Hogwarts rely on old-fashioned acquisitions of knowledge, through books or oral communication. Consequently, there is a greater possibility for the restriction and censorship of what students learn. Immense power resides with those who decide what is taught, something both Hitler and Voldemort realized. As a result, they sought entry into their respective educational systems in order to regulate knowledge, thereby gaining leverage over future generations, controlling people by controlling thought. This process evolved similarly in both worlds.

Under the Nazis, German education was rigorously regulated and reflective of Hitler's dominance. As author Susan Campbell Bartoletti writes, "For Hitler, education had one purpose: to mold children into good Nazis" (38). Therefore, schools were held to strict standards, with distinctive measures in place to ensure children only learned Nazi ideology. Often, this involved greatly limiting the freedoms of schoolteachers, requiring them to teach certain doctrine and use only what materials the Nazis permitted. An immense restructuring of the school system took place, during which Jewish instructors (or anyone who did not agree with Nazi ideas) were removed from their positions and old textbooks and works by Jewish authors were thrown out, often burned in large bonfires (Bartoletti 42–47). The Nazis completely rewrote the subject curriculum, eliminating what they thought unnecessary and adding what they felt was missing. History lessons were contextually changed to reflect Hitler and the Nazis as heroes and required children to write essays under such headings as "'Adolf Hitler, the Saviour of the Fatherland,' 'The Renewal of the German Racial Soul,' or 'What enables Adolf Hitler to be the German *Führer* and *Reichschancellor*'" (Lewis 73). New subjects included racial science and eugenics. As Bartoletti explains, "In racial science lessons, children were taught Aryans belonged to a superior master race that was intended to rule Europe. In eugenics lessons, children were taught that Aryans should marry only healthy Aryans. They were told not to 'mix their blood' by marrying non-Aryans" (42). This constant bombardment of Nazi ideology aimed to instill in children the same racist principles that guided the party. The Nazi way of life became all-encompassing, pervading every subject and every hour at school.

These teachings were further supplemented by the children's organization called the Hitler Youth. This social group promised the youth of Germany adventure and excitement in the form of weekly meetings, camping trips, and afternoon sports and games. It was structured as an army, with older leaders directing younger members and plenty of opportunities for advancement (Bartoletti 27). However, despite the potential the boys and girls saw in the Hitler Youth's activities, the founders of the organization had a different intent. As author Brenda Ralph Lewis writes, "What the Nazis meant to do was create a generation which knew nothing but Nazi principles and Nazi ideology" (7). The seemingly innocent activities of the Hitler Youth masked its function as a breeding ground for conformity, with the children all dressing alike and sharing the same values. Bartoletti states this principle clearly, writing, "the Hitler Youth did not tolerate originality or individuality. Through military drills and marches, the Hitler Youth learned to think and act as one. Most important, they learned to obey their leader, no matter what" (28). Though admission was voluntary toward the beginning of the group's creation, it soon became compulsory for all children. They were required to pass an examination to ensure they knew Nazi code and prove their racial background, as "[o]nly healthy boys and girls of proven 'Aryan' descent were permitted to join" (Bartoletti 25). Once admitted, these children became part of the system that perpetuated the Nazi regime, loyally following Hitler and growing up into faithful Nazis.

Through the school system and the Hitler Youth organization, both aimed at similar ends, children were immersed in the Nazi world. Hitler realized the power of the educational system in influencing youth, as did Voldemort. On several occasions, we see him attempt to insert himself into the system, but even when he is unable to do so, the system is adapted to his needs by others who share or comply with his objectives. This occurs most notably at the hands of Slytherin and Dolores Umbridge, individuals who both attempt to usurp the existing authority and structures of Hogwarts and replace them with people and ideas that support their efforts.

Slytherin perpetrates the earliest attempt to control education and pass on his line of thinking through it. One of Hogwarts's principle founders, Slytherin believed in educating only pure-bloods, a lesson he instilled deeply within his House restrictions. As the Sorting Hat tells in Harry's fifth year, "*Said Slytherin, 'We'll teach just those / Whose ancestry is purest'* . . . *Slytherin / Took only pure-blood wizards / Of great cunning, just like him*" (*Order of the Phoenix* 205). This legacy lives on in his House. Often, Slytherin students possess the same values as their founder, which gives them a negative reputation within the school and the larger world. As Hagrid tells Harry in the first book, "There's not a single witch or wizard who went bad who wasn't in Slytherin. You-Know-Who was one" (*Sorcerer's Stone* 80).

Through his actions, Slytherin creates a house of students predisposed to support Voldemort, though Voldemort comes many years after Slytherin. In the second novel, the password to the Slytherin common room is *"pure-blood,"* demonstrating that Slytherin's elitist message is still being transmitted years after he left (*Chamber of Secrets* 221). Because Voldemort rules by the same racial prejudices Slytherin advocates, the message Slytherin conveys is equally applicable to Voldemort's campaign. If Slytherins agree with the views of their House's founder, they are more likely to aid Voldemort. It is no surprise, then, that when Voldemort seeks fighters during the Battle of Hogwarts, Slytherin House supplies them.

In the fifth novel of the series, Hogwarts sees a more active form of educational reform at the hands of Umbridge. Umbridge is, in my opinion, one of the most detestable characters in the entire series. The Senior Undersecretary to the Minister of Magic, she is so blinded by her devotion to the minister and the establishment he heads that she propagates ideas that end up supporting Voldemort. Though Umbridge seems to believe otherwise, the changes she enacts at Hogwarts advance Voldemort's agenda and play right into his schemes for power. What she claims aligns students with the minister in reality weakens their defenses against the Dark Arts and limits their freedoms.

Umbridge begins her year at Hogwarts with a speech delineating what she expects out of the educational system, warning that there will be "pruning wherever we [the Ministry of Magic] find practices that ought to be prohibited" (*Order of the Phoenix* 214). She begins this process by restricting the school's subject matter. Within her Defense Against the Dark Arts class, Umbridge takes students back to square one with her revised curriculum and textbook, stating that they will be following a "carefully structured, theory-centered, Ministry-approved course" that eliminates the need to practice defensive magic, as "it is the view of the Ministry that a theoretical knowledge will be more than sufficient to get you through your examination" (239, 243). This change marks a major divergence from past classes, where practical applications of spells were at the center of the curriculum, and reveals the narrowing of knowledge to control the students. Students who have never practiced defensive magic are less likely to use it correctly and are therefore less likely to be a threat to either Umbridge or the Ministry.

Other limitations come in the form of the Educational Decrees Umbridge enacts once she is granted the position of Hogwarts High Inquisitor. This post, created by the Ministry of Magic, gives Umbridge the power to inspect other teachers and fabricate decrees to govern the goings-on at Hogwarts. She begins by immediately banning any clubs that are not sanctioned by the High Inquisitor, thereby giving herself the utmost control over what ideas she wants represented outside of the classroom at Hogwarts. Umbridge then proceeds to limit the flow of information from teachers to students by posting a decree that prohibits the giving of any knowledge "that is not strictly related to the subjects [professors] are paid to teach" (*Order of the Phoenix* 551). In this way, she keeps professors from sharing beliefs that may not agree with the Ministry. Further, she bans the magazine *The Quibbler* because she does not like what it reports, threatening to expel any student caught with it (581). Since no one outside of the Ministry can challenge the decrees, they effectively limit the freedoms of students and staff at Hogwarts. These limitations are highly reminiscent of those placed upon schools by the Nazis. By controlling subject matter, they sought to control the minds of the young, something Umbridge attempts as well. Her devotion to the principles of the Ministry, revealed as terribly misguided by the end of the novel, provide cause for the restrictions.

Just as repugnant as Umbridge's need for control is her astonishing willingness to use violence to enforce her decrees. Readers see this through Harry, whose defiance subjects him to many of Umbridge's punishments. After resisting Umbridge's Ministry-approved lessons and thus refusing to submit to her control, for example, Harry is forced to write lines in his own blood: "again and again the words were cut into the back of his hand, healed, and then reappeared the next time he set quill to parchment" (*Order of the Phoenix* 267). Lee Jordan is given the same treatment after he makes a joke about her Educational Decrees (551). To question students who are causing trouble, Umbridge makes use of the powerful (and restricted) Veritaserum potion, one "controlled by very strict Ministry guidelines" (*Goblet of Fire* 517). Umbridge, however, seems to have no problem using it whenever she pleases. Twice we see her try to use it on Harry, first in an attempt to coerce Dumbledore's whereabouts from him and again to try to force him into a confession. When she runs out of Veritaserum, Umbridge resorts to the Cruciatus Curse, perfectly aware that performing the spell is illegal; when challenged with this fact, she merely comments, "What Cornelius [the Minister of Magic] doesn't know won't hurt him" (*Order of the Phoenix* 746). When it comes to maintaining her control over Hogwarts, Umbridge has no qualms about using force. Umbridge and her rules irrevocably taint Harry's fifth year at Hogwarts, but in many ways, her actions provide an important warning for the students. The alterations to curriculum and the violence that she brings to Hogwarts serves as a precursor to the changes Voldemort enacts, a preview of what awaits students when Voldemort is in charge of wizarding education.

Voldemort's educational upheaval is revealed in the final novel of the series when he finally gains control of Hogwarts and alters its systems to his liking. Although the full effects of his changes are difficult to discern, as Harry is absent from Hogwarts his final year, the bits he picks up from Neville toward the end of the book provide an overview of its transformation.

Upon Dumbledore's death, Professor Severus Snape becomes headmaster of Hogwarts and the school is infiltrated by Death Eaters. Though Voldemort is physically absent from the school, his followers change the curriculum to suit his ends in his absence, turning Defense Against the Dark Arts into just the Dark Arts and requiring students to practice forbidden curses on one another as part of their lessons (*Deathly Hallows* 573). They also adapt Muggle Studies, making it a compulsory class and filling it with messages about how "Muggles are like animals, stupid and dirty, and how they drove wizards into hiding by being vicious toward them, and how the natural order is being reestablished" (574). This modification clearly parallels the Nazi effort to teach students about Aryan superiority and reflects Voldemort's ultimate goal of pure-blood dominance. Like Hitler, Voldemort saw the adaptation to the curriculum as a permanent change meant to support and perpetuate his ideas long into the future.

Once Voldemort controls Hogwarts, he leaves his Death Eaters in charge of maintaining that control, a task they accomplish using a variety of violent forms. To keep students within the school itself, there are "curses over the entrances and Death Eaters and dementors waiting at the exits" (*Deathly Hallows* 572). Amycus and Electo Carrow, two Death Eaters who teach the new subjects of Muggle Studies and the Dark Arts, are in charge of discipline, and according to Neville, they make Umbridge look tame (573). Neville is on the receiving end of many of their tactics, admitting, "they'll torture us a bit if we're mouthy but they won't actually kill us" (574). Once again, this torture includes the Cruciatus Curse. Students are punished for speaking out against Voldemort in any fashion, which leads several to find sanctuary in the Room of Requirement. Their safety, and that of the school, is only regained after a terrible battle, which takes place on Hogwarts's grounds, an additional indication of the school's significance.

Throughout the series, Hogwarts serves as the center of wizarding education. As the preeminent educational institution, it possesses immense influence; Voldemort knows that and sees it as a place to control the future. Hitler's programs sought a similar end, resulting in a force of young Nazis willing to die for him and his mission. In time, perhaps Voldemort could have achieved the same thing; he certainly realized the potential of youth. As Hitler once said, "I begin with the young. We older ones are used up. . . . But my magnificent youngsters! Are there finer ones anywhere in the world? Look at all these men and boys! What material! With them I can make a new world" (qtd. in Bartoletti 7).

Hitler did his best to remake the world as he saw fit, and although it has been seventy years since he and the Nazis were defeated, the consequences of their actions still resound throughout the ages, leaving a permanent stain on human history. By basing her villains on Nazi principles, J. K. Rowling taps into the enduring legacy of the Nazi machine, pulling Harry's story out of fantasy and linking it to brutal reality. Connecting Harry Potter to Nazism enables readers to recognize the misguided principles of Harry's enemies and the tactics they will pursue to promote the survival of their views. Through his racist ideas and actions, Voldemort embodies some of the worst principles of Nazism and reanimates some of the darkest days of the twentieth century. Our history is Harry's present. In overcoming the challenges offered to him, Harry fights as we once did for dignity and freedom, reminding us that good can prevail over evil.

Works Cited

Altman, Linda Jacobs. *The Holocaust, Hitler, and Nazi Germany*. Berkeley Heights, NJ: Enslow, 1999. Print.

Bartoletti, Susan Campbell. *Hitler Youth: Growing Up in Hitler's Shadow*. New York, NY: Scholastic, 2005. Print.

Hammer, Joshua. "Hitler's Children." *Newsweek* 135.12 (2000): 34–37. *Academic Search Premier*. EBSCOhost. St. Catherine University, St. Paul, MN. Web. 8 June 2011. http://web.ebscohost.com/ehost.

Hitler, Adolf. *Mein Kampf*. Trans. Ralph Manheim. Boston, MA: Houghton, 1971. Print.

Lewis, Brenda Ralph. *Hitler Youth: The* Hitlerjugend *in War and Peace, 1933–1945*. Osceola, WI: MBI, 2000. Print.

Reagin, Nancy R. "Was Voldemort a Nazi? Death Eater Ideology and National Socialism." In *Harry Potter and History*, ed. Nancy R. Reagin. Hoboken, NJ: Wiley, 2011. 127–152. Print.

Rhodes, Richard. *Masters of Death: The SS-Einsatzgruppen and the Invention of the Holocaust*. New York, NY: Knopf, 2002. Print.

Seven

The Nuances of Mastering Death

Murder, Capital Punishment, and
Assisted Suicide in Harry Potter

KALIE CAETANO

Six months after J. K. Rowling began writing the series that would become a global phenomenon, she experienced a traumatic loss—her mother died. During a candid interview with Oprah Winfrey, Rowling confessed how her mother's death profoundly transformed the course of Harry Potter's story—a seven-part saga constantly ruminating on mortality and human demise. "Her death is on virtually every other page," Rowling revealed, "At least half of Harry's journey is a journey to deal with death in its many forms, what it does to the living, what it means to die, what survives death . . ." (Harpo Productions). These themes seem relatively subdued at the outset of the series, but gradually the emphasis on dying ratchets up, beginning with Cedric Diggory's death and escalating until Harry soberly crosses the corpse-strewn Hogwarts grounds to meet his own end. By the final installment of the series the process of dying emerges as the chief preoccupation of the boy who lived.

Specifically, *Deathly Hallows* concerns itself with the *mastery* of death. In an interview with *Time* magazine, Rowling confesses that the "theme of the entire series" can be encapsulated in a biblical verse from First Corinthians: "The last enemy that shall be destroyed is death"—indeed this verse is the epitaph inscribed on the tombstones of James and Lily Potter

(Gibbs). Our hero, Harry, becomes the "master of death" by marshaling his Gryffindor courage and embracing his mortality. The moment in which he volunteers his life marks the crowning apotheosis of the series, more emotionally significant for the protagonist than the subsequent destruction of his lifelong foe, Lord Voldemort. Rowling asserts that Harry's freedom from the fear of his own mortality grants him mastery over death.

But Rowling's commentary on death's many forms—"what it does to the living, what it means to die, what survives death"—does not stop there. The books are rife with thoughts on the significance of what it means to take a life (or give one up) in myriad contexts—from the murderous rampages of the Death Eaters to the pivotal scene atop the highest tower of Hogwarts, in which Professor Albus Dumbledore takes his leave with a little help from the potions master. What lurks beneath the surface of dementor iconography and Horcruxology is a weedy and complex terrain in which Rowling implicitly moralizes on murder, capital punishment, and even assisted suicide, offering nuanced ethical hierarchies to interpret the moral culpability in how lives are taken and for what purpose.

Murder and the Ministry of Magic

It comes as little surprise that those who do the majority of life-taking are the villainous factions of the series: Voldemort, Death Eaters, dementors, Gellert Grindelwald, and so on. Murder is an instrument that they have a near monopoly on, while the "good" characters largely refuse to return fatal attacks in kind, despite temptation. Even though the stage is set for perpetual battle—between Harry and Voldemort, the Order and the Death Eaters, Dumbledore's Army (DA) and Dolores Umbridge—only under exceptional circumstances over the course of all seven books does any of our cast of heroes actually *kill* an enemy combatant. When Ginny Weasley and Remus Lupin give Harry an account of the Death Eaters' infiltration into Hogwarts in *Half-Blood Prince*, they describe a scene in which the DA and the Order hold their own with defensive spells (and a bit of Felix Felicis) while the Death Eaters hurl killing curses left and right

(618–619). Though *Avada Kedavra* is an incantation rarely uttered by any of Dumbledore's soldiers, the enemy exhibits no such restraint; Alastor "Mad-Eye" Moody sheds light on the dismal mortality rate of Order members when showing a picture of the organization's founders to Harry. His grim report details the murder of eight of the twenty-two original members, with two others (Alice and Frank Longbottom) being tortured into insanity. Compared to the voracious Death Eaters, the Order of the Phoenix's hands are largely clean of bloodshed. The exceptions to this rule, Molly Weasley (who murders Bellatrix Lestrange) and Professor Severus Snape (who kills Dumbledore), are isolated incidents that serve their own purposes (more on this later).

The obvious and predictable takeaway here basically boils down to a truth acknowledged by religious and state law the world over: murder is bad. But yet another, more interesting conclusion to derive may be the following: where evils exists it ought to be fought, but not *all* means are justified in doing so—particularly if those means will lower you to the level of your enemy. Thus, in order to maintain the moral superiority of her protagonists and their allies, Rowling takes murder out of their arsenal. That is not to say that "good" characters never encounter the temptation to kill—Lupin and Sirius Black intend to kill Peter Pettigrew (Wormtail) after discovering his treachery; Lupin says to him, "You should have realized . . . if Voldemort didn't kill you, we would" (*Prisoner of Azkaban* 375). Harry, likewise, hunts Bellatrix Lestrange through the Ministry after Sirius's murder, a chase that begins with a vow of fatal vengeance: "SHE KILLED SIRIUS . . . I'LL KILL HER!" (*Order of the Phoenix* 809). Both potential manslaughters are averted: first when Harry stays the hands (or wands, as it were) of the would-be murderers (Lupin and Sirius), sparing Wormtail's life; and later when, despite his threat to kill her, Harry only manages to unleash a feeble Cruciatus Curse on Bellatrix. In fact, never once in his seven-year quest to defeat evil does Harry ever aim to kill. Even in the final battle between the boy who lived and his mortal enemy, Harry shoots only to disarm Voldemort, and the Dark Lord ultimately destroys himself when his killing curse rebounds.

Rowling draws a clear line in the sand to divide the teams of good and evil, associating deadly aggression nearly exclusively with her less savory characters. Why? Maybe because she is, after all, writing a children's book—though this answer is unsatisfying, not only because it is too simple for a series that is so complex, but also because there is a third faction to consider in our analysis of who kills and why: the Ministry of Magic. If Voldemort and his Death Eaters kill and that makes them bad, and Dumbledore and his Order refrain from murder and that makes them good—then where does that leave the government?

The Ministry exists in a gray middle ground between the overtly good forces (Dumbledore and the Order) and the explicitly evil ones (Voldemort's followers). The magical government endowed with meting out justice all too often unwittingly finds itself the bedfellow of Voldemort's corrupt faction. The Ministry uses the dementors, who eventually free the Death Eaters from Azkaban, and they also employ a Death Eater, Weldon Macnair, as an executioner. Additionally, slippery Lucius Malfoy always seems to have his glib tongue wagging near the minister's ear. This government, initially introduced to the readers with the same whimsy with which the rest of the wizarding world is presented, eventually progresses into a sinister shade of the Third Reich, doling out arrests and executions according to bloodlines (see chapter 6 in this volume). Even before the seventh book, when the Ministry is overrun with Voldemort's puppets, evidence of the government's ethical waywardness crops up in *Prisoner of Azkaban*, when the Ministry wrongly attempts to prosecute and kill the titular character, Sirius, along with an unjustly arraigned hippogriff. Throughout the series Rowling slowly peels the Ministry's charming façade away until the magical government has progressed into a full-fledged dystopic state.

Rowling contrasts the Ministry against what she sets up as the true moral compass of the series epitomized in Dumbledore, Harry, and the Order. The novels, written in third-person semi-omniscient narration, generally afford the main characters a more accurate view of key realities—for example, Sirius's innocence in *Prisoner of Azkaban* or Voldemort's return in *Goblet of Fire*. As readers, we are privy to realities to which the third-party Ministry remains oblivious. The reader is uniquely positioned to hear

Sirius's heartfelt testimony when he pleads his case to Harry in the third book, just as there is no doubt in the reader's mind that Voldemort has returned after the eerie graveyard scene in book 4. However, the Ministry and its agents do not witness nor do they choose to believe in either Sirius's innocence or Voldemort's resurgence, and their subsequent action (or inaction) smacks of injustice (and cowardice). Of particular interest to me is Sirius's predicament with the Ministry. Despite Harry's willingness to verify his godfather's (truthful) version of events, the Minister of Magic is resolved to eliminate the convicted criminal. Dumbledore intervenes to subvert the minister's plans, sending Hermione Granger and Harry as emissaries into the past to save both the hippogriff, Buckbeak, as well as Sirius—who has been condemned to the worst penalty the wizarding government can administer: the Dementor's Kiss.

Technically, the kiss will not kill its victim—however, I think it safe to equate the Dementor's Kiss with a sentence tantamount to capital punishment. Once performed, the kiss leaves its recipient an empty shell of their former self in a permanent state of catatonia, soulless and absent of ego. Though the kiss's recipient may be alive—insofar as he or she could make a heart monitor beep—it is doubtful that they could be described as "living." When Sirius's sentence is not suspended, despite Harry's testimony, the reader is struck, along with our protagonist, by the injustice of the warped and ill-informed verdict.

In both Buckbeak's and Sirius's case the condemned are unfairly convicted as the result of a short-circuiting judicial system corrupted by malpractice and cronyism. Buckbeak's conviction is a consequence of Hagrid's lack of legal *savoir-faire*, particularly when pitted against the wealthy, influential, and cunning Lucius Malfoy, who has already used his power once at this point in the series to have Dumbledore ousted from Hogwarts after bribing and threatening the school governors (*Chamber of Secrets*). Malfoy's machinations before the trial lead to Buckbeak's execution order at the hands of (who else?) former Death Eater Macnair. Sirius, meanwhile, represents a more extreme case—he never committed the crime for which he served twelve years in prison—a consequence of never having been given a trial at all (*Goblet of Fire* 526). Despite this,

Minister of Magic Cornelius Fudge—the archetype of a political bungler, whose surname is appropriately a synonym for
"error"—erroneously judges Sirius guilty and sets his life as the
price. As a result, Harry and Hermione are bidden by the seemingly all-seeing Dumbledore to save two lives from Ministry-
ordained execution.

They succeed in their mission, granting Sirius a reprieve from
the kiss—a triumph that Dumbledore would later characterize
as Harry "snatch[ing]" his godfather from the "*jaws* of the Ministry" (*Order of the Phoenix* 839; emphasis added). Altogether,
Rowling's depiction of the Ministry—from the accuracy of its
intel to the keenness of its employees—is distinctly unflattering.
Naturally, when the government is permitted to lawfully wield
capital punishment, it becomes an ideal entry point for Voldemort's violent faction, particularly when the Ministry already
keeps dementors in its employ—creatures that Voldemort refers
to as the "natural allies" of the Death Eaters (*Goblet of Fire*
651). The association of the Ministry with a brand of monster so
intimately associated with death creates a tenuous alliance dis-
avowed by both Dumbledore and Lupin. The latter describes
dementors as being "among the foulest creatures that walk this
earth," an allegation justified by the strong links forged between
dementors, depravity, and death (*Prisoner of Azkaban* 187).

These creatures, depicted as doppelgängers of the Grim
Reaper, are symbolic of death and are unequivocally the most
monstrous of the Potterverse demons. Their image replicates
conventional depictions of Death, the shrouded, scythe-carrying
phantom that has haunted the Western imagination for centuries.
Rowling invests a lot of rhetoric in removing all human aspects
from the dementors to create a sense that they transcend humanity and radiate a vibe of inhuman aloofness—they are nonne-
gotiable and impassable—much like death itself. Homogenous,
ungendered, unspeaking, sightless, and faceless—these creatures
constitute a single-faceted mass of gloom and doom, representing not characters but a *force*. Rowling's depiction of dementors echoes a stanza from Edmund Spenser's *Faerie Queene* as
he introduces Death, describing him as "unbodied, unsoul'd,
unheard, unseene" (IIV.vii.46). Dementors are similarly soulless,
silent, and unseen (at least by Muggles). Dementors rob their

quarry of well-being with no concern for the pain they inflict and have no capacity for love or compassion. For example, when Harry is battling the dementors in Little Whinging in *Order of the Phoenix*, he unleashes his stag Patronus, the antlers of which catch the dementor "in the place where the heart should have been," suggesting that dementors, by nature, lack compassion, rendering them incapable of moral censure or remorse (18). Their *coup de grâce*, the Dementor's Kiss, conducted by pulling a person's soul out from her body through her mouth, is reminiscent of the colloquial phrase "to suck the life out of" something or someone, which is essentially what the dementors do with their much-feared smooch. Far removed from any humanizing or individualizing characteristics, they are defined by a single, solitary drive: *hunger*. When Lupin describes them to Harry, he characterizes the Hogwarts Quidditch match, full of jubilation and excitement, as being the dementors' "idea of a feast" (*Prisoner of Azkaban* 188). Couched in predatory terms, they need only one thing: to *feed*.

It is intriguing that dementors should be shrouded and heavily characterized with feeding terminology. Death Eaters, when convening with the Dark Load, are similarly enshrouded and masked. Their faces are obscured, their humanity hidden. They are dubbed "Eaters"—why? Of all the nouns that could complete that appellation: Death Bringers, Death Makers, Death Bearers, Rowling chose "Eaters." Perhaps, they are so named in order to pull their crimes into tight association with the voracious, devouring dementors. Death Eaters subordinate their compassion for their fellows, subscribing to a dogma of persecution in pursuit of the dubious goal of racial purity. This alienation of Muggle-borns and half-bloods liberates them from empathy and allows them to wage war against their own kind, employing murder frequently and flippantly. It is for this reason that murder is a weapon to be wielded only by Rowling's antagonists: the prerequisite to murder is the eradication of compassion, and this depravity undergirds all evil.

Because dementors and Death Eaters are framed as two related points on a sinister spectrum, the Ministry of Magic's association with the foul creatures stains its moral authority in the eyes of the reader. Why should such despicable

monsters—"natural allies" of Voldemort's forces—be working for the Ministry (*Goblet of Fire* 651)? The intimate linkage
between government and death creates a tension-riddled alliance
that makes our heroes, Harry, Ron, and Hermione, as well as
the reader, distrustful of the Ministry's weaponry—dementors
and their kisses—and raises the question: ought the Ministry
even have the authority to take life in the first place? I like to
think that Rowling suggests an answer to this query by offering
a scathing indictment of the Ministry's justice system and a symbolic execution in *Order of the Phoenix.*

By the fifth book, condemnation of the government becomes
unflinchingly explicit, and it's only fitting that one of the first
rituals performed in that novel is Moody's symbolic "disillu-
sionment" of Harry—a spell that presages the political disillu-
sionment that he and the readers will come to experience in the
ensuing chapters (*Order of the Phoenix* 54). In the course of the
book, the Ministry wages smear campaigns and courtroom cir-
cuses, and at the novel's end, fan favorite Sirius is killed in a setting that conspicuously reprises themes of execution.

While he survived *Prisoner of Azkaban* through an unofficial acquittal, organized by Dumbledore's and Harry's vigilan-
tism, Sirius's reprieve turns out to be more of a rain-check than a
real pardon. Until his death in *Order of the Phoenix*, Sirius lives
in hiding as an outlaw, dogged by crimes for which he has not
been legally cleared. Though his death eventually comes at the
hands of a Death Eater—not the Ministry—the setting for his
final stand is poignantly rife with subtext.

Killed in the halls of the Ministry, Sirius falls through the veil
in the Department of Mysteries. The veil is housed in a room
that is described as being structured like an "amphitheater"—
where in Roman times condemned criminals were hacked to
death by gladiators for the amusement of the public. The room
is also described as being reminiscent of a "courtroom" like the
one Harry had seen earlier in the same book, when he was tried
by the Wizengamot. There, he meets and narrowly escapes an
unjust conviction himself (*Order of the Phoenix* 773). Rowling
explicitly invokes these two connotations, subtly and yet con-
cisely linking the justice system (courtroom) with execution
(Romanesque amphitheater). The veil and the archway from

which it hangs—later revealed to be a portal to death—stand at the center of the foreboding room and may just as well be an electric chair. Fitting, then, that Sirius Black, of all the potential casualties at the Battle of the Ministry, is the one who falls through the veil—the faux criminal and perpetual victim of an imperfect justice system. If any ambiguity persisted *vis-à-vis* Rowling's implied distaste for capital punishment left over from *Prisoner of Azkaban*, the "Beyond the Veil" chapter of book 5 ought to have resolved it.

Horcruxes and Souls

Of course, Rowling's most explicit mechanism for condemning murder is delivered in the form of Horcruxes, magic rituals so dark and taboo that by the time Harry arrives at Hogwarts even the Restricted Section of the library yields no information about them. It is from Professor Horace Slughorn in *Half-Blood Prince* that the function and process of making a Horcrux is revealed to Tom Riddle. Horcruxes are inanimate objects in which fragments of a person's soul are embedded so as to evade death by fracturing blueprints of the self and stowing them away in unmarked items. The process of creating one involves "the supreme act of evil," namely, murder, which "rips the soul apart," cleaving it into pieces (*Half-Blood Prince* 498). In order to appreciate the gravity of this act, it's necessary to consider Rowling's presentation of the soul in a broader context. Souls, as Rowling presents them, represent the essence, the self and the humanity of a person. Dementors are "soulless and evil" creatures who reduce their victims to the same state by administering their kiss (*Prisoner of Azkaban* 187). A correlation between the absence of a soul and a predilection toward evil and emptiness emerges. In Christian theology, the soul represents the immutable vehicle by which humans transcend life into the afterlife. Similarly, "selling your soul to the Devil" is the pinnacle of taboo and typically done with evil intent. Voldemort's own Faustian bargain transforms him into a vampiric trope—a character who sustains his own immortality by killing others at the expense of his humanity and compassion.

Even the word association that Rowling plays with by coin-
ing the term "Horcrux" is telling of the feeling she intends to
inspire in the reader. The first syllable calls to mind adjectives
such as "horrible," "horrendous," "horrific," among others.
Meanwhile, *crux*, Latin for "cross," revives Christian symbolism in which the cross is the stand-in symbol for Christ's sacrifice. By this arithmetic "Hor-crux" can be broken down to
mean horrific sacrifice, a diabolical inversion of the Christian
story of self-sacrifice. As John Granger, author of *The Deathly
Hallows Lectures*, puts it, Voldemort "has divided his soul into
seven parts in a horrific attempt to ape alchemy and create an
egocentric rather than a spiritual immortality" (55). That is to
say, rather than trusting in an eternal afterlife, the Dark Lord
pursues a more literal immortality, privileging his obsession
with self and worldly power (egomania) over other human lives.
The mutilation of his soul in pursuit of this egocentric immortality is the crime that garners him the title of the series' most
despicable villain, while those who inversely sacrifice their own
lives for others—Lily for Harry and Harry for his comrades at
the Battle of Hogwarts—earn the title "masters of death." They
master death because they do not fear it—and in Rowling's view
this is a very sage attitude to take.

Dumbledore delivers an enduring aphorism as early as *Sorcerer's Stone*, when he says, "to the well-organized mind, death
is but the next great adventure" (297). His acceptance of death
precisely opposes Voldemort's desperation to preserve himself.
Tangentially, it has already been widely noted that the etymol-
ogy of the name "Voldemort" can be derived from the French *vol
de mort*, meaning "*theft* from death" or "*flight* from death" (*vol*
being a homonym in French). Dumbledore, contrarily, exhibits
no desire to fly from or steal himself away from death, which is
why an initial read of his pivotal exit scene in *Half-Blood Prince*
seems strangely uncharacteristic. In chapter 27 of *Half-Blood
Prince*, "The Lightning-Struck Tower," Dumbledore finds himself wandless and seemingly alone (though Harry, immobilized
and hidden beneath his Invisibility Cloak, silently witnesses the
entire scene). Cornered by Death Eaters (Draco Malfoy, Fenrir Greyback, Amycus and Alecto Carrow, and Snape), Dumbledore utters a whispered plea that deeply frightens Harry:

"Severus . . . Please . . ." (595). A cursory perusal leads the reader
to the natural interpretation that Dumbledore is begging Snape
to spare his life—to reveal his true allegiance to Dumbledore
and rescue him from the Death Eaters' murderous plot. But following this appeal, Snape executes the revered headmaster with
the killing curse, "hatred etched in the hard lines of his face"
(595). Of course, this bears all the marks of an odious betrayal,
but information revealed in the seventh and final book yields an
entirely different exegesis.

"The Prince's Tale" chapter of *Deathly Hallows* sheds light
on a more nuanced understanding, not only of Dumbledore's
death but also of the nature of killing and its implied effects
on the human soul. Before he dies, Snape gives Harry a few
key morsels from his memory to sift through in the Pensieve.
Among other insights, his memories reveal an insightful conversation that provide context for all of the unanswered questions
surrounding Snape, that most opaque of double agents. In the
memory, Snape confides in Dumbledore, telling him that Draco
Malfoy has been assigned the task of assassinating the headmaster. As glimpsed at the beginning of *Half-Blood Prince*, Snape
enters into an Unbreakable Vow with Draco's mother, Narcissa
Malfoy, assuming the responsibility of carrying out the execution himself, should Draco fail. Upon hearing this, Dumbledore
insists that Snape be the one to kill him, rather than the misguided, adolescent Slytherin boy—an order which prompts the
following dialogue:

> "If you don't mind dying," said Snape roughly, "why
> not let Draco do it?"
> "That boy's soul is not yet so damaged," said Dumb-
> ledore. "I would not have it ripped apart on my account."
> "And my soul Dumbledore? Mine?"
> "You alone know whether it will harm your soul
> to help an old man avoid pain and humiliation," said
> Dumbledore. "I ask this one great favor of you, Severus,
> because death is coming for me . . . I confess I should
> prefer a quick, painless exit to the protracted and messy
> affair it will be if, for instance, Greyback is involved . . .
> Or dear Bellatrix . . ." (*Deathly Hallows* 683)

Dumbledore's implication is a stunning one: "*You alone know whether it will harm your soul . . .*" In this single utterance Dumbledore introduces an entirely new dimension to the metaphysical rules Rowling establishes with Horcruxes. Through Voldemort's single-minded pursuit of eternal life, the reader learns that murder bears consequences to the perpetrator: it cleaves the killer's soul into pieces. Yet, Dumbledore suggests that Snape's soul may survive this particular killing unscathed— why? Because of his intent.

Perhaps one of the most hotly contested topics throughout the seven-part series is where Snape's true loyalty lies—with Dumbledore or Voldemort? Arguments on either side of the case jostle for the reader's attention until the matter is finally settled in "The Prince's Tale." The reader learns that Snape, still harboring a long-abiding, unrequited love for Harry's mother, Lily Potter, has been Dumbledore's man all along. Despite Harry's frequent doubts, Dumbledore exhibits unfailing confidence in Snape's loyalty and is able to bid him—with little reservation—to kill him. Because of this allegiance, Dumbledore dismisses Snape's fears that killing him will ravage his soul. It appears that the ends are not the only factor when considering the ethical integrity of taking another's life, but that intent—the why behind the killing—is of critical importance.

Snape's true allegiance determines his intent and thus frames the context of his execution of Dumbledore. If, as Dumbledore fervently doubts, Snape is Voldemort's agent, then killing Dumbledore is tantamount to murder; it is done with the intention of eliminating an enemy at Voldemort's behest, with the convenient permission of Dumbledore. However, if Snape is a true ally and he does this "one great favor" for the headmaster, his assassination is more akin to assisted suicide. Certainly the phrase "help an old man avoid pain and humiliation" recalls euthanasia rhetoric—proponents of which claim that the practice allows people to die with dignity, free from unnecessary suffering. At this stage of the novel, Dumbledore's health and mortality is already imperiled by his encounter with the cursed Resurrection Stone, the Horcrux that has mangled his arm and gradually saps his strength throughout book 7. Bound for the grave by both ailing health and a death warrant signed and sealed by Voldemort and

Draco, Dumbledore seeks death out voluntarily. Snape assumes the role of facilitator rather than murderer. Were Draco to perform the same task, he would commit an unambiguous murder, motivated by fear and self-preservation rather than mercy. He would assault his own soul—Snape would not. Thus Rowling strives to distinguish this sacrificial assisted suicide from cold-blooded murder.

Bearing this in mind, the reason Dumbledore pleads with Snape atop Hogwarts's Astronomy Tower becomes readily apparent. Consistent with his character, Dumbledore begs for *death*, not life, knowing that it will spare him an agonizing demise and preserve the soul of an (arguably) innocent boy. His volition, coupled with Snape's nonmalevolent intent, exonerates the greasy-haired pseudo-villain of any real crime and sets him apart from the other Death Eaters whose killing rampages are driven by a malicious desire to destroy an enemy.

Death and Maternal Instinct

Snape's execution of Dumbledore complicates cut-and-dried notions of what it means to murder, particularly by introducing a life-balance equation: taking Dumbledore's life saves Draco's life—might this redeem the killer somewhat? This premise may also lend insight into understanding the anomalistic "good guy" murder, perpetrated by the much-loved mother of seven, Molly Weasley. Her fatal attack on Bellatrix Lestrange comes from an unexpected corner, but few would argue that her actions are unjustified. Another question that the text does not explicitly address is Narcissa Malfoy's culpability in Dumbledore's demise. Her decision to make the Unbreakable Vow with Snape changes the game: it guarantees that *someone*—either Snape or Dumbledore—must die. Does this, in effect, make her a murderer? Snape might get off scot-free, but what are the consequences for *her* soul? She, the wife of a Death Eater, makes precisely the opposite bargain as the saintly Lily Potter, who, rather than killing for her child, dies in his place. These three women, Narcissa, Molly, and Lily—all mothers, all motivated to forfeit life for their child—fall onto a moral spectrum.

The same tenacious spirit undergirds Molly's manslaughter, Lily's sacrifice, and Narcissa's calculated plot. In each case the intent is the same: to save their children from impending destruction. As Bellatrix charges at Ginny Weasley, Molly intervenes, delivering a killing blow to the vindictive Death Eater. Her actions, impulsive and defensive, show a snap decision made under duress to eliminate a direct threat to her daughter's life. These factors distinguish her actions from Narcissa's—given that *she* uses other agents to save her son rather than throwing herself into the fray (she could have attempted to assassinate Dumbledore herself). She also designs this scheme well in advance of any immediate danger to her son. While Molly is moved by a sudden, unthinking impulse, Narcissa throws Snape under the bus in a premeditated strategy that smacks of cowardice and fear. Alternately, when Lily yields her own life to Voldemort to defend her son, not only does she achieve a martyr-like legacy in the series, but hers is the only sacrifice that provides tangible and lasting protection. The moral integrity of her decision to embrace death rather than deflecting it makes Harry literally *untouchable* for the first half of the series. The fallout of Lily's sacrifice still clings to Harry and burns Voldemort—not until he uses Harry's blood to resurrect himself is he able to bypass Lily's magical firewall.

Lily's love, her compassionate example, becomes the prototype for Harry's own role as savior at the end of *Deathly Hallows*. Her act of love is recycled and amplified through her son to rescue the combatants at the Battle of Hogwarts from the clutches of the Dark Lord and his followers. Following his mother's example, Harry learns what it means to live, to die—to master death, figuratively and literally. His love for others overwhelms his love of self, and his reward is resurrection. He destroys the last enemy and saves the day.

While the mastering of death in the series may be as simple as relying on the old biblical standby of fearing no evil while walking through that shadowed valley, the mastering of the *theme* of death in a broader context is slightly more nuanced. But Rowling equips her readers with partially omniscient narrators, juxtaposition, parallels, allusions, and more, in order to develop a message that not only lavishes admiration on the sacrificial lambs of Lily and Harry but also condemns both cold-blooded and state-sanctioned executions and tacitly validates assisted suicide in the face of an insurmountable and impending death. True to Dumbledore's adage, and to the chagrin of Voldemort, these three avenues of death—murder, euthanasia, self-sacrifice—and their consequences are representative of the various manifestations of love. Murder represents an absence of love and is condemned most effortlessly, but also most rigorously, throughout the series. Snape's act in taking Dumbledore's life, meanwhile, arguably constitutes an act of love by sparing him an even worse fate even at the cost of his own peace of mind. Yet the real trophy is, of course, reserved for those who sacrifice themselves for others, the absolute inversion of murder—the willing victim of death who could be motivated by nothing less than the deepest empathy and love.

Works Cited

Gibbs, Nance. "Persons of the Year 2007: Runners-Up." *Time*. 19 December 2007. Print.

Granger, John. *The Deathly Hallows Lectures.* Allentown, PA: Zossima Press, 2008. Print.

Harpo Productions, Inc. "Oprah Interviews J. K. Rowling." Online video interview. *YouTube*. YouTube, 25 Mar. 2013. Web. 23 June 2013.

Spenser, Edmund. *The Faerie Queene.* New York, NY: Penguin Group, 1979. Print.

Eight

The Wickedest of Magical Inventions

The Separable Soul in Harry Potter
and Medieval Folklore

SARAH SUTOR

In *Chamber of Secrets*, Harry Potter encounters the lost diary of Tom Riddle, a "small thin book . . . [with] a shabby black cover" (242). After an offer by the diary to reveal the events that occurred fifty years ago, Harry, hoping to end the Chamber of Secrets' threat, finds himself entering the diary's memory: "Before he knew what was happening, he tilted forward; the window was widening, he felt his body leave his bed, and he was pitched headfirst through the opening in the page, into a whirl of color and shadow" (242). Inside Riddle's diary, Harry is pulled into a world that appears to be reality. Outside the diary, Harry still has difficulty discerning the difference between truth and the story created by the diary. Later he (and we as readers) understands that the diary's story is false and that the diary itself is one of Lord Voldemort's Horcruxes, a separation of the Dark Lord's soul. Nevertheless, in this instance, we begin to discern the uncertain borders that demarcate fiction from truth and text from reality.

While Harry's plunge into Riddle's diary is the most literal metaphor for a reader's engagement with literature, where the interaction of text and consumer blurs the boundary between fantasy and reality, J. K. Rowling continually plays with uncertainty throughout her text, allowing Harry to doubt his perceptions and readers to experience an imagined reality. As Professor Albus Dumbledore famously notes, "Of course it is happening inside your head, Harry, but why on earth should that mean that it is not real?" (*Deathly Hallows* 723). More than just a commentary on psychology or a reader's response to literature, Rowling asserts that thoughts, dreams, and legends coexist with reality and, indeed, are perhaps the building blocks of truth, giving us devices and powers found only in literature that would otherwise be physically impossible to access. While engaged in the seemingly unremarkable act of reading a book, the reader exists in the middle of the ordinary and the extraordinary, where heroes, villains, and other mythical forces walk side by side with the humdrum. Even though people are often oblivious to the extent a text influences their "real" life, and still others attempt to dismiss a story's impact by labeling it imaginary, Rowling makes it clear that she does not envision a clear-cut divide between text and reader. As a result, literature possesses "a power beyond the reach of any magic" that leaves perceptible effects upon its audience (*Deathly Hallows* 709).

Although Rowling positions both Harry and the reader simultaneously within fantasy and reality multiple times in the Harry Potter series, I argue that Horcruxes are the most powerful example of this duality, integrating the novels into the tradition of separable souls. By examining Rowling's Horcruxes alongside earlier manifestations of the separable soul found in British folkloric tales from the Middle Ages, it is possible to gain further insight not only into Rowling's theory of reading but also into her thoughts about death. More specifically, the presence of Horcruxes in Harry Potter ushers readers into a world of myth while concurrently grounding them in the reality of the human condition, specifically, mortality. Through engaging with separable souls, readers are offered an otherwise impossible opportunity to create a Horcrux of their own and, at least symbolically, escape from death. Granting readers the fantastical possibility of immortality, Rowling empowers them to accept the actual alternative open to everyone: to face death without fear, as Ignotus Peverell in "The Tale of the Three Brothers" does: "And then he greeted Death as an old friend, and went with him gladly, and, equals, they departed this life" (*Deathly Hallows* 409).

Before tackling the reader's relationship with the legend, it is important to first understand the terminology and the specific aspects of the separable soul. The separable or external soul is an anthropological term with many names in various cultures and literary traditions, whose essential definition is the separation of someone's life, heart, essence, or soul from their physical body in order to defy death (MacCulloch, *Mythology* 118). Folklorist Katherine Briggs describes the separable soul as "a magical stratagem generally employed by supernatural wizards or giants . . . the giant or wizard removed his life, or soul, from his body and placed it in an egg which was concealed" (355). As long as the severed soul stays concealed and remains intact, then its original possessor is immortal. Medievalist and author J. R. R. Tolkien defines the separable soul in his famous lecture "On Fairy-Stories" as "an ancient and very widespread folk-lore notion, which occur[s] in fairy stories, the notion that the life or strength of a man or creature may reside in some other place or thing; or in some part of the body (especially the heart) that can be detached and hidden" (18). By definition, then, the concept of the separable soul is fairly direct. While Rowling invented "Horcrux" as a neologism for the separable soul, her basic definition stays true to previous tradition: "A Horcrux is a word used for an object in which a person has concealed part of their soul" (*Half-Blood Prince* 497). As the myth develops, the separable soul's nature becomes increasingly complicated.

In Harry Potter, separable souls have a shadowy, unnamed presence that directs the plot of the story. Rowling delays the revelation of their existence until the sixth book, where Dumbledore explains the nature of Riddle's diary and the other Horcruxes. The separable soul occupies a similarly ghostly position culturally, as readers largely remain unaware of the separable soul's existence in Western literature and of its significance, though it appears frequently across a variety of genres. Aside from being introduced as Horcruxes, "the wickedest of magical inventions," in *Half-Blood Prince*, some additional examples of separable souls include Davy Jones's heart in the film *The Pirates of the Caribbean: Dead Man's Chest*, the One Ring in Tolkien's *The Lord of the Rings*, and the undead lich's phylactery in *Dungeons and Dragons* and other role-playing games (381).

The genesis of the soul as a concept and the resultant split of people into spiritual and corporeal parts remains a mystery belonging to a period known only as "prehistory." The exact origins, geographically or chronologically, of the idea of a separable soul are unknown. The earliest known written record comes from the Egyptian D'Orbigny papyrus, *The Tale of the Two Brothers* (originally translated in 1852 by Vicomte De Rougé). The younger of the two brothers separates his soul from his body and commits it successively to an acacia flower, a bull, and a cedar tree: "I shall enchant my heart, and I shall place it upon the top of the flower of the cedar . . . when thou has found it, put it into a vase of cold water, and in very truth I shall live" (Tolkien 19). For the purposes of this chapter, the content of this tale from the ancient world is less important than the fact that it provides us with a clear sense of the long history of the separable soul. Thus, even without knowing the beginning of the separable soul's story, we know that Rowling's Horcruxes join a well-established tradition of avoiding death in favor of immortality.

Instead of trying to find the original tale, we can, alternatively, search for the belief that is the root cause of the myth—what essential need or desire it fulfills. By examining contemporary beliefs surrounding separable souls and the fears placated by these stories, we can begin to reconstruct earlier beliefs. This theory rests upon the idea that there are some aspects of the human condition that have remained relatively stable; so have the convictions that emerge from these conditions. This attempt must be approached with caution since, as postmodernism tells us, we cannot presume the existence of essential, eternal human qualities. Nevertheless, I find it a risk worth taking. The story of the separable soul really begins with the fact of mortality, which is a constant of the human condition. Everyone dies, yet nobody knows what happens after death; it is the greatest mystery and the one humans most fear. As Dumbledore explains, "It is the unknown we fear when we look upon death and darkness, nothing more" (*Half-Blood Prince* 566).

Furthermore, death is the one human journey we must take alone. As Harry walks into the Forbidden Forest to make the ultimate sacrifice, he comes to understand that he is unable to bring Hermione Granger and Ron Weasley with him this time: "This was a journey they could not take together" (*Deathly Hallows* 693). Not only can Harry not make a mortal decision for Hermione and Ron, but also, in dying, he must leave behind the ones he loves and continue on alone. Since nobody can experience the exact same feelings and thoughts, and since these thoughts are impossible to share, dying is inevitably an individual experience. As Dumbledore responds to Harry's suggestion that limbo is in King's Cross Station, "My dear boy, I have no idea. This is, as they say, *your* party" (*Deathly Hallows* 712).

Humans, both Muggles and wizards, must find a way to cope with and accept mortality. Nevertheless, even for the bravest, fear remains; out of this terror comes the desire to escape. Faced with the pain, loss, and uncertainty "that is part of being human," circumventing death becomes increasingly attractive (*Order of the Phoenix* 824). Today, with everything from wrinkle cream to medical procedures, our culture is obsessed with delaying the Grim Reaper. Considering our intense anxiety of morbidity and decay, paired with the highly alluring prospect of immutability, it is not so difficult to imagine earlier people and cultures might have sought a way to escape death as well. Furthermore, it is fairly easy to believe that someone like Voldemort—whose name literally means "flight from death" (see chapter 7 in this volume)—might exist, one so "determined to evade death" that he would be willing to forcibly "tear" his soul from his body (*Half-Blood Prince* 500). The unnatural severing of the soul from the body is a terrible choice to contemplate, yet as Dumbledore points out, "The trouble is, humans do have a knack of choosing precisely those things that are worst for them" (*Sorcerer's Stone* 297). Mortality and the fear of death, then, are where the original idea of the separable soul emerged, and the concept has remained with us ever since, because the original cause, the desire to escape death, has never been eradicated.

In both Harry Potter and medieval folklore, an evil wizard or a giant is almost always responsible for the creation of a separable soul, and his wickedness is consistently established prior to dividing his soul and body. The preexistence of evil before the production of a separable soul is important, as almost all the characters in Rowling's Harry Potter series are wizards and witches. Writers in the Middle Ages, in general, may have understood witchcraft to be synonymous with sin, but in Harry Potter, only Lord Voldemort commits the greatest evil, murder, in order to split his soul and create a Horcrux. Still, Voldemort holds true to the precedent of committing crimes, including serial murder, genocide, and tyranny, before choosing the existence offered by a separable soul. As for the Middle Ages, stories featuring an evil wizard or giant with a separable soul usually begin with the abduction, rape, and murder of the hero's wife or fiancée followed by other depraved acts. For example, the giant in "The Bare-Stripping Hangman" begins by capturing four princesses, murdering several knights who attempt a rescue mission, and, finally, stripping the corpses and hanging them from the rafters like hams for future meals (MacDougall 78). The fact that this giant is sexually aggressive, murderous, and even anthropophagus is neither unique in medieval representations of monsters nor particularly noteworthy for Harry Potter scholarship except that it helps to characterize the nature traditionally assigned to those who make use of a separable soul. Since fleeing from death is cowardly and hubris seems inherently connected with immortality, every being that resorts to divorcing soul from body in order to gain indestructibility is portrayed as evil. Certainly Rowling and medieval folklorists agree that deathlessness is wrong and those who pursue it are monstrous. And having gone so far, these individuals are not above committing any act no matter how horrible.

Now knowing the dark wizards and giants involved, the question, then, is what purpose does the separable soul serve? In Harry Potter, we learn from Professor Horace Slughorn that the entire purpose of removing a part or all of your soul is to protect against death: "Well, you split your soul, you see . . . and hide part of it in an object outside of the body. Then, even if one's body is attacked or destroyed, one cannot die, for part of the soul remains earthbound and undamaged" (*Half-Blood Prince* 497). In a haunting twist, Rowling not only provides us with the theory behind imperishability, but she also offers Volde-mort's "spectral existence" and subsequent resurrection as a poignant example of the power of separable souls (*Half-Blood Prince* 503). Of course, Voldemort's Horcruxes are only the lat-est in a long history of defying death. Again, in the medieval tale "The Bare-Stripping Hangman," a group of knights besieges the giant's castle in order to rescue a captured princess. Once inside, they attempt to slay the Hangman:

> They found the way to the Den of the Giant, and saw that he was in a heavy sleep. They said to each other that that was the time for them to have revenge for the King's daughter, and to take the head off the giant. . . . But scarcely had they got outside through the gate of the castle than they saw the Giant coming after them, and his head on him as it was before. (MacDougall 87)

Naturally, in the few moments before their deaths at the hands of the angry giant, the knights are quite bewildered as to how the decapitated villain lives. Only later is the secret to the giant's survival revealed as his separable soul, which renders him essen-tially invincible.

The giant temporarily loses his head and Voldemort is bodi-less for a time, consisting of only spirit, but neither are destroyed, only weakened. Even when they are both incapacitated, com-pletely incorporeal in Voldemort's case, both are still dangerous because of their Horcruxes. Beheading barely slows the giant, and Tom Riddle's diary manages to possess and almost kill Ginny Weasley at the end of *Chamber of Secrets*: "The longer Riddle stood there, the more life was dwindling out of Ginny . . . and in the meantime, Harry noticed suddenly Riddle's outline was becoming clearer, more solid" (316). A Horcrux, then, not only fortifies its maker from death but also serves as a weapon, and those who have the misfortune of encountering a separable soul or the violence unleashed by one will be irrevocably altered by its presence. And it is clear in the novels that both the creators of Horcruxes and their victims will be changed in the encounter.

More importantly, the doom that befalls those associ-ated with Horcruxes also reveals the treacherous nature of the

separable soul. For a moment, let us forget that every wizard or
giant who creates a Horcrux is defined as evil. Then, what is so
wrong with creating a Horcrux in order to protect your life? Is
it not actually the intelligent move? Maybe, as Voldemort suggests, those who denounce the practice are actually afraid. Perhaps, as he contends, "there is no good or evil . . . only power
and those too weak to seek it" (*Sorcerer's Stone* 291). According to this logic, the creation and use of a separable soul makes
perfect sense, and that is why the practice is so deceptive. On
the surface, the Horcrux is designed to preserve life and protect
the soul, but the problem is that its very creation permanently
damages the soul: "you make the rest of your soul [unstable]
by ripping it" (*Deathly Hallows* 103). Voldemort's soul becomes
so "unstable that it [breaks] apart," creating another Horcrux in
Harry even when he did not intend to (*Deathly Hallows* 709). A
comparable situation to the state of a split soul is a condemned
building. You start removing bricks and after a while, the building becomes so structurally unsound that it will collapse without any further interference. In a terrible inversion, the object
that is supposed to make a wizard strong and immortal actually makes him weaker and more open to attack. As Voldemort
laments, "See what I have become. . . . Mere shadow and vapor.
I have form only when I can share another's body" (*Sorcerer's
Stone* 293).

Then, due to its weakened state outside of the body, the separable soul can actually be destroyed. As Hermione explains:
"Look, if I picked up a sword right now, Ron, and ran you
through with it, I wouldn't damage your soul at all . . . whatever
happens to your body, your soul will survive untouched. . . . But
it's the other way round with a Horcrux. The fragment of soul
inside depends on its container, its enchanted body, for survival"
(*Deathly Hallows* 104). If Voldemort had kept his soul inside his
body, then he would have been mortal, but his soul would have
been safer. Finally, if the Horcrux is destroyed, what remains
of its creator is less than the original whole. Dumbledore tells
Harry that "[w]ithout his Horcruxes Voldemort will be a mortal
man with a maimed and diminished soul" (*Half-Blood Prince*
509). During Harry's time in limbo at King's Cross Station, we
catch a glimpse of the condition in which Voldemort will spend

eternity: "It had the form of a small, naked child, curled on the ground, its skin raw and rough, flayed-looking, and it lay shuddering under a seat where it had been left, unwanted, stuffed out of sight, struggling for breath" (*Deathly Hallows* 706–707). Seeing this pathetic being, it becomes overwhelmingly evident that the practice of the separable soul only appears alluringly beneficial but is actually figured as extremely dangerous. For this reason, every writer from the Middle Ages to Rowling who has contemplated separable souls has reaffirmed the strength and righteousness of a soul whole and intact.

Inevitably, as a natural result of the vulnerability of the soul outside the body, the wizard or giant cannot just leave his separated soul lying around. Although the specific reasoning of a wizard or giant is usually omitted, medieval stories repeatedly detail the extensive methods of protection surrounding separable souls in order to prevent their discovery and destruction. Likewise, Rowling shows how carefully Horcruxes must be protected. Each of Voldemort's Horcruxes is concealed by secrecy, an impenetrable location, or powerful magic. As Dumbledore tells Harry, "I stumbled across the ring hidden in the ruin of the Gaunts' house. It seems once Voldemort succeeded in sealing a piece of his soul inside it, he did not want to wear it anymore. He hid it, protected by many powerful enchantments" (*Half-Blood Prince* 504). The security surrounding Voldemort's Horcruxes varies from simple misdirection, as in Rowena Ravenclaw's diadem hidden in the clutter of the Room of Requirement, to the dangerous, multistep ordeal Harry and Dumbledore face at the cliffside cave in *Half-Blood Prince.*

As clever as Rowling is, the Middle Ages were truly the golden age of hiding separated souls. As seen in the Basque pastorals of Malbrouk, the most popular safeguard was a concealment technique that resembled Russian nesting dolls: "You must kill a terrible wolf which is in the forest, and inside him is a fox, in the fox is a pigeon; this pigeon has an egg in his head" (MacCulloch, *Childhood* 133). Additionally, in certain cases, time constraints or specific weaponry limited the opportunities for annihilation, as in "The Tale of Cú Chluainn": "Cúroi's soul was in an apple, and this in a salmon, which appeared every year in a certain well, while the apple could be split only by Cúroi's sword" (MacCulloch, *Mythology* 151). Where exactly this salmon hangs out the rest of the year, nobody knows, but it is clear that it only makes an appearance at this well one day a year, and this is the only time it can be caught. A similar yet alternative means of protection to the nesting doll style is used in the tale "Greensleeves," which consists of concealing the separable soul in the most likely location: "go to the top of a high hill as fast as possible, and there . . . find an egg in a certain bird's nest" (Buchan 45). By far, the most popular container for the separable soul in the Middle Ages was an egg, and the most natural place to find an egg is in a nest. If there are no specific directions as to the type of egg the soul is housed in or the location of the nest, let alone which hill, a person could search indefinitely. After all, exactly how many nests would you estimate existed in continental Europe, and how much time would it take to check each and every one? So, due to the nondescript nature of an egg in a nest, the separable soul left there is almost perfectly camouflaged.

One final, clever method of concealment involves constant movement. This could be achieved by relocation, as with the moveable salmon in "The Tale of Cú Chluainn." A separable soul that migrates may be external like Salazar Slytherin's locket, which moves with the individual who wears it. The conveyor of a separable soul, however, may not always be aware of the fragment's presence, as the Horcrux is not always located in a separate, exterior container; sometimes, as in Harry Potter, a body is the Horcrux. Similarly, in "The Bare-Stripping Hangman," the separable soul is housed inside a "swift-footed hind" that roams many forests (MacDougall 105). Since the deer is capable of movement, the soul never has a single hiding place and is more challenging to find, as we learn in the "Hangman": "I cannot tell thee where the soul of the Bare-Stripping Hangman is now, for it fled out of the place where it was four days ago" (MacDougall 103). Additionally, at least in the case of the hind, the nesting doll technique is also employed, which makes it twice as hard to capture. When the deer is slain, a green duck flies out and you have to start the chase all over again. In most cases, this pattern repeats itself several times until there are finally no more animals stuffed inside other animals to let loose.

Rowling makes memorable use of this strategy. First, Volde-mort's pet snake, Nagini, is made into a Horcrux and is espe-cially favored, considering that she always accompanies her master. The second living Horcrux is, of course, Harry himself. We learn, finally, that when Voldemort attempts to kill one-year-old Harry, "A fragment of Voldemort's soul was blasted apart from the whole, and latched itself onto the only living soul left in the collapsing building. Part of Lord Voldemort lives inside Harry" (*Deathly Hallows* 686). Apparently, Harry being turned into a Horcrux was unintentional, and Voldemort was not even aware it happened. Nonetheless, Harry also turns out to be a very powerful receptacle for Voldemort's soul, since he can defend himself and because other witches and wizards, like Dumbledore, go to great lengths to protect him. They don't care about Voldemort's soul, but their love for Harry causes them to keep him safe, and, consequently, the Horcrux is secure as well.

All living vessels for separable souls are unquestionably formidable, yet Rowling complicates the idea in ways that the Middle Ages never imagined. When Harry asks if animals can be Horcruxes, for example, Dumbledore replies, "Well, it is inadvisable to do so . . . because to confide part of your soul to something that can think and move for itself is obviously a risky business" (*Half-Blood Prince* 506–507). Medieval hinds and birds lack an active will and the ability to make decisions. They do flee when they are being hunted, but this is more from sur-vival instinct rather than actual awareness of the separable soul. Rowling reverses this lack of consciousness and gives her living Horcruxes the ability to choose. In the case of Harry, the bearer can purposefully elect to sacrifice himself in order to eradicate the Horcrux he carries. Voldemort would never consider this radical decision, and yet it is a very real possibility when your Horcrux has the ability to decide its own fate.

In a related vein, when the soul is encased in an inanimate or nonliving container, that container sometimes takes on human properties. In an unknown process, perhaps because the soul is the very essence of life, inanimate objects seem alive. Hold-ing Slytherin's locket, for example, Harry wonders, "Was it his own blood pulsing through his veins that he could feel, or was it something beating inside the locket, like a tiny metal heart?" (*Deathly Hallows* 276). Objects without any discernible means of movement are suddenly mobile: "The Egg gave a bounce out of his fist, and sprang three heights of a man in the air" (Mac-Dougall 109). As Horcruxes, articles with no mouth or any other means of producing noise can begin to communicate. When Harry discovers Riddle's journal and writes in it, "Ooz-ing back out of the page, in his very own ink, came words Harry had never written. 'Hello Harry Potter. My name is Tom Riddle. How did you come by my diary?'" (*Chamber of Secrets* 240). When Harry and Ron destroy the locket, the communication is audible: "There was a clang of metal and a long, drawn-out scream" (*Deathly Hallows* 377). That same locket also manages to communicate through thoughts alone, as when it convinces Ron, "I have seen your dreams . . . and I have seen your fears" (*Deathly Hallows* 375).

Finally, these animated inanimate objects also gain a sense of self-preservation. When Harry retrieves Godric Gryffindor's sword, the locket "sensed the presence of the sword and tried to kill Harry rather than let him possess it" (*Deathly Hallows* 373). Not only can the Horcrux apparently feel and perceive its surroundings, but it is also aware of the danger present in the sword and takes action to save itself. Ominously, a separable soul not only looks after itself, but it is also so powerful that the traditional relationship of owner and property is reversed. As a living Horcrux, Harry struggles to control his thoughts: "I think I am going mad . . . for a couple of seconds there I thought I was a snake, I felt like one—my scar really hurt when I was looking at Dumbledore . . . I wanted to attack him" (*Order of the Phoenix* 480–481). Though Harry undoubtedly has the most intense relationship with Horcruxes, separable souls exert unwholesome power over everyone, and they change a possess-or's personality for the worse. Ron confesses, "That [locket's] bad for me . . . I can't handle it . . . it made me think stuff—stuff I was already thinking anyway, but it made everything worse" (*Deathly Hallows* 374). Ron, who is a good person and loyal friend, finds himself acting extremely out of character. While he generally keeps his doubts in check, Ron wears the Horcrux and suddenly his thoughts become poisonous and his mentality shifts. As Riddle so astutely observes when he possesses Ginny,

"I grew stronger and stronger on a diet of her deepest fears, her darkest secrets. I grew powerful, far more powerful than little Miss Weasley. Powerful enough to start feeding Miss Weasley a few of my secrets, to start pouring a little of my soul back into her" (*Chamber of Secrets* 310). Thus when Ron is close to the Horcrux, "a bit of the soul inside" left the magical container and temporarily flitted inside him (*Deathly Hallows* 105).

Considering the nature of the wizards and giants who create Horcruxes, it is not surprising that even a small part of their soul would be malevolent and that its effect would be detrimental to others. Essentially, even the best of individuals, if they become emotionally intimate with a separable soul, appear to open themselves up to its power. They lose a part of themselves and begin to resemble the creator of the Horcrux. Throughout Rowling's series, for example, Harry shares Voldemort's thoughts and emotions: "He often felt lurches of annoyance or cheerfulness that were unrelated to what was happening to him at the time" (*Order of the Phoenix* 553–554). Harry sometimes even progresses to assuming Voldemort's consciousness:

> "What are you talking about?" said Ron, sounding scared. "D'you mean . . . did you see You-Know-Who?"
> "I was You-Know-Who," said Harry and he stretched out his hands in the darkness and held them up to his face to check that they were no longer deathly white and long fingered. (*Order of the Phoenix* 586)

The result of this transformation process is usually physical death and the destruction of the bearer's soul. Harry is one of the few literary characters to survive an encounter with a separable soul and certainly the only wizard ever to have been a Horcrux and survived, but his good fortune does not mean that he is free from the physical and emotional scars inflicted by his experiences.

Faced with the pestilence of separable souls, we are left with the dilemma of how to destroy them and defeat their creators. Ironically, when a separable soul is discovered, it is usually not due to poor security measure but rather to loose lips. In the stories "How the Great Tuairisgeal Was Put to Death" and "The Young King of Easaidh Ruadh," the giants involved have a particular weakness for flattery, and when the women they imprison decorate the purported sites of their souls, they are immensely pleased (MacKay 23). Of course, the original locations were a ruse, but after seeing the beautiful ornamentation, the giants disclose the real sites of their separable souls to their own detriment. In the case of the giant in "The Bare-Stripping Hangman," his vanity apparently extends to compliments about his physique and sexual prowess: "When the giant went to bed, the woman began to say to him: 'Thou canst not be killed, as thou art so strong'" (MacDougall 63). By a combination of false praise and seduction, the giant's prisoner cajoles the true location of the separable soul from the giant. Of course, as soon as the giants in these stories confess, these women or their male rescuers immediately unearth the separable souls and obliterate them, thereby killing their captors: "The queen caught the egg . . .when she crushed the egg, he [the giant] fell down dead" (Campbell 11). Though Voldemort does not imperil his Horcruxes for the sake of flattery or sexual gratification, he does make thinly veiled references to their existence and believes that nobody will be able to understand him or discover their hiding places. As with Voldemort's literary forbearers, his inability to remain silent is what allows Dumbledore and Harry to discover and destroy his Horcruxes.

If a separated soul can be found, then it is possible to eradicate it, but the destruction of its casing is rarely as easy as breaking eggs, because "ripping, smashing, or crushing" will not normally do the job (*Deathly Hallows* 104). Usually a powerful magical method, such as a certain sword, basilisk venom, or Fiendfyre is required. After the soul is obliterated, the life of the wizard or giant is ended, but destroying the Horcrux does not undo all the damage that was wrought by its presence. Harry, Ron, and Hermione, not to mention the wider wizarding world, will never be free of the Horcruxes' legacy.

In the end, there is only one way to completely defeat a separable soul. A separable soul, whatever name it goes by and whatever physical form it takes, always returns to the same issue: death. A Horcrux, and all its incumbent evil, exists because a wizard or a giant wants to escape death. They hunger for power so intensely that they cannot stand to be vulnerable in the face of death, so they make a desperate bid to circumvent universal fate and brutally damage their souls in the process. Somewhat simply, the way to counter the power of the separable soul is to accept death. As Dumbledore points out, "The true master of death does not seek to run away from death. He accepts that he must die, and understands that there are far, far worse things in the living world than dying" (*Deathly Hallows* 720). Not only does acceptance of mortality destroy any allure that a Horcrux might have, but it also eliminates its original motivation—fear of death.

Ultimately, there is no evidence to support the existence of the soul, nor the fact that you can separate it from the body and encase it elsewhere. Nevertheless, the insistent presence of this concept throughout the mythology and literature of Western civilization cannot be denied. Thus, there must be a need for this story—human beings need to construct a choice to escape death. For us, this must be tied to the fact that we are mortal and must die. Maybe, as a species, we need help coping with the inevitability of death. Perhaps we need to warn ourselves of the dangers associated with trying to be like the gods. The brave and wise accept death and, consequently, the unknown. Meanwhile, it is the wicked, weak, and cowardly who seek to circumvent nature. Interestingly, the use of the separable soul in literature goes one step further. As hard as I might try, I cannot cause my soul to take up residence in my copy of *Deathly Hallows*. In the real world, it is both physically and spiritually impossible to create a Horcrux. Yet, in the land of legends, in the imaginary, literary world, it is a very real possibility. And since by reading we can manage to blur the distinctions between reality and fantasy, we can dream up our own Horcruxes and we can make the choice to relinquish them and accept death. By having the separable soul in our stories, we give ourselves the choice that life denies us.

Works Cited

Briggs, Katherine. *Encyclopedia of Fairies: Hobgoblins, Brownies, Bogies, and other Supernatural Creatures*. New York, NY: Pantheon, 1976. Print.

Buchan, Peter, ed. *Ancient Scottish Tales*. Peterhead: Buchan Field Club, 1908. Print.

Campbell, John Francis, trans. *Popular Tales of the West Highlands*. London, UK: Alexander Gardner, 1890. Print.

MacCulloch, John Arnott. *The Childhood of Fiction: A Study of Folk Tales and Primitive Thought*. London, UK: John Murray, Albemarle Street, 1905. Print.

———. *The Mythology of All Races: Celtic*. New York, NY: Cooper Square, 1964. Print.

MacDougall, J., ed. *Folk and Hero Tales: Waifs and Strays of Celtic Tradition*. New York, NY: AMS, 1973. Print.

MacKay, John G., trans. *More West Highland Tales*. Edinburgh, Scotland: Birlinn, 1994.

Rowling, J. K. *The Tales of Beedle the Bard*. New York, NY: A. A. Levine Books, 2007. Print.

Tolkien, J. R. R. "On Fairy-Stories." In *Essays Presented to Charles Williams*, comp. C. S. Lewis. Grand Rapids, MI: Eerdmans, 1966. Print.

Nine

WWHPD

What Would Harry Potter Do?

CALLIE KNUDSLIEN

> In *The Lord of the Rings*, J. R. R. Tolkien fused his ardent Catholicism with a deep, nostalgic love for the unspoiled English landscape. C. S. Lewis was a devout Anglican whose *Chronicles of Narnia* forms an extended argument for Christian faith. Now look at Rowling's books. What's missing? If you want to know who dies in *Harry Potter [and the Deathly Hallows]*, the answer is easy: God.
> —Lev Grossman, *Time*

Almost since its debut in 1997, the Harry Potter series has faced opposition from religious leaders and authority figures. At a school in Kent, a principal banned the series from being incorporated in activities or the classroom, saying that "[t]he Bible is consistent in its teaching that wizards, devils, and demons exist and are real and dangerous, and God's people are told to have nothing to do with them" (Grossman). In other places, worried parents petitioned school boards to withdraw the series from libraries and reading lists. Even my friend's mother, a well-read woman, forbade him and his sister from reading the series when they were children. Since turning eighteen, he has read the entire series and is quite the enthusiast, all while remaining a devout Christian. Most people's concerns come from the dark themes of "death, hate, lack of respect, and sheer evil" present in the books and in their focus on magic and witchcraft (Bridger 9). Other individuals argue that the characters of the series are bad examples—children who lie, break rules, and are otherwise disobedient. The general sentiment boils down to an insistence that the books undermine Christian values. In his article in *Time* magazine, Lev Grossman categorizes J. K. Rowling as having "more in common with celebrity atheists like Christopher Hitchens than she has with Tolkien and Lewis." What many of these religious fundamentalists seem to be forgetting is that the Bible does not present untarnished characters or stories devoid of evil. Many of the best-known Bible stories or best-loved biblical characters are ones of sin and redemption. For example, King David, regarded as the greatest Israelite king, committed adultery with a married woman and then had her husband killed (NIV, 2 Sam. 11). He later realized the sinfulness of what he had done and repented—and Harry Potter is similar. The characters we regard as "evil" in the series are hardened to wrongdoing and feel no remorse, but those we regard as "good," rather than being sterling examples of character at all times, choose their actions in response to their conscience and accept punishment when they know they've done wrong (Neal 187—188).

The Harry Potter series has more similarities to the Bible than closed-minded fundamentalists would like to think. In an interview with Rowling following the release of *Deathly Hallows*, the author revealed that she very intentionally modeled the series and our hero's journey on "the greatest story ever told." Rowling stated, "To me, [the religious parallels] have always been obvious. . . . But I never wanted to talk too openly about it because I thought it might show people . . . where we were going" (Adler).

In fact, Harry Potter serves as a Christ figure in the series. In literature, a Christ figure is a fictional character that demonstrates some of the qualities of Jesus Christ but is not necessarily a perfect allegorical substitute. Some examples include Gandalf and Frodo in Tolkien's Lord of the Rings trilogy and Aslan in Lewis's *Chronicles of Narnia* (Roper 83, 84—87). Harry's position among them as a Christ figure is evidenced through rampant symbolism, through his similarities to Jesus in moral values, and through the blatant connection between his death experience and Christ's Passion and Resurrection.

Rowling has scattered Christian symbolism throughout her entire series. Even from the opening chapter of *Sorcerer's Stone*, we can find connections between Christ's story and Harry's. First of all, their births and eventual destinies were prophesied. A passage of Isaiah refers to a servant that will be crushed for the sins of humanity, saying that he will be led like a sheep to the slaughter and will not protest (Isa. 53). Christians often maintain that this servant is Jesus, as he voluntarily suffered and died for the redemption of humankind from sin. Harry's birth and fate are similarly prophesied by Professor Sibyll Trelawney (one of the few accurate predictions she makes): *"THE ONE WITH THE POWER TO VANQUISH THE DARK LORD APPROACHES . . . HE WILL HAVE POWER THE DARK LORD KNOWS NOT"* (*Order of the Phoenix* 841; emphasis in original). The fact that both Jesus and Harry lived to fulfill these destinies was a testament to their mothers' love. Mary was approached by an angel and asked to take on a responsibility that would change her life forever, and she said yes out of love for God and, consequently, the son whom she was to bear (Lk. 1:38). Lily Potter has an opportunity to be spared by Lord Voldemort if she hands Harry over to him, but refuses, begging, *"Not Harry, please no, take me, kill me instead"* (*Prisoner of Azkaban* 179; emphasis in original). This act of love and sacrifice is what then protects Harry from Voldemort's killing curse and enables his survival. It is also a scene highly reminiscent of Herod's "Slaughter of the Innocents," in which King Herod sought to kill all boys under the age of two in the vicinity of Bethlehem upon hearing the prophecy that the newborn Christ would be king over the Jews (Mt. 2). In a similarly vicious quest to maintain his authority and power, Voldemort sought to kill the child that, according to prophecy, will have the power to destroy him.

When Jesus was born, his arrival was heralded by unusual occurrences—prophecies, appearances by angels, extraordinary gifts from magi, and an astonishingly luminous star—while Harry's survival and delivery to Privet Drive is accompanied by strange occurrences such as wizard sightings, shooting stars, hordes of owls zooming about in broad daylight, and flying motorbikes (Killinger 13). In both cases, a young child slept out-side in the night as "residents of another realm broke through the skies to proclaim their unrestrained joy to the world" (Neal 7).

Indeed, both Harry and Jesus were of two realms. Both had humble origins in the natural world—the son of a carpenter, the unwanted nephew of a family of Muggles—and enormous status in the supernatural realm. Both realized that these two worlds affected one another and that it was the responsibility of those with knowledge of the supernatural realm to help those of the natural realm in times of need (Neal 174–175). Similarly, both Jesus and Harry seemed to come to a realization of their natures when on the cusp of adolescence. In a well-known story from the Gospel of Luke, a twelve-year-old Jesus was found in a tem-ple speaking with the elders after his parents had undergone sev-eral days of frantically searching for the missing boy. When he was chastised, he responded, "Didn't you know I had to be in my father's house?" (Lk. 2:42–51). This is the first gospel story suggesting that Jesus is aware of his dual nature. Harry, on the other hand, is told that he is a wizard on his eleventh birthday by the half-giant Rubeus Hagrid, a conversation that occurs after the Dursleys have been frantically fleeing for several days from the onslaught of letters sent to their residence (*Sorcerer's Stone* 50).

Shortly after his baptism, Jesus journeyed out into the desert for forty days, during which he fasted and was tempted by the devil: to make stones into bread to assuage his hunger, to test God by throwing himself off a cliff, and to worship the devil in return for dominion over all the kingdoms of the world. Jesus refused all of these temptations and sent the devil away (Lk. 4:1–13). Harry, when battling Professor Quirrell and Volde-mort for the Sorcerer's Stone, is tempted by Voldemort, who tells Harry that he will help him bring his parents back from the dead—something Harry desperately longs for, the thing he sees when looking into the Mirror of Erised—in return for the Stone. Despite his longing to know his parents, Harry adamantly refuses, provoking Voldemort to a battle in which Quirrell dies and Voldemort flees. After this ordeal, Harry wakes up three days later in the Hospital Wing. "It should have been crystal clear to anyone familiar with the story of Jesus!" John Killinger insists. Indeed, the skirmish with evil followed by a three-day coma is reminiscent of Jesus's three days in the tomb following his crucifixion (75).

Christian symbolism continues in the next book of the series, *Chamber of Secrets.* The tale climaxes as Harry and Ron Weasley descend into the Chamber of Secrets and Harry battles the deadly basilisk. He is aided by Fawkes and the Sorting Hat, the latter of which provides him with the sword of Godric Gryffindor. With the sword, he manages to kill the basilisk and ultimately thwart Voldemort's attempt to reclaim his body. The sword is frequently likened to a silver cross in the series, and it is with this "cross" that Harry destroys the serpent, a traditional biblical symbol of Satan. Furthermore, the fact that the sword belonged to Godric Gryffindor is highly relevant. *Godric,* derived from Old English, means "power of God," and *Gryffindor* is like *griffin d'or*, meaning "griffin of gold" in French. The griffin is a symbol of Christ, for it combines the eagle (a creature of the heavens) with the lion (a creature of the earth) to create an animal of dual natures (Roper 25). The sword is later used to destroy Salazar Slytherin's locket and the snake Nagini, both of them Horcruxes.

As time passed, both Jesus and Harry develop a greater awareness of and dedication to their respective missions. They both have their share of believers and nonbelievers: Jesus had many disciples and followers but also people who scorned his message or doubted him. Harry has some close friends who believe him in *Order of the Phoenix* when he claims that Voldemort has returned, but there are also many students—even the Ministry of Magic—who do not believe him and who ridicule him as a result. Even when the Ministry finally realizes that Voldemort is back and joins the Order of the Phoenix in trying to oppose him, Harry stands up to the authorities and will not condone their wrongdoings. Despite working toward the same eventual goal, Harry will not ally himself with Minister of Magic Rufus Scrimgeour and the Ministry: "So basically . . . you'd like to give the impression that I'm working for the Ministry? . . . No, I don't think that'll work . . . You see, I don't like some of the things the Ministry is doing. Locking up Stan Shunpike, for instance" (*Half-Blood Prince* 345–346). Likewise, Jesus and the

religious leaders of his time were working for the same goal—
the spiritual well-being of the people—but Jesus allied himself
with fishermen, sinners, and tax collectors rather than the Phari-
sees and Sadducees: "Woe to you experts in the law, because you
have taken away the key to knowledge. You yourselves have not
entered, and you have hindered those who were entering" (Lk.
11:52).

Eventually, Harry departs to seek and destroy Voldemort
along with Ron and Hermione Granger, ever the loyal compan-
ions. This "Golden Trio" reflects the three human powers of the
soul: the spirit, mind, and will. The objects they receive in Professor Albus Dumbledore's will reflect their natures. Harry (the
spirit) receives the Golden Snitch and Resurrection Stone, which
he uses later to reunite briefly with the souls of his deceased family. Hermione (the mind) receives *The Tales of Beedle the Bard*,
written in runes and containing a hidden mystery. Ron (the will)
receives Dumbledore's Deluminator, with which he relocates his
friends and saves Harry's life (Granger qtd. in Roper 87). Peter
Kreeft, a theologian, explains that the human powers of the soul
correspond with the "threefold nature of the Messiah as Priest
[the spirit], Prophet [the mind], and King [the will]." These trip-
tychs are also sometimes classified as "head, heart, and hands"
or "mind, emotions, and the will" (qtd. in Roper 87).

As the trio nears their goal of collecting all of the Horcruxes
and defeating Voldemort, their quest brings them back to Hogwarts, where students loyal to Harry and to Dumbledore have
been leading a resistance movement against the new regime at
the school. When they see Harry, they are certain that it means
they are going to overthrow the Death Eaters stationed at the
school and restore Hogwarts—a revolution. When Harry tells
them that he has a different plan and purpose, they ask, "You're
going to leave us in this mess?" Harry is not coming to "conquer" in the way they had expected him to (*Deathly Hallows*
581). Similarly, Jesus's followers believed that the Messiah's purpose was to overthrow the Roman regime as a champion and
conqueror. Even after his resurrection, Jesus's disciples asked
him, "Lord, are you at this time going to restore the kingdom
to Israel?" (Acts 1:6). The answer was no, for he had a different
plan than his followers expected.

There are plenty more parallels and instances of Christian symbolism in the Harry Potter series that connect Harry to Jesus and suggest that he is a Christ figure. Such examples have been uncovered by priests, theologians, or perceptive individuals; others have yet to be discovered and are known only to Rowling. However, Harry's similarities to Jesus do not end with mere symbolism; Harry also demonstrates Christian values in many of his actions and decisions throughout the series.

From almost the very beginning, Harry demonstrates care for the marginalized. Just as Jesus befriended tax collectors, beggars, sinners, lepers, women, and other individuals on the fringes of society, Harry befriends those on the fringes of wizarding society. Ron, the very first friend Harry makes, comes from a family regarded by wizard purists as "blood traitors." When encouraged by the pure-blooded Draco Malfoy to drop Ron's friendship and join him instead, Harry replies, "I think I can tell who the wrong sort [of wizards] are for myself, thanks" (*Sorcerer's Stone* 109). They befriend Hermione not long after, a Muggle-born witch (sometimes referred to by the vulgar term "Mudblood" by wizard purists). Also among Harry's group of friends are Neville Longbottom, a self-dubbed "almost Squib," Hagrid the half-giant, the eccentric Luna Lovegood, Remus Lupin (a werewolf), and Dobby the house-elf. Harry's friendship with Dobby is especially relevant, since house-elves are servants, practically slaves—the very least of society—with no rights. House-elves are usually regarded with no respect and with no concern and are forced to punish themselves painfully if they disobey or speak ill of their masters. Harry frees Dobby from enslavement to the Malfoys in *Chamber of Secrets* and interacts with him throughout the rest of the series. In *Deathly Hallows*, Dobby saves the lives of Harry and his friends at the expense of his own life. As a final tribute to Dobby, Harry toils to dig a grave by hand with a spade rather than using magic and carves a headstone to mark the place where the elf was laid to rest. This instance is "the epitome of love" in the series—a scene demonstrating love for "the least of these," as Jesus advocated in his ministry (Killinger 148).

In the final Battle of Hogwarts, all of these marginalized unite against Voldemort and the purist regime: "blood traitors" and "Muggle lovers," Muggle-borns, house-elves, Hagrid and his full-giant brother, the centaurs—all those disregarded in the wizarding world. Just as Saint Paul stated, "There is neither Jew nor Greek, slave nor free, male nor female, for you are all one in Christ Jesus," all those that were separated by diversity were united with Harry in the fight against evil (Gal. 3:28).

Just as Harry demonstrates love for the marginalized, he also shows love and mercy to his enemies. Jesus preached forgiveness and loving one's neighbor and demonstrated such love as he forgave those that crucified him. Harry shows mercy to his rival Draco Malfoy, risking his life to save Draco and his friends from a dangerous fire caused by dark magic, and then again from a Death Eater during the siege at Hogwarts. Harry quickly forgives Ron on several occasions and ultimately forgives even Professor Severus Snape. In the final moments of the Battle of Hogwarts, in his face-off against Voldemort, he tries to help Voldemort redeem himself: "It's your one last chance . . . I've seen what you'll be otherwise . . . Be a man . . . try . . . Try for some remorse" (741).

Harry has a tendency to help people. In *Order of the Phoenix*, Hermione suggests he has "a bit of a *saving-people thing*" (733). According to Gospel writers, Jesus came "to seek and save what was lost" (Lk. 19:10). Both were similar in that they put themselves in peril to save the ones they loved—not just once but repeatedly. The virtue of self-sacrificial love, advocated so strongly by Jesus in his public ministry, is a recurring theme in the series: "Greater love has no one than this, that he lay down his life for his friends" (John 15:13). This biblical verse is practically a mantra for Harry and his friends. In *Sorcerer's Stone*, Harry and Ron rush headlong into danger to save Hermione from a mountain troll rather than taking the time to find an adult and running the risk that the delay might mean Hermione's death. Later in the same book, the trio faces the perils beyond the trapdoor to save the wizarding world. Harry and Ron brave the Chamber of Secrets to save Ginny; Harry throws himself in the way of Sirius Black and Remus Lupin to stop Wormtail (Peter Pettigrew) from being murdered; Harry faces hordes of dementors intent on taking his soul in order to save Sirius and Hermione (as well as his other self, as he was time-traveling);

during the Triwizard Tournament, Harry remains in the lake longer than necessary to save all hostages during the Second Task, repeatedly puts himself in harm's way to help the other champions during the Third Task, and risks his life to bring Cedric Diggory's body back from the graveyard; in *Order of the Phoenix*, Harry travels to the Ministry of Magic with his friends to save his godfather, Sirius. Certainly more examples exist, but it is clear that Harry has lived a life of self-sacrificial love. Love is a powerful force in the world of Harry Potter. It is the power that "the Dark Lord knows not," that Voldemort underestimates and cannot understand (*Half-Blood Prince* 509–511). Love is the reason that Voldemort was unable to kill Harry as a baby and unable to possess him as a young man. In his *Time* magazine article, Grossman simplifies this profound message, calling it a "mere human emotion" rather than a power coming from God or nature: "In choosing Rowling as the reigning dreamer of our era, we have chosen a writer who dreams of a secular, bureau-cratized, all-too-human sorcery, in which psychology and tech-nology have superseded the sacred." What Grossman seems to be forgetting is that love is much more than a "mere human emotion"—it is the very heart of the Gospel message, the cen-tral focus of Jesus's parables and teachings. In his Sermon on the Mount and parable of the Good Samaritan, Jesus explained the ways in which we are called to love our neighbors; in the par-able of the Prodigal Son, he illustrated the love that God has for humankind; when asked what the greatest commandments are, he replied, "Love the Lord your God with all your heart and with all your soul and with all your strength and with all your mind, and Love your neighbor as yourself" (Lk. 10:27). Love is not a *mere human emotion*: it is the reason that God sent Jesus to teach and redeem humankind and the reason Jesus went will-ingly to the cross to suffer and die (John 3:16). It is in this action that the concept of self-sacrificial love is most clearly seen—and it is upon this action that Harry's ultimate fate is modeled.

Harry's fate at the end of the series is quite obviously mod-eled on Christ's Passion and Resurrection—if Rowling's refer-ences to Christianity weren't clear before, they definitely are following *Deathly Hallows*. Nearly every step of Jesus's journey to the cross is reflected somewhere in the Harry Potter series.

Both went through a period of being revered, then suddenly reviled: Jesus, shortly before the Passover, entered Jerusalem to acclaim and shouts of joy and blessing. A week later, he was put on public trial, at which the crowds of people demanded that he be crucified. Harry is likewise regarded as the "Chosen One" by much of the wizarding community, their hope for the defeat of Voldemort. As soon as the Ministry falls, however, he is labeled as "Undesirable Number One" with a price on his head (*Deathly Hallows* 252). Even beyond this betrayal by the general public, both suffered the betrayal of a close follower. The apostle Peter denied knowing Jesus when asked, and Ron leaves Harry and Hermione midway through their quest to find Horcruxes. However, both Peter and Ron repent and return, Peter thrice insisting on his love for Christ and Ron rescuing Harry and destroying a Horcrux (Killinger 148; Neal 237).

Harry becomes frustrated during his quest, not only because of Ron's defection, but because he feels abandoned by Dumbledore, his mentor. Stories and rumors about Dumbledore are running rampant, and Harry is beginning to realize how little information he has been given. Dumbledore leaves him to grope in the darkness, to wrestle with unknown and undreamed-of terrors, alone and unaided. Nothing is explained: "Look at what he asked from me, Hermione! Risk your life, Harry! And again! And again! And don't expect me to explain everything, just trust me blindly, trust that I know what I'm doing, trust me even though I don't trust you! Never the whole truth! Never!" (*Deathly Hallows* 362).

Jesus suffered similar feelings of abandonment, crying out from the cross, "My God, my God, why have you forsaken me?" (Mt. 27:46). Despite these feelings of betrayal and abandonment, both Jesus and Harry face their deaths willingly, though with trepidation. The Agony in the Garden paints a picture of Jesus as agitated and hesitant but willing to follow the Father's plan: "Yet not my will, but yours be done" (Lk. 22:42). Harry is also fearful in his walk to the Forbidden Forest, wishing he had a final chance to speak to or even see his friends and loved ones: "This cold-blooded walk to his own destruction would require a different kind of bravery. . . . He wanted to be stopped, to be dragged back, to be sent home. . . . At the same time he thought that he would not be able to go on, and knew that he must" (*Deathly Hallows* 692, 697–698). However, he is not alone in his walk to death: he faces it with the presence and encouragement of Sirius, Remus, and his parents. Those who had gone before him have come to fetch him. Likewise, Jesus was with Peter, James, and John in the Garden, and Moses and Elijah (the law-giver and the prophet) came down to him at the Transfiguration "to encourage Jesus as he was about to take his last determined steps toward the predestined death that he would have to choose to carry through" (Neal 266).

Harry follows the path modeled by Christ, called the Via Dolorosa, into the Forbidden Forest to face Voldemort. He is fearful but determined to save his friends and the wizarding world, even though it means his death. He does not attempt to defend himself, just as Jesus put up no resistance in his arrest and is quickly killed. However, things do not go as Voldemort planned. Harry ends up in a sort of limbo, a place that looks like King's Cross Station, where he is met by Dumbledore and receives the full truth at last. The reason Harry is not dead comes down to a matter of blood: his blood in Voldemort's veins ties him to life. Conversely, Christians understand Christ's blood to be that which connects them to Jesus and eternal life. At the Last Supper, Jesus established himself as the sacrifice of the new cov-enant, stating that his blood would be "poured out for many for the forgiveness of sins" (Mt. 26:28). Furthermore, when most Christian faiths partake in Communion, the celebration of the Last Supper, they do so with the understanding that it ties them to Christ and the entire community of believers. Likewise, Har-ry's sacrificial action protects and unites all those gathered to fight for the side of good during the Battle of Hogwarts. Fol-lowing Harry's death, none of the spells Voldemort or his Death Eaters cast keep their hold on those Harry died to protect, and none of the individuals fighting for the side of good die from this point in the story onward.

Harry is presented with a choice when speaking with Dumbledore at King's Cross: he could return to the world of the living and complete the battle with Voldemort, or he could board a train that would take him on. Harry chooses to leave the comfort of the place where he was and return to life, much like Jesus's resurrection, solidifying his journey as a "Christian story," despite the fact that it was not identical. Jesus rose in the glory of Easter Sunday, taking away death's hold over humanity. Humans still die in this world, but death has been disarmed of its power for Christians, since humanity can be brought to eternal life in Christ. As Saint Paul writes in his letter to the Corinthians, "Where, O death, is your victory? Where, O death, is your sting? . . . But thanks be to God! He gives us the victory through our Lord Jesus Christ" (1 Cor. 15:55, 57). This pattern is repeated in Harry's victory over Voldemort. While the Dark Lord aims to kill with his curse, Harry responds with *Expelliarmus*—the Disarming Charm. Harry simply aims to disarm Voldemort, rather than deal a killing blow. Voldemort destroys himself and falls to the ground at the same time as the sun breaks through the morning sky and onlookers began to cheer and shout their joy—the glorious image brings to mind the dawn of Easter morning, after a nightlong vigil in the dark, ended at once in a flood of light and celebration (Neal 290; Killinger 122).

If it was not clear to religious fundamentalists and overwrought parents before, it certainly should be after the conclusion of the final installment of the Harry Potter series: Harry's tale is modeled on Christ's journey. He may not be a pure, sinless character as Christ was, but evidence throughout the series indicates that he is a literary Christ figure. There is abundant symbolism throughout the series, Harry exemplifies many of morals and values central to Christ's teachings, and he dies and rises again as an act of self-sacrifice, just as Jesus did in the redemption of humankind. As Kreeft states, "This should not surprise us . . . Christ is the central point of the whole human story from the beginning in the Mind of its Author" (qtd. in Roper 83). It is apparent through her interviews following the completion of the series that Rowling wrote the novels with deliberate Christian connections. "If you want to know who dies in *Harry Potter*, the answer is easy: God." In a sense, Grossman was right—Harry, as a Christ figure, dies of his own free will at the hands of Voldemort to save the Muggle and wizarding worlds, just as Jesus of the triune God died of his own free will to save humankind.

Works Cited

Bridger, Francis. *A Charmed Life: The Spirituality of Potterworld.* New York, NY: Image, 2002. Print.

Grossman, Lev. "Who Dies in *Harry Potter*? God." Editorial. *Time* magazine US. 12. July 2007: n.p. Web. 15 Aug. 2012. http://www.time.com/time/magazine/article/0,9171,1642885,00.html.

"*Harry Potter* Author J. K. Rowling Opens Up About Books' Christian Imagery." Interview by Shawn Adler. MTV.com. *MTV News.* 17 Oct. 2007. Web. 15 Aug. 2012. http://www.mtv.com/news/articles/1572107/jk-rowling-talks-about-christian-imagery.jhtml.

Holy Bible, New International Version, NIV. Biblica, 2011. Biblegateway.com. Web. 15 Aug. 2012. Web.

Killinger, John. *The Life, Death, and Resurrection of Harry Potter.* Macon, GA: Mercer UP, 2009. Print.

Neal, C. W. *The Gospel according to Harry Potter: The Spiritual Journey of the World's Greatest Seeker.* Louisville, KY: Westminster John Knox, 2008. Print.

Roper, Denise. *The Lord of the Hallows: Christian Symbolism and Themes in J. K. Rowling's Harry Potter.* Denver, CO: Outskirts, 2009. Print.

Ten

Doubting Dumbledore

JENNY MCDOUGAL

I am going to begin with a question that makes me nervous: as readers of the Harry Potter series, is our loyalty to Professor Albus Dumbledore undeserved? What I mean to say is this: Dumbledore, in the service of his endgame, uses lies, manipulation, and blind loyalty to coerce Harry Potter into a role he doesn't choose: saving the future of the wizarding world and destroying Lord Voldemort. Nowhere else was this theory met with as much derision and confusion as in a course on Harry Potter at St. Catherine University. The class, consisting of thirty-one students; two teaching assistants; our professor, Cecilia Konchar Farr; and one graduate student (your esteemed author) met once a week over the course of fourteen weeks to talk of nothing but Harry Potter, its legacy, and its sociocultural themes. After we finished *Sorcerer's Stone*, I came to class with one question scribbled in a small corner of my notebook: "Loyalty to D—why?" Our professor asked the room for our thoughts regarding this novel, and since it was one of the first classes, and because I always enjoy leaping into a discussion on literature, I offered my question. Silence followed, and then the most exciting discussion I ever witnessed erupted, one in which most everyone had something to say in defense of this beloved character.

Albus Dumbledore is the stuff of legend, the all-knowing, well-meaning hero who not only can save you, but who does so while being heroic and deft, cunning and charming. And *righteous*. I get it; it's the story we love, the one that parents tell their children: there are people out there who are good and strong and will save you—all you have to do is have faith in them. Even I, in my stuffy, feminist tower, love who Dumbledore is in Harry Potter. Even I want to be saved by his benevolent patriarchy. In the series, Dumbledore is ostensibly Harry's savior. He is responsible for rescuing him from the destroyed remains of his dead parents' home, and he later saves him from a life of torment and neglect with the Dursleys. Dumbledore is the series' veritable knight—that wizened guide who takes you into his tutelage, shows you how to brandish a sword, solve the puzzle, follow the footsteps, and who inducts you into the ways of this maladjusted world. And he does. He takes Harry away from the pains of his childhood, certainly with the best intentions, and grooms him to be the hero the wizarding world needs. Dumbledore fights and lives while plucking the heartstrings of each reader, and when he dies at the end of *Half-Blood Prince*, everyone is gutted.

So on this fateful day, my question of undeserved loyalty to Dumbledore was an abomination. I was outnumbered and outmatched by a band of college women, and it was very clear that I had hit on something primal. Why are we so eager to conceive of Dumbledore as the bastion of morality and goodness? Why do we read past Dumbledore's failings?

Certainly, Dumbledore is capable of good deeds and moral actions—the novels are full of them—but the beginning and end of Dumbledore isn't moral purity; these are not the kinds of characters J. K. Rowling writes. Essayist Veronica Schanos writes in "Cruel Heroes and Treacherous Texts" that the nature of Rowling's narrative articulates a "uniquely complex understanding of morality," one that allows for multidimensional characters and themes (131). A cursory scan of many characters in Harry Potter offers proof of Rowling's ability to build characters that operate within both good and bad schemas.

As in real life, Rowling's fictional world is made up of good people who do bad things and bad people who are capable of mercy and goodness. Take, for example, a member of the Order of the Phoenix, Remus Lupin. Described as slovenly, shabby, and gray-tinged, Lupin has all the outward signs of being untrustworthy. For most of *Prisoner of Azkaban*, he is cagy, unreliable, and mysterious. But we discover that Lupin is not only part of the original Order of the Phoenix, but he is also a member of Dumbledore's inner circle. However, like Rowling's other characters, Lupin isn't morally pure. He, along with Sirius Black, attempts to execute Peter Pettigrew at the end of *Prisoner of Azkaban*. And, most notably, Lupin attempts to abandon his pregnant wife, Nymphadora Tonks, to go glory-seeking in *Deathly Hallows*. Draco Malfoy is another example. The son of Lucius and Narcissa Malfoy, Draco plays the role of antagonist in nearly every novel of the series. He's crass, racist, disrespectful of authority, and willing to lie and scheme to get what he wants; he itches to join the Death Eaters. But the end of *Half-Blood Prince* sees Draco unable to perform the task Voldemort has asked of him—the execution of Dumbledore. Draco tells Dumbledore, "No you can't [help me]. . . . Nobody can. He told me to do it or he'll kill me. I have no choice" (591). Ultimately, Draco doesn't kill Dumbledore. He is unable to, and in that moment a glimmer of humanity is apparent in a character that in hundreds of pages before appears to have none.

And there are countless others: Cornelius Fudge, Professor Quirrell, Narcissa Malfoy, Petunia and Dudley Dursley, Sirius Black, Mundungus Fletcher, Mad-Eye Moody, Xenophilius Lovegood, and others. Every character inhabiting Rowling's universe operates in shades of gray, and readers *see* those dimensions in her characters. Thus, those characters become human; they become real. We understand at the end of *Deathly Hallows*, finally, that Professor Severus Snape's hatred of Harry is not because he is evil or working with Voldemort, but because Snape is motivated by his profound and lasting love for Lily, Harry's mother. It turns out that the one person who the reader and Harry believed to be thoroughly evil and duplicitous is one of the people most reliably working in Harry's favor.

If this is all true, that Rowling's characters can be more than they appear, that they can operate in more than one mode of being, than why isn't Dumbledore the same? The class at St. Catherine was willing to keep Dumbledore safe from the same kind of analysis they brought to other characters. Whole shouting matches erupted in response to my prodding. What could it mean other than we desperately want our heroes to be good, through and through? I argue that those kinds of heroes are feeble and without merit, and most importantly, don't exist in our world. Heroes worthy of our loyalty should be complex and conflicted—they should be human.

It does a disservice to the complexity of Dumbledore to refuse a dissection of his choices and behaviors; the hero of the story deserves more. Dumbledore is the epitome of Rowling's complex understanding of morality and offers a profound lesson: that each of us is capable of both good and bad deeds, but we are measured against the choices we make and the things we believe in. Dumbledore says it perfectly when he proclaims in *Chamber of Secrets*, "It is our choices, Harry, that tell us who we are, far more than our abilities" (333).

What follows is a hindsight argument about the nature of Dumbledore's character, moments in the narrative that I found clearly indicative of who and what Dumbledore is working for and toward. I've considered the narrative as a whole, not seven novels of a series, and have isolated the five most telling examples of Dumbledore's manipulation and deceit, scenes that explicate his larger endgame. To set up Harry as the sacrificial lamb, Dumbledore must create the hero the wizarding world needs. He does this in three significant instances: first by stripping Harry of his agency, placing him with the Dursleys, and withholding information in *Sorcerer's Stone*; then by removing his power in *Order of the Phoenix*; and later by playing on the loyalty Harry feels for Dumbledore and his family in *Half-Blood Prince*. All of these instances reveal Dumbledore's worldview of a kind of utilitarian morality for the greater good. They prove that his aim isn't always the protection of Harry; yet like Harry himself, the reader looks past Dumbledore's manipulations and lies (yes, lies). Most importantly, all of his "blunders" exist in stark relief against his righteous, moral, and supremely kind actions. Like most of Rowling's creations, he is a balanced and nuanced character until the very end.

The nature of Rowling's narrative is complex and intricately woven, yet her use of point of view is ingeniously simple. Using third-person limited, Rowling places the reader with Harry, with only a few exceptions. Because we are situated with Harry, we tend to read as he does, overlooking the actions made by Dumbledore that explicate his endgame and the nature of his character. Each of these moments further Dumbledore's plans for the demise of Voldemort.

Throughout the novels, we learn of Voldemort's abuse of other children in the orphanage, his harming of animals, and his propensity to take tokens from those he hurts.[1] After his education at Hogwarts, Voldemort mounts a campaign to weed out those he terms "Mudbloods" and to create a pure wizard race. Learning of a prophecy that could mean the end of him, Voldemort sets out to destroy the one he thinks the prophecy references: Harry Potter. After hunting down the Potters, Voldemort kills James and Lily and attempts to murder one-year-old Harry. He fails and is stripped of physical form—Voldemort is defeated. But, as the events of *Sorcerer's Stone* show, Voldemort was able to resurrect himself, and he vowed to destroy Harry Potter for good.

Clearly, in the context of the narrative trajectory of the series, the destruction of Voldemort is an important task that needs completing. But to coerce a small child into assisting in this dangerous work isn't something an entirely moral adult would do—particularly the Dumbledore the students in our class championed. To achieve the destruction of Voldemort, Dumbledore needs a working theory about why, on the night he tried to murder Harry, Voldemort was reduced to a shell of his former self. To generate this theory, Dumbledore must have known three key factors: what the prophecy given to him by Professor Sybill Trelawney meant, why Harry survived a killing curse, and what Horcruxes are, including how they are made.

The prophecy, given to Dumbledore a year before Harry Potter was born, illuminates two important pieces of information regarding Voldemort. It foretells the birth of a child capable of defeating Voldemort by "[marking] him as his equal, but he will have power the Dark Lord knows not . . . and [the second] either must die at the hand of the other for neither can live while the other survives" (*Order of the Phoenix* 821). Dumbledore deduces from this prophecy that Harry, marked as an equal by the scar left from his attempted murder, will have to be the one to destroy Voldemort once and for all.

In addition to the prophecy, Dumbledore must have also known how Harry survived the night Voldemort came for him. Since Dumbledore is often described as being one of the greatest and wisest of wizards, it is plausible to assume that he is also aware of old, mysterious magic and how it can work. Lily Potter's sacrificial death at the hands of Voldemort marked Harry with the protection of love, an old magic and ultimate protection. However, Lily's sacrificial death to protect Harry created something that Voldemort didn't intend: an accidental Horcrux, the cause of his lightning bolt scar.

I am unsure whether we are to understand that at the time of the Potters' deaths Dumbledore deduced the nature of Harry's scar, but I am positive that Dumbledore later had a working hypothesis about why Voldemort survived that night and what it might mean for Harry. The first time readers catch a glimpse of Harry's scar, Professor Minerva McGonagall asks if Dumbledore could "do something about it." Dumbledore remarks, "Even if I could, I wouldn't. Scars can come in handy" (*Sorcerer's Stone* 15). Later Rubeus Hagrid tells Harry, "That was no ordinary cut. That's what yeh get when a powerful, evil curse touches yeh" (*Sorcerer's Stone* 55). It isn't until the end of *Order of the Phoenix* that Dumbledore elucidates the connection between Harry and Voldemort. He says, "I guessed, fifteen years ago, when I saw the scar on your forehead, *what it might mean*. . . . For it became apparent, shortly after you rejoined the magical world, that *I was correct*, and that your scar was giving you warnings when Voldemort was close to you" (*Order of the Phoenix* 826–827; emphasis mine]. It was clear to Dumbledore that Harry's scar was more than a leftover artifact of Voldemort's killing curse. Having this last piece of the puzzle, Dumbledore's quest to destroy Voldemort was affirmed. All he needed was someone willing to take up the mantle.

Agency in *Sorcerer's Stone*

Harry was stripped of agency the moment Dumbledore gave Hagrid the order to retrieve the newly orphaned boy from the rubble at Godric's Hollow. For Dumbledore, placing Harry with the Dursleys not only ensures his safety—from Voldemort or his gang of Death Eaters—but also indicates what kind of life he will have. After meeting Dumbledore outside of the Dursleys, McGonagall asks where Harry will live now that his parents have died. Dumbledore tells her that Harry will live here with the Dursleys, as they are his only remaining family. Horrified, McGonagall cries, "You don't mean—you *can't* mean the people who live *here*? . . . You couldn't find two people who are less like us . . . Harry Potter come and live here!" (13). Readers are just as horrified that Harry will be living with the Dursleys until he's old enough to go to Hogwarts. After all, we start the series with a declaration of the kind of people the Dursleys are: "The Potters knew very well what [Vernon] and Petunia thought about them and their kind" (8). Like McGonagall, we cannot conceive of any reason why Harry Potter must live with people who hate wizards.

Unconvinced after Dumbledore's assurances, McGonagall presses him further, arguing that Harry would be better off in a wizarding home where loving guardians would be able to explain everything to him. McGonagall announces that Harry will be famous in their world, that there will be books written about him. Unmoved, Dumbledore says, "Exactly . . . It would be enough to turn any boy's head. Famous before he can walk and talk! Can't you see how much better off he'll be, growing up away from all that until he's ready to take it?" (13). Placing Harry with the Dursleys, Dumbledore resigns Harry to a life of mistreatment that includes verbal and emotional abuse and severe neglect. Harry spends his formative years unaware of who he is, where he's from, and why his parents died. He grows up marginalized from his family and arrives at his eleventh birthday ready for some answers to his questions about why he has a curious scar, why he can make things happen as if by magic, and why he keeps getting mysterious letters addressed to *Mr. H. Potter, Cupboard Under the Stairs.*

Answers come at the stroke of midnight on his eleventh birthday. In the living room of the little cottage on the sea, Hagrid is livid that the Dursleys have kept Harry from knowing about his past. He exclaims, "Do you mean to tell me . . . that this boy—this boy!—knows nothin' abou'—about ANYTHING" (49). Indignant, Hagrid tells Harry about his parents and the wizard who brought about their deaths. He tells Harry that he is, in fact, a wizard; that he came from a loving family; and that he will be joining others like him at a school for witchcraft and wizardry. Harry feels as though a balloon is swelling inside of him, Rowling writes, that this is the happiest he's ever felt, and it's all thanks to Hagrid, Dumbledore's proxy. None too keen on letting Harry go with Hagrid, the Dursleys attempt to keep Harry from leaving—culminating in Vernon's insult of Dumbledore. Hagrid responds with a roar: "NEVER—INSULT—ALBUS—DUMBLEDORE—IN—FRONT—OF—ME" (59). From this moment on, Harry is clear about where his loyalties should lie, and we readers are as well.

Harry leaves for Hogwarts with a sense of excitement, and Hagrid, acting on directions from Dumbledore, fills Harry in on the details of the night Voldemort came for Lily and James Potter and for Harry himself. At school, Harry encounters many trials and troubles from both fellow classmates and from Professor Snape. Throughout *Sorcerer's Stone*, Harry is consistently berated by Snape during daily potions lessons and is taken to task, due, apparently, to his less than stellar performance in class. It is clear that Snape is set up to act as the villain, described as an overgrown bat with greasy hair whose ethics are more than dubious. (Not only does Snape favor students from his House, but he also shames, yells, and awards detentions to those who are not in Slytherin.) Throughout *Sorcerer's Stone*, Harry constantly schemes against Snape, convinced that Snape's loyalties lie with Voldemort, and the reader is keen to agree with Harry. Viewing Snape through his point of view, we see a villain.

However, events unfold that discredit Harry's theory that Snape is evil and working for Voldemort. *Sorcerer's Stone* culminates in Hermione Granger, Ron Weasley, and Harry's search for the titular stone. After coming to the (false) conclusion that Snape is, in fact, after the stone, Harry devises a plot to find the stone first. Both Ron and Hermione are unconvinced that going after the stone will amount to anything. Hermione is concerned that Harry could be expelled. To that, Harry responds:

> Don't you understand? If Snape gets hold of the stone, Voldemort's coming back! Haven't you heard what it was like when he was trying to take over? There won't

be any Hogwarts to get expelled from! . . . If I get caught before I can get to the stone, well, I'll have to go back to the Dursleys and wait for Voldemort to find me there, it's only dying a bit later than I would have, because I'm never going over to the Dark Side. (270)

Harry resigns himself to going after the stone, aided in part by the Invisibility Cloak found underneath his pillow bearing a simple message: "Just in case," scribbled in Dumbledore's hand.[2] Committed to Harry, Ron and Hermione accompany him through the six fail-safes protecting the stone. Arriving at the seventh fail-safe, Harry encounters Voldemort in the guise of Professor Quirrell, not Snape. Quirrell explains to Harry just how misguided he was to suspect Snape of treachery. Quirrell tells a stunned Harry, "Of course [Snape was trying to protect you]. . . . Why do you think he wanted to referee your next [Quidditch] match? He was trying to make sure I didn't [try to kill you] again" (289). Just like Harry, readers are stunned to learn that our perception of Snape is faulty. What is curious and rather shortsighted of Harry is that he doesn't recalibrate his opinion of Snape afterwards. Having thought one thing—that Snape is *so very evil*—and having that knowledge up-ended, Harry cleaves illogically to his conclusion that Snape is not to be trusted.

Clearly, Harry lacks mature judgment, and shouldn't we, dear reader, have a better grasp on who Snape is and who Dumbledore is? There is a disconnect between what Harry sees and what is actually occurring, and his perceptions of both Dumbledore and Snape are, ultimately, flawed. *Sorcerer's Stone* is proof that we cannot completely trust what Harry sees and thinks about any one character in the series. Yet the students in my class disregarded Harry's flaccid deductive reasoning, standing behind the contention that Dumbledore is above criticism.

"What about the conversation between Harry and Dumbledore at the end?" I asked in class. At first, Dumbledore praises Harry's courage: "I arrived in time to prevent [Quirrell from getting the stone], although you were doing very well on your own, I must say" (296). Praising Harry's abilities subtly reinforces the behaviors Dumbledore values in Harry—bravery,

passion, and the need to save others. Dumbledore offers amazing compliments to Harry, things he's never heard before from
the Dursleys or anyone. Importantly, the reader is comforted
that Dumbledore believes the tale Harry has told, because adults
in children's literature are rarely counted as confidants. Here in
the hospital wing of Hogwarts, Harry, and the reader, associate
safety and comfort with Dumbledore.

However, Dumbledore complicates this sense of safety and
comfort by reminding Harry that there is no reason to believe
that Voldemort won't find another way to either possess someone else or achieve his own resurrection. Harry asks Dumbledore if he thinks Voldemort is gone for good, and Dumbledore
offers this answer: "Harry, while you may have only delayed his
return to power, it will merely take someone else who is prepared to fight what seems a losing battle next time" (298). Not
only does Dumbledore evade an answer to Harry's question, but
his non-answer ramps up the fear in both the reader and Harry
that Voldemort can (and most likely will) return. Keeping Harry
in a state of perpetual fear of the wizard who wants him dead,
Dumbledore succeeds in maintaining some kind of hold on this
young boy. It's quite upsetting to see Dumbledore manipulate
a child as young as Harry, and I think our growing affection
for Dumbledore is the reason we read past his manipulation in
this scene. Like Harry, we see Dumbledore's evasion as part of
the larger goal: protecting Harry, that is, keeping him alive and
destroying Voldemort for good.

Dumbledore evades larger truths when he denies Harry
answers about why Voldemort wants him dead. Instead of considering that Harry has a right to information that could shape
his future and his past, Dumbledore withholds an answer, saying only this: "Alas, the first thing you ask me, I cannot tell you.
Not today. Not now. [When] you are ready, you will know"
(299). This passage troubles me and has since the first time I
read it. Since Dumbledore later confesses in *Order of the Phoenix* that it was a mistake to think that Harry was too young to
know why Voldemort wants him dead, it is safe to assume that
Dumbledore, perhaps, has other reasons for withholding this
crucial information; perhaps he wants to avoid the ugly business
of acknowledging that he considers Harry his sacrificial lamb.

Praising Harry's tenacity and bravery in facing and prevent-
ing Voldemort's return, Dumbledore decides that Harry is much
too young to hear information that will help him process both
the deaths of his parents and the reasons Voldemort wants him
dead. Instead of liberating Harry from the bonds of ignorance,
Dumbledore resigns Harry to the dark and places him in thrall
to the will of his headmaster. By the end of the first book, Harry
has become Dumbledore's loyal, and ultimately blind, servant, a
boy without power or privilege of his own.

Power and Privilege in *Order of the Phoenix*

Arguably the most poignant and powerful novel of the series,
the *Order of the Phoenix* not only changes the way the characters operate throughout the narrative, but it also changes how
the reader interacts with the series; in essence, we grow up with
Harry. Rowling pushes her characters through the challenges of
heartache, puberty, death, a fanatical professor, and destruction,
without deference to her youngest readers. Harry experiences
his first kiss, his first crush, and, after dealing with the death of
a fellow classmate in *Goblet of Fire*, he experiences the deeper
loss of a loved one. And the reader experiences all of it with
him. Harry is also plagued by increasingly troublesome dreams
of a long corridor and locked door—the culmination of these
nightmares leads Harry on a quest to save Sirius Black. Arriving in the Department of Mysteries, Harry finds no trace of
Sirius and is, instead, ambushed by Voldemort's Death Eaters.
After a long battle, Bellatrix Lestrange murders Sirius. The cli-
max of the battle occurs when Voldemort possesses Harry and
attempts to control him, only to be thwarted, at the last minute,
by Dumbledore.

Harry arrives back at Hogwarts and spends the first few
moments alone in Dumbledore's office, ruminating painfully
on Sirius's death. Rowling writes, "The silence and the stillness,
broken only by the occasional grunt or snuffle of a sleeping
portrait, was unbearable to him. If his surroundings could have
reflected the feelings inside him, the pictures would have been
screaming in pain" (820). Unable to reconcile his feelings with

the calm of Dumbledore's office, Harry casts about for some measure of relief; he does not find any. Instead, Harry must wait for Dumbledore. The arrival of Dumbledore, and their subsequent conversation, articulates the power and privilege within their relationship and throughout the narrative. In the entire series, no other conversation between them is as important. This is a perfect illustration of the moral complexity of Dumbledore.

In the face of Harry's grief, Dumbledore remains calm, a tactic that appears to heighten Harry's emotional state. When Dumbledore tells him he knows how he feels, Harry erupts in anger, exclaiming that Dumbledore knows nothing about how he is feeling. Dumbledore seems to disregard Harry's claim and presses further, telling Harry that he should feel no shame, that this ability to feel is his "greatest strength" (823). Dumbledore tells Harry that pain is a part of being human; the fact that he cares is an important part of being alive. This distinction proves to be an important piece of knowledge for Harry, because it's a way to differentiate himself from Voldemort. Harry fears that because Voldemort has marked him as an equal, there is only so much difference between them.

Throughout the events in *Order of the Phoenix*, Harry is concerned because he can enter Voldemort's mind via his dreams and see what he sees, and the distance between them isn't much distance at all. Harry, growing older and more mature, experiences feelings he hasn't really expressed before—anger, hatred, fear. These emotions tie him to Voldemort, and, Harry believes, *come from* Voldemort. Harry finds other disturbing similarities between Voldemort and himself, such as the ability to speak Parseltongue, a history of childhood abuse and neglect, and parentage that is both wizard and Muggle. Knowing that these similarities exist is a constant source of anxiety for Harry. That Dumbledore recognizes this fear and attempts to quell it is a kind gesture on the part of the headmaster.

However, in the same scene, Dumbledore capitalizes on Harry's emotional state. Rowling writes, "'Oh yes, you do [care],' said Dumbledore, still more calmly. 'You have now lost your mother, your father, and the closest thing to a parent you have ever known. Of course you care'" (824). Harry, in anger, attempts to leave Dumbledore's office after hearing this but is denied that privilege; he is literally forbidden to leave the office. Harry tells Dumbledore to let him out, and after each rebuke, Harry asks again. Dumbledore refuses Harry's requests again and again, finally telling Harry that he must listen to what he has to say. At last, Dumbledore admits to Harry that he's made terrible mistakes and that Harry is not as angry as he should be (825).

"Finally," I said in class, "finally we have an admission of guilt from Dumbledore." Over the course of a couple of weeks, I had managed to convince one student that Dumbledore was not the morally pure character that everyone had decided he was—and that was after reading through four books. Groans followed and, I'm sure, eye-rolls from the other thirty students when I called for a discussion about this scene in *Order of the Phoenix*. "He felt bad," one girl said, casting around, "he obviously felt bad because Sirius had just been killed, and Harry was so distraught." Which meant what—that Dumbledore was arbitrarily offering a confession because Harry was sad?

Dumbledore never does anything in the novels without weighing the consequences and outcomes, and this admission of guilt is no different. This character obviously knows in his bones he was wrong to withhold information from Harry, and after the battle at the Ministry and Sirius's death, it is never more clear than when Harry is in his office. So Dumbledore confesses: there is a specific reason Harry was sent to live with his aunt and uncle, and the reason isn't because of their generosity or that the Dursleys were his only remaining family. Dumbledore was determined that Harry remain alive because of the prophecy made about him and because Harry was and is the only person who can ultimately defeat Voldemort. Dumbledore says, "Five years ago, then . . . you arrived at Hogwarts, neither as happy nor as well nourished as I would have liked, perhaps, yet alive and healthy. . . . *Thus far, my plan was working well*" (837; emphasis mine). Here is an admission that Dumbledore has made a plan for Harry's life, one that was constructed long before Harry was capable of making his own choices; certainly, this is proof of Dumbledore exercising his privilege and power over a very young boy.

Dumbledore understands the situation he has placed Harry in, which makes his plan that much more egregious and Dumbledore that much more culpable. Such sadness permeates the *Order of the Phoenix* that readers can't help but feel resigned to the task laid out for Harry at the end of Dumbledore's story. After hearing the prophecy, Harry asks Dumbledore the question that has plagued him since the events in *Sorcerer's Stone*: "'So,' said Harry, dredging up the words from what felt like a deep well of despair inside him, 'so does that mean that . . . that one of us has got to kill the other one . . . in the end?'" (844). Solemnly, Dumbledore answers, finally, the question Harry has asked with a simple *yes*. The journey Harry must embark on was conceived and put in place well before he was old enough to understand and accept his fate in the larger scheme of things. Dumbledore knows the kinds of choices Harry must make, and he keeps secret most, if not all, of the reasons why—until Harry is so beaten down and tired, until he has no other choice but to submit.

Later, with Ron and Hermione, Harry must decide whether to tell his best friends that he either must kill or be killed, and it is a painful moment when he considers this. Even later, Harry is described as feeling isolated and alone since the talk in Dumbledore's office. Rowling writes, "It was sunny and the grounds around him were full of laughing people, and even though he felt as distant from them as though he belonged to a different race, it was still very hard to believe as he sat here that his life must include, or end in, murder" (856). This is such a burden for Harry, for anyone, who is young and kind, and his total acceptance of his fate is quite heartbreaking. Dumbledore has constructed Harry to accept the role of a sacrificial lamb, to be the one to end Voldemort in any way he can, and Harry must comply. The end of *Order of the Phoenix* shows us a boy who is resigned to the path chosen for him so long ago.

Trust and Loyalty in *Half-Blood Prince*

Harry's path from the boy who lived to the man who must die in order to save the wizarding world begins when the prophecy is revealed and Voldemort marks Harry as his equal. Yet Harry's growth from a wide-eyed eleven-year-old to a young man ready to take on the perilous journey ahead of him by the end of *Deathly Hallows* is Dumbledore's construction, one that begins when Dumbledore leaves Harry on the Dursleys' doorstep. The end of *Order of the Phoenix* sees Harry accepting his fate as the only person who can really destroy Voldemort, and the events of *Half-Blood Prince* reinforce the trajectory Dumbledore has set him on. There is no going back.

Half-Blood Prince begins with Harry back at the Dursleys for the summer and greeted by a letter from Dumbledore that asks him to attend to a matter of much importance. Harry replies to Dumbledore that he would be happy to help him. Arriving at Number Four Privet Drive, Dumbledore finally admonishes the Dursleys for their treatment of Harry since he came to live with them. It is interesting that Dumbledore chooses to say this now when he had fifteen previous years to do so. Dumbledore says, "You did not do as I asked. You have never treated Harry as a son. He has known nothing but neglect and often cruelty at your hands" (55). Dumbledore is indignant at the Dursleys' treatment of Harry, but he also seems to admonish them in order to tighten the bond Harry has to him and to reinforce the loyalty readers have to Dumbledore. Since Harry and Dumbledore are about to embark on a perilous journey to find and destroy Voldemort's Horcruxes, Dumbledore wants to be sure that Harry is with him until the end.

Half-Blood Prince is key to the series because readers are privy in this novel to the way Dumbledore uses those who can be of service to him. Peppered throughout the book are moments when Dumbledore capitalizes on his ability to manipulate those around him. Probably the saddest casualty of Dumbledore's ability to control those who are of use is Severus Snape. Using his love for Lily, Dumbledore makes Snape into a vigilant guardian for Harry. Readers discover later, at the death of Snape, just how much control Dumbledore asserted over his life, entreating him to act as a double agent and ultimate protector of Harry. Dumbledore also commands Snape to act as executioner at the end of the sixth book, even when Snape doesn't want to. Snape's enduring guilt over Lily's death makes him incredibly useful in Dumbledore's quest to destroy Voldemort.

We first glimpse overt manipulation when Dumbledore finesses Professor Horace Slughorn to return to Hogwarts. Using Slughorn's need to "collect" famous and influential people, Dumbledore brings Harry to where Slughorn is hiding. Harry wonders how he can be of any help persuading this man to return to Hogwarts, and Dumbledore tells him, "Oh, I think we'll find a use for you" (60). Being of use to Dumbledore is important for Harry, who has known no other way to relate to his headmaster. As for most people in Dumbledore's life, being useful is an important quality.

After Harry and Dumbledore find Slughorn, and after Slughorn talks with Harry, Slughorn agrees to return to Hogwarts. On their way back, Dumbledore tells Harry he did a good job of showing Slughorn how much he "stands to gain by returning to Hogwarts" (74). Dumbledore says that Slughorn will attempt to woo Harry, and that it would be in their best interest to let him. Slughorn is in possession of an important piece of information about Voldemort's Horcruxes, and Harry must know what Slughorn knows. Again, the reasons are kept from Harry, and Dumbledore offers only vague answers to sustain his student's questions and to perpetuate his loyalty. Constant evasion of certain topics keeps Harry unaware of what is actually going on, a tactic that Dumbledore uses throughout the series.

The action of *Half-Blood Prince* revolves around Dumbledore and Harry's excursions through memory and landscape. On their first journey, Dumbledore tells Harry, "I have decided that it is time, now that you know what prompted Lord Voldemort to try and kill you fifteen years ago, for you to be given certain information" (197). Harry, naturally, seems taken aback by Dumbledore's statement since, during their last conversation in *Order of the Phoenix*, it appeared that Harry was told the entire truth about what happened fifteen years ago. Dumbledore admits to Harry that everything he was told was what Dumbledore "knew to be true," and the information he is gaining will be situated "comfortably in the land of speculation" (197).

"As a reader of the series," I said in class, "I'm curious why Dumbledore claims that he *doesn't* know what he's about to share with Harry. Obviously, Dumbledore knows more than he's willing to share." Couching his considerable knowledge in the guise of guesswork reinforces Harry's loyalty to both Dumbledore and to his mission. It is also a great way to keep Harry from making the *choice* to follow Dumbledore or to demand the information at the beginning.

However, just moments after this scene, Dumbledore asks Harry to keep his secrets close but to share whatever he knows with Ron and Hermione. Not only does this give Harry the opportunity to build a necessary support system, but it also indicates that Dumbledore knows Harry's limitations as a wizard. Harry needs Hermione for her cleverness and Ron for his loyalty and heart. This gesture demonstrates Dumbledore's benevolence and kindness. It also reinforces the way Dumbledore consistently and constantly shifts between these modes—one moment he is evasive and stoic, another he is kind and considerate. But his moods are not the only shift in balance. His whole demeanor can change. In one scene, he's willing to share information; in another he can shut down inquiry with no more than a few words. During Dumbledore's meeting with the Dursleys in *Half-Blood Prince*, Harry is curious about the state of Dumbledore's hand. Rowling writes, "As he replaced his wand in his pocket, Harry saw that his hand was blackened and shriveled; it looked as though his flesh had been burned away. 'Sir—What happened to you—?' 'Later Harry,' said Dumbledore. 'Please sit down'" (48). It is not surprising that Harry isn't sure how to feel about his headmaster during the series, and especially during *Half-Blood Prince*.

Harry continues his lessons with Dumbledore in this novel, discovering Voldemort's past, his parents, and how he came to be a student at Hogwarts. At the end of each lesson, Harry has gained more knowledge about Voldemort the man, but Dumbledore continually thwarts him when he asks for further information. Instead of telling Harry outright about Voldemort's Horcruxes, Dumbledore decides to withhold this information. Dumbledore maintains Harry's interest and loyalty precisely because of this secret-keeping. Given the chance, I wonder if Harry would continue to humor Dumbledore's lessons, especially if he knew the whole truth. Since he is never given the chance, Harry willingly follows Dumbledore into the depths of memory and history.

In this pursuit, the return of Slughorn to Hogwarts is important for Dumbledore. Slughorn possesses a memory that will confirm Dumbledore's hypothesis about Voldemort, and Harry is tasked with retrieving it. Acting on Dumbledore's orders, Harry sets about finding a way to get Slughorn to give up the actual memory. Failing on numerous occasions, Harry returns again to Dumbledore's office, embarrassed at his failure, to find a disappointed headmaster. Instead of acknowledging that Harry is under considerable pressure, Dumbledore shames his student and insists that he make retrieving the memory his top priority (428–429). Harry and the reader have never witnessed this kind of behavior from Dumbledore, and it is a bit distressing. It is clear from this scene that destroying Voldemort is all-consuming and that nothing else is more important to Dumbledore.

Dumbledore's myopic vision is never more apparent than after Harry coerces Slughorn to give up his memory. Harry immediately heads for Dumbledore's office and, with Dumbledore, witnesses Slughorn's conversation with Tom Riddle. Discovering the last piece of the puzzle energizes Harry, and it is here that he finally commits to the path laid out for him by Dumbledore. Harry, too, wants retribution for the deaths of his parents, Cedric Diggory, Sirius Black, and others who have fallen at the hands of Voldemort and his Death Eaters. After impelling Harry to understand the gravity of Voldemort's choice to split his soul and attain immortality, Dumbledore tells him why he is a threat to Voldemort: Harry has the ability to love. Not until the events of *Deathly Hallows* does Harry finally understand that it's not his soul that is a threat to Voldemort, but the fact that Harry is an unintentional Horcrux. By marking Harry as his equal, Voldemort splits his soul seven ways and part of it resides in Harry.

Much as he does at the end of *Order of the Phoenix*, Dumbledore uses the deaths of Lily and James to influence Harry's decision to go after Voldemort. Dumbledore says, "Got to [try and defeat Voldemort]? Of course you've got to! But not because of the prophecy! Because you, yourself, will never rest until

you've tried! *We both know it!*" (511; emphasis mine). Harry
is moved, both by the knowledge that Voldemort has murdered
those he cared for most and that Dumbledore has shown how
much confidence he has in Harry's abilities. This is an important moment in the trajectory of Dumbledore's plan: it is not
the prophecy but the personality that Dumbledore has created.
Ironically, because of *who* he has been constructed to be, Harry
accepts his task just as Dumbledore wants him to.

Once Harry has committed to going after Voldemort and
ending him, we finally see the man Dumbledore has crafted him
to be since his infancy. Rowling writes that Harry finally understands what Dumbledore was trying to tell him all this time, that
there was a "difference between being dragged into the arena
to face a battle to the death and walking into the arena with
your head held high" (512). But Harry has been dragged for six
books; Dumbledore has seen to it that there would be no other
way. The end of *Half-Blood Prince* sees the death of Dumbledore at the hands of Professor Snape and a distraught Harry
trying to understand the journey ahead of him. He remarks to
Ron and Hermione that going after the remaining Horcruxes is
"what [Dumbledore] wanted me to [do], that's why he told me
all about them" (651). And so he does.

This is what I was waiting for, the end of *Half-Blood Prince*
and our subsequent discussion on *Deathly Hallows*. Harry's quest to find and destroy Voldemort's Horcruxes and the
events of *Deathly Hallows* were my ace, all the proof I needed
to convince these women that Dumbledore is, indeed, an agent
of mixed morality—just like the rest of us. *Deathly Hallows*
is Rowling's final revelation of the fascinating complexities of
Dumbledore because we are finally privy to a comprehensive
history of the man to whom so many are loyal. Dumbledore is
a man with a tricky past, with his share of heartache and death,
destruction and love.

Dumbledore is deeply influenced by his youthful and passionate relationship with Gellert Grindelwald, a wizard with
the means and guile to force Muggles into subservience, to gain
power, and to unite the wizarding world "for the greater good."
This also appeals to the young Dumbledore, but Grindelwald
pushes too hard and Dumbledore's brother, Aberforth, pleads

too loudly, and an argument that erupts between the three culminates in the death of Dumbledore's sister, Ariana. Dumbledore remembers:

> Well, Grindelwald fled. . . . He vanished, with his plans
> for seizing power, and his schemes for Muggle torture,
> and his dreams for the Deathly Hallows, dreams in
> which I had encouraged him and helped him. He ran,
> while I was left to bury my sister, and learn to live with
> my guilt and my terrible grief, the price of my shame.
> (*Deathly Hallows* 716–717)

Dumbledore's painful past epitomizes his propensity to over-
look the pawns while contemplating the endgame; Dumbledore
always works in the interest of the greater good. Can we blame
Dumbledore for the mistakes he made in his youth? The end
of *Deathly Hallows* shows Harry and the reader—most importantly the reader!—that Dumbledore is no different from the
rest of us: misguided, angry, joyful, selfish, loved, powerful,
smart, and wishing for a life better than the one we have. We are
all wishing to be saved or to be the savior, looking for one who
can show us the way, trying to find the hero.

"Dumbledore's past makes him so much more human to
me," I said on one of the last nights of discussion. "I can forgive him his arrogance, his grief, and his will to power, but I
can't forgive what he did to Harry." The women sighed audibly.
I think I had worn them down. And truly, it was alright with me
by then. I was content to sit with my own ideas about this character we all love—and it's true, I love Dumbledore as a literary
character, but I hate his coercive actions. And isn't that the more
important thing? That Dumbledore is a complex character with
human flaws and strengths? Dumbledore is proof that no matter
who our family is, with whom we associate, or what we've done
that has harmed others, our choice to *do better* is the worthier
action. But no choice will make Dumbledore perfect; Rowling
thwarts our desire for an omniscient father figure.

Rowling is an astounding writer. Spending fourteen weeks
with these books, these characters, and the women in my class
strengthened my love for the series and my admiration for

Rowling. Each discussion brought new insights and illuminations about even the smallest characters, the most mundane of passages. Above all, Rowling's series demonstrates that no one is born into one way of being, that we all have choices. Reading Harry Potter is an act of awareness: it shows us that if we strip away the artifice, we get to see the human thriving underneath; in all that darkness, light.

Notes

1. A lot can be said about how Voldemort's severe neglect and family history contributed to his ultimate hatred of Muggles and those who sympathize with witches and wizards of mixed parenting. Personally, I think Tom Riddle's behavior and ideology can be attributed to undiagnosed mental illness—to wit, I believe Voldemort is a sociopath (see chapters 12 and 13 in this volume). But, that's another chestnut altogether.

2. One could spend a lot of time and page space examining why Dumbledore leaves the Invisibility Cloak for Harry with such a curious note pinned to it. "Just in case" assumes that Dumbledore knows Harry would go after the stone. After all, Dumbledore has said that he is present at the school even when he's physically not there, so it's safe to assume he knew what Harry was up to. Dumbledore returning the cloak to Harry after he left it in the topmost tower, clearly breaking the school rule of being out of bed in the middle of the night, suggests that he wanted Harry to go through the trapdoor.

Work Cited

Schanos, Veronica. "Cruel Heroes and Treacherous Texts." In *Reading Harry Potter*, ed. Giselle Liza Anatol. Westport, CT: Praeger, 2003. Print.

My Harry Potter Story

MARION BASILIO AND CARRIE MATHEWS

Marion Basilio, twenty-two, Oxon Hill, Maryland. Plays the drums and guitar, and is pursuing a degree in business. Photo by Maria Ignacio.

Marion Basilio: Many Harry Potter fans grew up reading the series as part of their childhood. I, however, wasn't really a big reader as a kid. I would always avoid reading books thicker than the width of three of my fingers. As soon as pictures left the inside of books, my motivation to pick up another book gradually decreased.

It was at the end of my freshman year of high school that I became hooked on Harry Potter (better late than never), and it was because of my best friend. I always knew my best friend was into Harry Potter. She used to have email addresses and screen names referring to phoenixes and Ravenclaw. One day, I finally asked her, "Does this stuff really entertain you?" She told me that I would have to read it to understand. That made sense, but I wasn't sold. The following week, she came up to me and handed me a hardback book with a picture of a boy in a striped shirt and red cape riding a broomstick. *Harry Potter and the Sorcerer's Stone* it read. Automatically, I judged the book by its cover. It looked so childish, although the thickness did intimidate me at the time.

So I took the book home, and that is where it stayed for a week until my best friend wanted it back. Given the time I had left with the book, I finally gave the first three chapters a try. Even as an inactive reader, the plots and the creatures of the wizarding world intrigued me. I kept going and actually finished the book in three days, which wasn't bad for someone who hated reading. I gave the book back to my friend and asked for the next one.

Ever since then, I've caught up with all the books and the movies and fallen in love with J. K. Rowling's unbelievable imagination. I have even been to a couple of midnight premieres of the Harry Potter movies, which I never imagined myself taking part in. I also bought a wand made of holly wood and an exact replica of an acceptance letter to Hogwarts (with her name on it) for my friend as a thank-you gift. My friend, by introducing me to the wizarding world of Harry Potter, rejuvenated my imagination. Harry Potter ignited the spark I have for reading and improved my confidence in actually finishing a book. In fact, I'm pretty sure I would never have overcome my laziness to tackle thick hardback books if it wasn't for Harry Potter.

Carrie Mathews, twenty-seven, Arlington, Texas. Student at the University of Texas in Arlington, majoring in social work. Photo by the author.

Carrie Mathews: Most devout fans began their journey with Harry Potter when they were young, but I started a little late in the game. My mother introduced Harry Potter to my younger brother just as the third installment hit stores. Of course, I was the older sister and was very uninterested in anything my brother liked. Little did I know these books would later have a profound effect on my life.

When I graduated high school in 2004, I decided to start school at a community college, and to my disappointment, I was completely unprepared. Out of four classes, I had to drop two. I was completely discouraged and did not go back for my second semester. I didn't feel intelligent enough for school, so I thought I would try my hand at full-time work. Then, in 2007, I became increasingly depressed. It was also the same year I went with my friend to see the movie *Harry Potter and the Order of the Phoenix*. I identified with Harry's loneliness and depression in this movie, because it was ever present in my life at this time. I slept ten to twelve hours a day and cried myself to sleep almost every night. After a few weeks, I picked up *Half-Blood Prince*. I was completely mesmerized by how much insight these books originally defined as "children's books" had. They not only have adult subjects such as good versus evil, death, and violence embedded in the story lines but also some of the most striking words of wisdom.

My favorite quote from all seven books is when Albus Dumbledore says to Harry, "It is our choices, Harry, that show what we truly are, far more than our abilities." Harry, throughout this series, must make some of the most impossible choices, like choosing to save the school and risk being expelled or even killed. This quote had a bigger impact on me while reading of the difficulties Harry faced. The choices I had to make at the time I was reading these books weren't of the same magnitude as Harry's, but I was just as terrified.

I was a part of the population laid off from work because of the Recession. I tried for months to find a job with no luck. For several years, my parents urged me to go back to school. Since my first attempt at college in 2004, I was reluctant to go back because I didn't feel like I was college material. I've never been much of a reader, but since reading the Harry Potter series, I have been reading more than I ever had. It would have been much easier for me to curl up with depression and give up, or possibly settle with a job at the local supermarket. However, in the summer of 2010, I made the decision to enroll in the fall semester at my local community college. I knew it wouldn't be easy, but I felt I was in a better position this time around.

As September got closer and closer, I began to get increasingly nervous, and I thought of Neville Longbottom. Throughout the series, I watched this boy with very low self-esteem slowly grow into the courageous young man he becomes in *Deathly Hallows*. This young man, fictional though he may be, has a lack of confidence and awkwardness that is very relatable. Slowly with the encouragement of friends, he begins to stand up for himself and perseveres through being the target of many bullies. Neville never stops trying, even when he is completely terrified. Here I was living with my parents, unable to find a good-paying job, completely without direction, and terrified. J. K. Rowling's Harvard commencement speech really hit me hard because I had hit my "rock bottom" the year before and was slowly trying to find my way. As she said, "So my rock bottom became the solid foundation for which I rebuilt my life." I began to think that starting over wasn't such an impossible thing, and maybe, just maybe, I am smarter than I think I am. What I realized was that I was so afraid of failing that it was holding me back. So, I took school head on and surprised myself and everyone around me when I accomplished a 3.5 GPA my first semester back. I don't think I have ever been as happy as I have been these past four months. For the first time in years, I am seeing all these possibilities I couldn't see before.

I believe everything happens for a reason, and the Harry Potter books came into my life at the perfect moment. They not only provided an escape from my uncomfortable reality, but, because of my age, I noticed all the moral and insightful lessons embedded in the stories. I don't think that there are enough words in the English language to fully describe how much J. K. Rowling and her books have impacted my life today. My journey wasn't *with* Harry Potter, because, by the time I found my way to the books, his journey was over, and mine was just beginning.

PART III

Transfiguration

Eleven

Harry Potter and the Wizard's Gene

A Genetic Analysis of Potterworld

COURTNEY AGAR AND JULIA TERK

As Warren G. Bennis once explained, "The most dangerous leadership myth is that leaders are born—that there is a genetic factor to leadership. This myth asserts that people simply either have certain charismatic qualities or not. That's nonsense; in fact, the opposite is true. Leaders are made rather than born" ("Genetics Famous Quotations"). In the Harry Potter series by J. K. Rowling, we see a true leader grow into his position, overcoming treacherous obstacles with a combination of love, trust, strength, and unwavering courage. These characteristics cannot be genetically inherited, and they are what allow Harry Potter to save the wizarding world. However, in addition to the personal traits that make him the hero that he is, there is still a necessary genetic component that allows him to take action throughout the novels: the ability to do magic. It is not only Harry's character strengths that lead to his conquering of evil, but also the genes that he inherits that make him a wizard.

We have come to understand that every living thing is a compilation of cells that perform all essential tasks in our body for growth and survival. At the root of everything are chromosomes, which are made up of sequences of nucleotides composed of nucleic acids, and they make up our genetic material (Klug et al. G-1-9). This genetic material codes the production of every functioning cell in our body. Differing genetic material leads to variations within the same species and to the vast differences that occur across species. With this knowledge of life's basic blueprint, it is interesting to consider whether differing genetic material was contemplated and implemented throughout the Harry Potter novels. If that is the case and genetics is a factor in the books, are we to imagine wizards and witches as a completely different species from Muggles, or is wizarding power a result of something as simple as a mutated gene? We hypothesize that wizarding power does not originate from a species different from *Homo sapiens* but rather from specific modes of inheritance that affect, most importantly, the heritability and expression of the gene that codes for wizarding ability.

In order to comprehend the mechanism through which wizards inherit their power, one must first understand the basics of heritability in genetics. Most importantly, our varying genetic material is what is responsible for the differences of every individual within a species, including those who express wizarding power. The sequences of nucleotides that encode our traits, particularly through the production and expression of a specific protein, are called genes. Each differing sequence, or gene, is specific for a different protein, all of which are involved in various roles throughout our bodies. We inherit genes from both parents. Each gene equates to half our mother's genetic material and half our father's genetic material. Due to this fact, geneticists describe a gene as being composed of two alleles.

These alleles (expressed as any letter for one gene in genetic analyses) are the subunits of a gene. One is inherited randomly from one of the mother's two alleles for that gene and one is from the father's two alleles. The genetic combination of these alleles is termed the genotype, and the expression of the trait is termed the phenotype, which is seen as the observable characteristic. In most genes, an individual's expressed phenotype is determined based on dominant (written as a capital letter) or recessive (written as a lowercase letter) alleles. An example would be in Labrador Retrievers that have either black (B) or brown (b) fur. In this case, those that are BB or Bb would be black, where those that are bb would be brown, as the B (said "big B") is dominant over the b (said "little b"). Thus, when the dominant B is present in the genotype, it is the one expressed, but only when the B is completely absent is the b shown in the phenotype (Wygal). Individuals expressing both of the dominant alleles (e.g., AA) are considered homozygous (having the same two alleles for a single trait) dominant, where those that have both of the recessive alleles (e.g., aa) are homozygous recessive. If an individual has one of each allele (e.g., Aa), they are heterozygous for the gene (Klug et al.).

With the genetic modes of inheritance in mind, we hypothesize that the inheritance of the wizarding power in the Harry Potter series occurs in an autosomal (non-sex chromosomes) dominant gene that has yet to be discovered by either the wizarding or Muggle world (Klug et al. G-1). This gene, which we have assigned a W, will give a person magical ability if he or she is homozygous dominant (WW) or heterozygous (Ww). If a person is ww for this gene, they will be a Muggle or a Squib, both of whom do not have magical ability. However, the w allele is extremely rare in the general population, and for that reason, we would rarely encounter an individual with a Ww (heterozygous) genotype for the wizarding gene, much less ever see someone who is ww (homozygous recessive). This hypothesis is based on a comment Rowling made during an interview with *Hilary Career*, a woman's magazine, during which she said, "magic is a dominant and resilient gene" (Riccio). This being said, how is it that Muggles are as common as wizards with the ability to perform magic? We hypothesize that another form of inheritance called epistasis is affecting the expression of the wizarding gene itself.

When epistasis is present, the expression of one gene is masked or modified by another (Klug et al.). When this occurs, it can appear that the individual lacks the genotype necessary for the characteristic to show, when, in actuality, the *phenotype* is simply being suppressed. In the Muggle world, this can be seen in the coat color of Labrador Retrievers mentioned previously. Affecting the deposition of color, epistasis produces yellow Labradors. With the presence of a dominant E (EE or Ee) in the modifier gene, the black or brown color will be deposited into their fur, but if the dog is ee, it will be yellow (Wygal). In Harry's world, it is the *expression* of magical ability that is the key attribute when being considered a wizard. The expression of the wizarding ability is directly influenced by the modifier gene, which we have termed as E for expressivity. In those whose genotypes are WW and Ww in the wizarding gene, the W gene can only be expressed with a dominant E; thus, those with wizarding ability who are also EE or Ee would express magical ability. However, those who are ee would have their magical ability masked despite being WW or Ww for the wizarding gene. Therefore, even though they possess the gene to have magical ability, no expression of it would result, and that individual would not display any magical power.

With the genetic phenomenon of epistasis, we can account for why so many Muggles and Squibs exist in the world of Harry Potter. Neither possesses magical ability, or at least, neither expresses it. Rowling explains that "[a] Squib is almost the opposite of a Muggle-born wizard: he or she is a non-magical person born to at least one magical parent. Squibs are rare" (Rowling "SQUIBS"). For a Squib to result, the modifier gene masks the wizarding gene. The Squib must have at least one magical parent, but both parents could be magical as well. In this case, both parents would be Ee for the modifier gene. This would result in each of their children only having a 25 percent chance of inheriting a e (pronounced "little e") from both parents to be a ee genotype. However, in the case of only one magical parent, he or she must then be Ee while the Muggle parent is ee, masking his or her power. Both parents must have a e to pass on for an offspring to be ee.

In order to view and predict what possible genotypic combinations could result for the offspring of two parents, we can use a Punnett Square (Klug et al. 41–42). An example of how a Squib could arise can be seen in figure 15.1. The mother is WW for the wizarding gene while the father is Ww (WW is more likely, but it will produce the same results). This gives the parents a 100 percent chance of passing wizarding ability on to their offspring. The mother is Ee for the modifier gene, which will express her powers and she will be considered a witch. However, the father is ee, so his wizarding ability is masked and he is seen as a Muggle. Thus, although the probability (P) of their children having the ability to be a wizard is 4/4 or 100 percent, each child's chance of inheriting the ee genotype that will mask that ability is

MATERNAL			
		W	W
P A T E R N A L	W	WW	WW
	w	Ww	Ww

MATERNAL			
		E	e
P A T E R N A L	e	Ee	ee
	e	Ee	ee

P(offspring having wizarding ability) = 4/4 = 100%   P(offspring expressing wizarding ability gene) = 2/4 = 50%

FIGURE 15.1. Squib inheritance and expression of wizarding ability.

2/4 or 50 percent. Subsequently, the couple's children have a 50 percent chance of appearing to be nonmagical Squibs.

As seen in figure 15.1, in order for a Squib to be born, one parent could be a Muggle (or even a Squib as we now understand that they are genetically the same), one a wizard or witch, or both parents could be magical. However, with such a high probability of becoming a Squib, how are they so rare? We believe this to be a result of the e allele being so uncommon in the wizarding world. Although the reasons for this are unknown, we believe it is a combination of a few factors, one of which is pure-blood breeding between many wizard families. Sirius Black explains this to Harry in *Order of the Phoenix* when he says, "The pure-blood families are all interrelated. If you're only going to let your sons and daughters marry pure-bloods your choice is very limited; there are hardly any of us left" (113). Pure-blood breeding in Harry Potter is the mating of two individuals from family lineages that contain only expressible magic, so all would be either EE or Ee. With this, two heterozygotes (Ee) could produce a ee Squib, but he or she would quickly be outcast and denied as family. This occurred in the pure-blood Black family when Marius Black was born a Squib. The Black family were so disgusted by Marius that they burned his name off the family tree tapestry to completely deny his existence (Bunker). This is not only the case for pure-blood families, though, as Squibs tend to be rejected throughout the entire wizarding population. Subsequently, a Squib child would not be allowed to attend Hogwarts, work for the Ministry of Magic, or be involved in the normal daily life of other wizards. Thus, it is unlikely that they would meet another wizard and have children to continue passing on the e allele, causing the social situation of Squibs to be another factor in the decreased prevalence of e. Rather, it is more likely that the Squib would live the life of a Muggle, marry a Muggle who also has the ee genotype, and have all nonwizard children. This was seen with Molly Weasley's second cousin, the accountant, who was a Squib and married a Muggle. When Ron Weasley and Harry meet in *Sorcerer's Stone*, Harry asks if all of Ron's family is wizards, and he replies, "Er— Yes, I think so. . . . I think Mom's got a second cousin who's an accountant, but we never talk about him" (99). This is an indicator of how disconnected Squibs can become from their wizarding families. In the Harry Potter series, there are only two other known Squibs: Argus Filch and Mrs. Figg ("Harry Potter Universe"). We know nothing about their parents or their potential siblings for certain, but we could assume that their siblings could have been either wizards or Squibs. Regardless, due to negative views toward Squibs in the wizarding world, it would be understandable that most wizard parents who give birth to a Squib would no longer have children for fear of another Squib. Thus, parents who are heterozygotes (Ee) are less likely to continue reproducing than the homozygote parents (EE) are, decreasing the likelihood that ee Squibs will be born. Furthermore, when wizards procreate only with other wizards (EE or Ee), such as in the case of pure-blood families, this again decreases the likelihood of Squib births. Often ostracized, Squibs have a decreased likelihood of continued reproduction by heterozygotes, so the e allele has most likely been almost bred out of the wizarding population. This has resulted in a vast majority of those expressing their wizarding ability to be EE, making it unlikely for a wizard to be a Ee genotype in the first place, much less happen to reproduce with another Ee or a Muggle to give the ee possibility. It is for this reason that almost all children produced by one wizard and one nonwizard lead to a half-blood wizard and not a Squib.

According to Rowling's official site, half-bloods are wizards with one magical and one nonmagical parent; however, if either one of their parents is even a Muggle-born wizard, according

MATERNAL				MATERNAL		
		W	W			E	E
PATERNAL	W	WW	WW	PATERNAL	e	Ee	Ee
	W	WW	WW		e	Ee	Ee

P(offspring having wizarding ability) = 4/4 = 100%   P(offspring expressing wizarding ability gene) = 4/4 = 100%

FIGURE 15.2 Half-blood inheritance and expression of wizarding ability.

to pure-blood supremacists such as the Death Eaters who view Muggle-borns as "bad" as Muggles, these wizards would also be considered half-blood. In this view, Harry would be a half-blood although both of his parents were magical. Regardless of supremacist attitudes, true half-blood offspring are produced when a wizard mates with a Muggle. An example of a true half-blood is Lord Voldemort, whose mother was a witch and father was a Muggle. He admits this to Harry in *Chamber of Secrets* when he points out all of their similarities: they are "[b]oth half-bloods, orphans raised by Muggles" (317). These true half-bloods always express their wizarding ability by inheriting the Ee genotype, and they are common, as procreation between a wizard and Muggle does occur outside of pure-blood families. Due to the extreme unlikelihood of a Ee wizard reproducing with a ee Muggle, we would most likely see half-blood wizards produced by a couple whose genotypes were WW and ee for the Muggle, and WW and EE for the wizard (one could be Ww, but w is an unlikely allele, so we assume WW). The offspring would then result with a WW and Ee genotype that would allow for expression of their magical ability (see fig. 15.2). Both parents are WW for the wizarding gene giving them both the wizarding ability that they will then pass to all of their children. More importantly, the wizard parent is a EE genotype where the Muggle parent is a ee. This results in their children having a 100 percent chance of being a Ee and expressing their magical power.

In the wizarding community, both Squibs and Muggle-borns are unaccepted by some, especially those who believe in pure-blood breeding. The irony in this is that half-bloods and Squibs alike contain the same "magical ability" as pure-blood wizards if they are WW or Ww for the wizarding gene; a completely unrelated gene affects their ability to perform magic. Muggle-born wizards, however, are viewed much more negatively by pure-blood supremacists, who refer to them as "Mudbloods." Muggle-borns are wizards born to nonmagical parents. Their deprecation by supremacists is seen explicitly throughout the novels. Draco Malfoy's comments after the Chamber of Secrets is opened are relatively tame when he says, "Father says to keep my head down and let the Heir of Slytherin get on with it. He says the school needs ridding of all the Mudblood filth" (*Chamber of Secrets* 224).

Far from filth, Muggle-born wizards gain their magical abilities in the same way all wizards do. As all Muggle-borns have two nonwizard parents, it seems impossible that a wizard could be one of their offspring. One could say the milkman had a hand in it, but what would a wizard be doing delivering milk? As we know, the w allele in the gene for wizarding ability is very rare, so we can still assume that both of the Muggle parents are WW, or maybe one could be Ww. Moreover, both parents must then be ee genotypically as their wizarding power is masked, so the child cannot inherit the dominant modifier allele E in order for their power to be expressed. Thus, we hypothesize that the only way a Muggle-born wizard can be an offspring of two Muggle parents is when a germline mutation occurs at the modifier gene locus (the specific location of a gene on its chromosome) resulting in the encoding for a E allele's genetic material rather than that of a e. A germline mutation occurs in the cells that specifically lead to sexual reproduction, and subsequently, this causes a change in the genetic material that will be passed on to offspring (Klug et al. 322). Subsequently, the two Muggle parents who are both ee could end up with a child whose genotype in the modifier gene is Ee, who would then express their wizarding ability. In the Harry Potter series, some well-known Muggle-borns are Hermione Granger, Colin Creevey, Moaning Myrtle, and Lily Potter. Harry's mother, Lily, is a great example, as both of her parents—Harry's grandparents—were Muggles. We can use her in order to see the probabilities of a Muggle-born wizard/witch

	LILY'S MOTHER				LILY'S MOTHER	
	W	W			e	e
LILY'S FATHER W	WW	WW		**LILY'S FATHER** E	Ee	Ee
LILY'S FATHER W	WW	WW		**LILY'S FATHER** e	ee	ee

P(offspring having wizarding ability) = 4/4 = 100%   P(offspring expressing wizarding ability gene) = 2/4 = 50%

FIGURE 15.3. Lily Potter's (Muggle-born) inheritance and expression of wizarding ability.

from two Muggle parents in the Punnett Squares of figure 15.3. A germline mutation occurred in the modifying gene, E, resulting in a modification of the ee genotype passed on from Lily's father, allowing her to inherit either a E or e. As she had the wizarding ability through her WW genotype (100% chance), she then had a 50 percent chance of expressing it by receiving the E.

Because Lily was a witch, she must have inherited a E to express the WW for wizarding ability. The modifier gene would not mask the wizarding gene in that case, since she would have been Ee. Although Lily's powers were not masked, her sister Petunia's were; Petunia was quite resentful of this and made it clear when she talked about her sister, saying, "for my mother and father, oh no, it was Lily this and Lily that, they were proud of having a witch in the family!" (*Sorcerer's Stone* 53). As germline mutations occur in the germline of a particular sex cell (such as a sperm), they will result in only the one offspring with that mutation. Subsequently, it is unlikely that two Muggles would have more than one magical child, as this rare mutation would have to occur twice. This did occur once in Harry Potter, though, as Colin Creevey's brother, Dennis, was also a wizard. Lastly, Mafalda, the Weasleys' cousin who was the daughter of Mrs. Weasley's second cousin, a Squib, and his Muggle wife could also be considered a Muggle-born. As we have come to understand, both Muggles and Squibs are genetically the same when they both possess the genotype for wizarding ability, as their powers are simply masked in the same manner by a homozygous recessive genotype for the modifier gene (ee). Thus, although her extended family still had wizards throughout, a germline mutation still would have had to occur to give her the Ee that would allow the expression of her wizarding gene.

We now understand that the existence of the autosomal dominant wizarding gene and its modifier gene are responsible for the existence and expression of wizarding ability. These components make up the world of the Harry Potter series that we have all been so enthralled by, for without a dominant genotype in both the wizarding gene and its modifier, Harry could not possibly be the hero that he is for us now. Furthermore, being that the w allele is so rare in the general population, it is most likely that we are all a WW or a Ww. So these are not just the genetics of Potterworld but of our world. There is quite possibly a bit of wizard in all of us.

Works Cited

Bunker, Lisa W. "The Noble and Most Ancient House of Black." *The Harry Potter Lexicon*. 26 June 2003. Web. 25 May 2010. http://www.hp-lexicon.org/wizards/blackfamilytree.html.

"Genetics Famous Quotations." *Famous Quotes Inspirational Motivational Friendship Quote Website QuotesDaddy.com*. 2010. Web. 25 May 2010. http://www.quotesdaddy.com/tag/Genetics/1.

"Harry Potter Universe." *Wikipedia, the Free Encyclopedia*. 25 May 2010. Web. 27 May 2010. http://en.wikipedia.org.

Karki, Kedar. "Mule Genetics." *scribd.com*. 2008. Web. 5 Jan. 2010. http://www.scribd.com/doc/3748491/Mule-Genetics.

Klug, William S., Michael R. Cummings, Charlotte A. Spencer, and Michael Palladino. *Essentials of Genetics*, 7th edition. Upper Saddle River, NJ: Benjamin Cummings, 2010.

Riccio, Heather. "Interview with J. K. Rowling, Author of Harry Potter—HILARY MAGAZINE." *HILARY Magazine—The I Love Fashion Celebrity Blog*. Web. 3 April 2014. http://hilary.com/career/harrypotter.html.

Rowling, J. K. "Section: Extra Stuff Mafalda (*Goblet of Fire*)." *J. K. Rowling Official Site*. Web. 27 May 2010. http://www.jkrowling.com/textonly/en/extrastuff_view.cfm?id=3.

———. "Section: Extra Stuff SQUIBS." *J. K. Rowling Official Site*. Web. 27 May 2010. http://www.jkrowling.com/textonly/en/extrastuff_view.cfm?id=19.

———. "Section: F.A.Q." *J. K. Rowling Official Site*. Web. 27 May 2010. http://www.jkrowling.com/textonly/en/faq_view.cfm?id=58.

Wygal, Deborah. "Mendelian Modes of Inheritance." Genetics class. St. Catherine University, St. Paul, MN. March 2010. Lecture.

Twelve

Give Nature a Wand and It Will Nurture Magic

KIAH BIZAL

It is widely agreed in the psychological community that a combination of nature and nurture make up who we are and who we become, both the genetics our parents gave us as well as how we were raised. Yet each individual is unique. Even identical twins have distinctly different characteristics, despite sharing the same genes and often the same home environment. Cases like these have stumped psychologists and researchers for decades. Surely they also would be stumped by how Tom Riddle and Harry Potter turned out so differently despite having similar upbringings. However, upon closer investigation, there are definite differences in genetic predispositions and early development that set the two fictional boys apart. Family history, relationships with peers, behaviors that are reinforced or punished, temperament and personality, and secure attachment all play a critical role in the development of children, especially when considering Tom and Harry.

A Brief Psychological History

During the 1920s, research in developmental psychology and personality theories and disorders had only just begun (Grusse 13). Virtually nothing was known about how to treat psychological disorders, so most "treatments" were inhumane and untested. There was no universal standard of how research was to be conducted or how data should be interpreted. Many early studies ran experiments with little obligation to moral codes and interpreted findings based mainly on Freudian psychoanalysis. At this same time, behaviorism was becoming quite popular in the United States, so much so that it began to be preferred over Freudian analysis; it was, however, less popular in Europe (Grusse 18). Behaviorism gained popularity in the United States because the progress and efficacy of therapy could easily be observed and measured. Individual behaviors could be studied, and then therapy could focus specifically on them. As innovative as this type of therapy was, Europe preferred Gestalt psychology, which examined the mind as a whole rather than its various parts. In Gestalt theory, one explanation could account for multiple symptoms, instead of each individual problem creating separate symptoms. Both Gestalt psychology and behaviorism had their benefits, but both also were relatively new in the 1920s, with the pioneers in the field still improving their theories and techniques.

The history of psychology is important in this case because J. K. Rowling sets Tom Riddle's birth in the 1920s, when any psychological help that could have been given to a boy like him was severely limited. Treatments were rare, and those that worked were hard to come by. If someone could have recognized early warning signs in Tom, it is possible that intervention could have prevented his eventual demise as Lord Voldemort. It is also possible that the early modes of intervention would not have helped at all or that they would have come too late to change the psychological abnormalities rooted deep in his childhood.

Biological Origins

Observations of family history can offer some insight into how Tom was genetically predisposed to develop, as certain personality traits, behaviors, and cognitive processes can be traced in families, passed down like heirlooms no one wants but cannot throw away. When the reader is first introduced to Tom's ancestors, the Gaunts, it is clear that they are unpleasant people, to say the least. They believe themselves superior to everyone purely on the premise of their ancestry—to them, no one is of equal status—so they treat others poorly as a result. Professor Albus Dumbledore describes them as "[a] very ancient wizarding family noted for a vein of instability and violence that flourished through the generations due to their habit of marrying their own cousins. Lack of sense coupled with a great liking for grandeur . . . with a nasty temper, a fantastic amount of arrogance and pride" (*Half-Blood Prince* 212). Lack of diversity in the gene pool does not allow for much variation in the display of recessive genes that would normally be hidden by dominant ones; this lack of genetic diversity could also cause some phenotypes to become more severe. If what Dumbledore says is true, the Gaunts' predilection toward violence and other psychological tendencies have likely been passed down for several generations in their family. Tom apparently inherits these behaviors as well, since it would take much more than one generation to breed them out.

While less is known about Tom Riddle Sr.'s family, we do know he came from a wealthy family of Muggles. From how he addressed the Gaunts' house, it is safe to assume he probably had narcissistic tendencies of his own (*Half-Blood Prince* 209). He apparently thought he was better than the Gaunts, whose small, ragged cottage contrasted with his family's grand estate. He also used his good looks to his advantage; readers recognize that Tom Riddle Jr. likely inherited both his father's looks and some of his manipulative behavioral tendencies. As much as he would hate to admit it, Tom was predisposed to multiple behavioral and psychological tendencies from both of his parents, which unfortunately left him extremely vulnerable to the environment he was raised in (Quinsey 44).

From the information readers have about Harry's parents, it can be inferred that they did not have any psychological abnormalities or violent behavioral tendencies. His father, James, did tend toward arrogance, but as Sirius Black tells Harry, "[He] was the best friend I ever had, and he was a good person. Many people are idiots at the age of fifteen. He grew out of it" (*Order of the Phoenix* 671). Although his father had a bit of an ego, he was simply a teenager who allowed popularity to go to his head.

Sirius and Remus Lupin admit that Harry's father jinxed people for fun, but there was never any serious harm done; it was generally a joke to get onlookers to laugh, and he eventually grew out of that as well (671). Rowling has said herself that jinxes are mainly used to annoy, irritate, embarrass, or poke fun at their victims and do not have lasting harmful side effects ("Spells and Definitions" 2).

Even more, James hated the Dark Arts and would go to any lengths to avoid using spells or aligning himself with anyone who used them. Harry expresses his adamant rejection of the Dark Arts as well, but that's likely a result of the Dark Arts causing his parents' deaths (*Half-Blood Prince* 488). Overall, however, Harry grows up to be a very fine young man who has mature morals for his age. He is certainly his parents' son, amazingly so when he had such little time to know them and was raised in a less than ideal environment.

Peer Relationships

As a boy, Tom has no friends at the orphanage where he is raised. Mrs. Cole, the matron, reveals that he bullied the other children and that they are afraid of him (*Half-Blood Prince* 267). She also tells Dumbledore that Tom is an odd boy, which likely means that the other children reject him and never accept him into any peer groups. As he gets older and discovers he has power over his peers and enough cunning to deceive authority figures, he becomes a bully, expressing his aggression through magic. Despite his young age, he is highly intelligent and figures out that he can intentionally control the magic within him. He then uses it on his peers as revenge for their early rejection of him. Perceiving himself a victim, he completely loses the need to communicate his true emotions. These clear characteristics of victimization and externalization of negative emotions toward others are manifest in Tom from a very early age, and psychological research supports the idea that rejection by peers in early childhood can have detrimental consequences later in life.

Peer rejection can serve as a catalyst for aggression and cause children either to see others as a threat or to seek revenge for their own victimization (Grusse 363). Without proper bonds or friendships, children often become aggressive and easily pro-voked. Their emotions are not well regulated, and for this reason, they will likely live in an eternal cycle of aggressive behaviors. The rejection by peers leads to aggressive behaviors, and these behaviors lead to further rejection. Doomed to the outer circles of social groups, these aggressive children sometimes find com-panions in other rejected peers, but this can lead to just as many future delinquencies as remaining alone. Forming their own social group, these older rejected children align with others who have the same antisocial tendencies.

Tom's school years at Hogwarts suggest that he still had no friends. Admirers and followers were plentiful, but he had no affection for them, and many of them, in turn, only sought per-sonal gain in aligning with Tom (*Half-Blood Prince* 361–362). Many later become the first Death Eaters, continuing their school social group into their adult lives. At Hogwarts, Tom continues to manipulate others and to hide his true emotions to get what he wants. His aggressive actions are never directly perceived by authority figures, but readers observe his habit of bullying oth-ers when he orders his Death Eaters around. He is more care-ful than most antisocial youth in controlling his emotions, but there are instances when he simply cannot hide his true nature. Whenever he is overcome with rage, he finds something to break or someone to torture or even kill. He is also extremely patient and methodical when it comes to getting revenge. He waits for the opportune moment to strike back, perhaps to get the best, or worst, effect. His antisocial behaviors appear throughout his lifetime, and while he tries to suppress them, there is no denying that they are still there.

Harry's case of peer rejection is slightly different from Tom's. It seems that the peers at his Muggle school were not friends with him only because Dudley Dursley and his gang had bullied them into keeping their distance: "Everybody knew that Dudley's gang hated odd Harry Potter and his baggy old clothes and broken glasses, and nobody liked to disagree with Dudley's gang" (*Sorcerer's Stone* 30). They had nothing against him per-sonally, other than the strange way he dressed, but they feared that Dudley's gang would bully them as much as they bullied Harry if they befriended him. Because of this, Harry develops protective mechanisms that allow him to hope for something better ahead; he just had to survive until he could get there (Starr 133). Harry finally sees a glimmer of hope in going to a different school than Dudley; it becomes a brilliant gleam of excitement when he learns that he is a wizard and will be going into a different world entirely. At Hogwarts, he is free to start over and finds that he can make friends quite easily. He never lacked the ability; he had simply been the victim of a dominant bully who controlled the social hierarchy of the school.

Harry not only forms friendships with people he finds forthcoming, but he also rejects invitations from those he identifies as controllers. He doesn't want to become what Dudley had been to him, so he immediately rejects the overtures of Draco Malfoy. To Harry, Draco represents everything he had learned to dislike from his childhood—people who acted superior to him and who sought to control the social interactions of those around him. Harry doesn't want to be a part of this manipulation, either by causing it or once again succumbing to it, and chooses instead to make true, genuine friendships, the kind of which he had been previously deprived.

Behaviorism: Reinforcement and Punishment

In the early twentieth century, B. F. Skinner developed a method to categorize and measure observable behavior known as *operant conditioning* (Grusse 188). He described an increase in the occurrence of a behavior as *reinforcement* and a decrease in the occurrence of a behavior as *punishment*. He also used the terms *positive* and *negative*, not in the popular sense indicating the nature of the action but to indicate presentation of a stimulus or the removal of one, respectively. A related term based on Skinner's research, though he did not coin it himself, is *avoidance learning*, used to describe a situation in which an individual has learned to avoid painful stimuli altogether. All of these terms are used in close conjunction with parenting and teaching children acceptable behavior.

Much of Tom's behavior, such as stealing and bullying the other children, can likely be attributed to a lack of effective punishment. The immediate gratification of stealing comes from the positive reinforcement of possessing a desired item (Kuczynski 134). If no punishment is given, then the behavior will be repeated. Since his caretakers never actually witness him committing any rule-breaking, they never properly punish him for his wrongdoings. Instead, they do nothing, and the behavior continues.

Tom's temperament as a child could also play a role in how his caretakers treated him. Tom's escalating pattern of behavior was clearly unnerving to the matron of the orphanage, who seemed to know there was nothing she could do to help the boy. Again, she found him "odd" and knew that he was different from the other children (*Half-Blood Prince* 267). This oddness left her unsure of how to handle him. Unprepared and unqualified as his caretakers were to raise such a problematic child, they likely gave up any attempt to socialize him and seemed relieved when Dumbledore comes to take him to Hogwarts.

Harry's behavior, on the other hand, is based primarily on survival instinct. As a child, he did what he could to survive in an abusive home, and his mind was frequently in the fight-or-flight response state. Though he more often acted on the flight impulse, he found that avoidance learning worked in his favor in that he was faster than Dudley, who frequently tormented him (*Sorcerer's Stone* 24). Since Dudley was fat and slow, both physically and mentally, Harry could both outrun and outsmart him. In short, he protected himself by finding ways to escape physical pain, either by running away from Dudley or by hiding where Dudley could not find him. Similarly, he was able to escape his aunt and uncle when they sent him to his cupboard under the stairs; in reality, this was negative reinforcement for Harry, since he no longer had to be in the presence of the people he did not want to be around.

Secure Attachment

Possibly the biggest difference between Tom and Harry lies in the concept of "secure attachment." Secure attachment refers to the bond of trust and love between a child and his or her primary caregiver (Grusse 77). Unattached children have no such bond. They may have had inattentive care, a lack of physical and emotional contact, or multiple caregivers with no connection to any child in particular. Dr. Foster Cline, a leading expert in unattached children, developed a list of fourteen symptoms exhibited by such children: lack of ability to give and receive affection, self-destructive behavior, cruelty to others or to pets, phoniness, stealing or hoarding and gorging, speech pathology, extreme control problems, lack of long-term childhood friends, abnormalities in eye contact, unreasonably angry parents, preoccupation with blood or gore and fire, superficial attraction to and friendliness with strangers, learning disorders, and crazy lying (Magid and McKelvey 80). At some point during his life, Tom displays every one of these symptoms. For this essay, however, I focus specifically on his inability to give and receive affection, his self-destructive behavior, and his extreme cruelty to others.

The first symptom, the lack of ability to give and receive affection, is fairly self-explanatory and is apparent from the first time readers meet Tom. Again, he is not close with any of the caregivers or the other children at the orphanage where Dumbledore finds him. Along with Harry, readers of Rowling's novels discover Tom's inability to comprehend love and can clearly see he has no experience with what it means to be loved. Later, he fails to see why Lily Potter gives her life for her only son, why Professor Severus Snape is never truly on his side, and why Harry lives after the numerous times he tries to kill him. The reason for all of these things, of course, is love, something Tom neither feels nor understands. The closest thing to love he ever feels is toward his snake, Nagini; he seems to genuinely care about her. However, it is quite possible that he feels a connection with her because he can talk to snakes, and, being that she is an animal, she does not have the complex human emotions that he finds so bothersome. Even if his affection for Nagini is love, Tom lives for seventy years without ever knowing the love of another human being. He never feels it, nor receives it: "[He] has never had a friend, nor I do believe that he has ever wanted one," Dumbledore tells Harry (*Half-Blood Prince* 277).

Tom's cruelty to others is ruthless; self-destructive behavior refers not only to self-harm but also to a general disregard for life, or to reckless behavior and risk-taking (Magid and

McKelvey 82). He terrorizes and bullies the other children in the orphanage, and he continues these vicious acts for the rest of his life. Harry learns that young Tom had taken two children from the orphanage to a cave where he likely tortured them (*Half-Blood Prince* 268). When Harry visits the seaside cave, it seems impossible that anyone without advanced mountaineering skills and equipment could have reached it, let alone three small children (*Half-Blood Prince* 556). The journey to such a dangerous place probably thrilled Tom as much as it terrorized the other children. The more dangerous the task, the more fulfilling the reward would be for the emotionally damaged child. Later, Tom tortures or kills those who disobey him, betray him, refuse to join him, interfere with his plans, and annoy him. Most horribly, though, he tortures and kills some purely because he can (or for his enjoyment), without ever showing remorse.

The deprivation of secure attachment has detrimental effects on developing children. They can grow up without morals, emotions, or love. The fact that Tom displays all fourteen symptoms of unattached children is clear evidence that he was not loved as an infant. Therapy for these children works only if they are quite young when the intervention begins; most cases become unsuccessful once the child reaches school age, and few are successful in adolescence (Magid and McKelvey 216). No one has been successful in treating adults. By the time Tom reached Hogwarts, it was too late to reverse the psychological damage that had been done. He had already become too enamored of his own cruel power and had the means to achieve even more power. Even if he could change, he would not. He liked that he could manipulate others into doing his bidding without punishment or consequence. He liked avoiding any real emotion. He used these things to his full advantage, making him the most feared wizard of all time. It was not only his power that frightened people, but also how cunning and ruthless he could be with it. This created terror among the masses since they could not predict his behavior and never knew if they could trust him. Tom was terrifying because he could not love. He could not love because he had never known love.

Harry had known love. For the first year of his life, his parents had loved him dearly and he shared a deep bond with them. The reader gets a glimpse of this when Harry finds among

Sirius's possessions a letter from his mother. Lily's affection for
her son was clear from the letter, as she described how he flew
around on his toy broomstick (*Deathly Hallows* 180). The photograph that came with it showed young Harry zooming about
on his new toy, having the time of his life. His father's legs were
also in the picture, chasing Harry about, playing along with
him, and probably trying to prevent him from breaking anything. Children learn substantially through play, especially when
it involves social interaction (Kuczynski 135). Harry's parents
apparently played with him often, giving him the social stimu-
lation that he needed to develop his own social and emotional
competency. Despite being torn from this attachment so young,
Harry retained what it taught him: that there was love in the
world and that he was capable of feeling it. He longed to be res-
cued during the dreadful decade of his life that he endured with
the Dursleys, but no one ever came. He had no other family
members (*Sorcerer's Stone* 30). He knew there was something
better in the world; he only needed to find it.

How much Harry desired love and a family is shown in the
Mirror of Erised, when he sees himself surrounded by family.
Dumbledore later explains to Harry the true importance of what
he sees in the mirror. Where other wizards would see riches or
fame, Harry only sees his family (*Sorcerer's Stone* 209). His ability to love and his desire for a loving family gives him what he
needs to protect himself from the terrible suffering he endures
in his life. He remains pure of heart and is never tempted by the
Dark Arts, all due to the love his parents gave him.

The "What-if" Factor

There are a few loose ends to be tied up if a valid argument is
to be made about why Harry and Tom turned out the way they
did. There are still several questions that arise, most of them
starting with "what-if?"

First, *what if one of the other children in the orphanage
became a mass murderer?* Would we then credit environmental factors for Tom's behavior? The answer to this question
remains that no one can be sure. We know nothing about the

other children in the orphanage and their backgrounds. Wizards are notorious for not caring about what goes on in the Muggle world, so perhaps one of them could have turned out to be a serial killer, but no reader would ever know about it. This is an unlikely possibility however, since every child's backstory is unique. It is probable that most of the other children were not born in the orphanage but were left or brought there when their parents died or were unable to care for them. Therefore, there is a possibility that they had secure attachment already and only viewed the orphanage as a temporary home. The orphanage was Tom's only home and the sole environmental influence on his early development. He also had a less than ideal genetic predisposition for such an environment, which is also something we can't know about the other children. It is probably safe to assume that the other children at the orphanage did not come from a limited gene pool with narcissistic and violent tendencies. Tom did have these predispositions, and that set him back even further when put in an environment that could stimulate the worst in him. Assuming that the orphanage was the sole cause of how he turned out is made invalid from what we know and do not know of the other children. There simply is not enough evidence to categorize it as a creator of mass murderers and sociopaths.

What if someone had recognized Tom's symptoms and he had received intervention and therapy? The answer to this question relies heavily on the time in which fictional Tom was born. In the 1920s, no such treatment existed, and Tom's caregivers were clearly baffled by him. They had no explanation for his behavior, because no research had yet been published on children like him. The only solution for people with mental illness was for them to live their lives isolated in an asylum. Tom fears this, as he accuses Dumbledore of being sent from an asylum to bring him there (*Half-Blood Prince* 270). There was no hope for treatment in this period, but perhaps another time would have produced different results.

If a child such as Tom had been born within the last thirty years, it is possible that intervention could have helped. Now that the early signs of personality disorders have been established, it has become much easier to diagnose cases like Tom's.

He likely would have been diagnosed with conduct disorder, defined by a lack of social skills and delinquent tendencies, and treated with intense behavioral therapy (Quinsey et al. 99). To deal with his attachment issues, much more complex therapy would be needed. He would have to be forced to express his emotions, including his internal rage (Magid and McKelvey 205). This type of therapy can take several long, expensive sessions that an orphanage could not afford, so even if Tom could be "cured," he may not have been able to receive this treatment. He would be another victim of the mental healthcare system in both the Muggle world and wizarding world.

In fact, the wizarding world does not appear to have any system for mental healthcare at all. All they can do is lock people up in the St. Mungo's equivalent of a psych ward and hope for the best. There is little communication between the magical medical community and the nonmagical medical community, so they also have limited knowledge of what techniques Muggles use to treat mental illness. If the wizarding world had some sort of system for treating mental illness in magical children, perhaps this would have helped Tom even more than the nonmagical treatments outlined here. He could have been taught how to develop positive relationships with peers, how to identify the rules and boundaries of magic (such as the fact that being magical does not make one invincible to death); he might also have learned not to use his magic in aggression. The wizarding world could have intervened had they not waited until it was time for him to come to Hogwarts, when it was already too late.

A Recipe for Disaster

All of the factors that had a function in the development of Tom determined who he ultimately became. If one were to take the metaphorical cauldron containing the potion of his biological predispositions, such as narcissism and violence, add the ingredients of his environment, like peer rejection and lack of punishment or mental health care treatment, and put it over the blazing fire that was a lack of secure attachment, the catastrophic result would almost guarantee that Tom would turn out the way he did. As a child, he was doomed by the situation, biological and environmental, that he had been set in by fate. What matters however, is what he chose to do with that situation. Tom clearly had the intelligence to know that something was wrong with him, and he could have chosen to get help at any time. Granted, help would have still been limited in his time, but his personal choice to change would have made all the difference. He knew what he was doing was wrong; he just lacked the capacity to care. When Harry gives him one last chance at remorse, Tom acts as if he cannot even comprehend what Harry has asked of him (*Deathly Hallows* 741). It is quite likely that he could not. By that point in his life, Tom had lived for so long without emotions like remorse or love, he was so far from intervention having any effect at all, and he had distorted his soul so much that it was not possible for him to feel remorse. This led to his downfall and Harry's triumph. What a difference love made in Harry's life. It protected him from the cruelty of the world both with and without magic.

Works Cited

Grusse, Joan E. *Handbook of Socialization Theory and Research.* London, UK: Guilford, 2007.

Kuczynski, Leon. *Handbook of Dynamics in Parent-Child Relations.* London, UK: SAGE, 2003.

Magid, Ken, and Carole A. McKelvey. *High Risk Children without a Conscience.* New York, NY: Bantam, 1987.

Quinsey, Vernon L., Tracey A. Skilling, Martin L. Lalumiere, and Wendy M. Craig. *Juvenile Delinquency: Understanding the Origins of Individual Differences.* Washington, DC: American Psychological Association, 2004.

Rowling, J. K. "Extra Stuff: Miscellaneous: Spells and Definitions." Web. jkrowling.com.

Starr, Raymond H., Jr., and David A. Wolfe. *The Effects of Child Abuse and Neglect: Issues and Research.* London: Guilford, 1991.

Thirteen

A Nursing Care Plan for Tom Riddle

KARI NEWELL

SECTION I—Background Information:

Patient: Tom Riddle (Lord Voldemort)
Age: Eleven (and sixty-something)
Health Status: Patient/Family Stated Concern: Tom Riddle is a troubled young wizard who needs psychological examination in order to better understand his character.

SECTION II—Analysis:

Empirical Knowing: Psychosocial Data Analysis:

a. Role-Relationship:

Tom Riddle is the antagonist of Harry Potter in J. K. Rowling's Harry Potter series. Tom and Harry are enemies, yet they have similar backgrounds. They were both orphaned very young, can't remember their parents, are adept in the Dark Arts, and speak Parseltongue. Tom has no relationships with other characters. He keeps himself at a distance and is unable to love anyone. Even though, later, as Voldemort he is surrounded by his Death Eater "friends," they aren't truly friends. When Lucius Malfoy allows the prophecy to be destroyed in *Order of the Phoenix*, Voldemort doesn't care that Malfoy was imprisoned in

Azkaban, even though he has been one of his most loyal followers. Voldemort easily dismisses his so-called friend Lucius Malfoy. While the Malfoys once held a position of power among the
Death Eaters, their status falls because Voldemort clearly does
not feel any love or affection toward his followers.

b. Self Perception:

Tom Marvolo Riddle is an orphan. On his maternal side, his family are the pure-blood descendants of Salazar Slytherin, as identified by Tom's grandfather, Marvolo Gaunt, who said, "Salazar
Slytherin's! We're his last living descendants" (*Half-Blood Prince*
208). Even though the Gaunts are pure-bloods and should, by
tradition, marry only other pure-blood wizards, Merope, Marvolo's daughter, falls in love with a Muggle. Merope loves her
neighbor, Tom Riddle Sr.

Morfin, Merope's brother, talks about how she swoons over
him: "*She likes looking at that Muggle. . . . Always in the garden
when he passes, peering through the hedge at him, isn't she? And
last night— . . . hanging out of the window waiting for him to
ride home, wasn't she?*" (210). Tom Riddle Sr. is not smitten with
ragged Merope, so she gives him a love position to make him fall
in love with her and marry her. Eventually, Merope stops giving
Tom the love potion, believing he had, by then, naturally fallen
in love with her, but she was wrong. Tom leaves Merope while
she is pregnant with his son. Merope is so heartbroken and weak
that she dies right after her son, Tom Marvolo Riddle, is born.
Tom is left to grow up at an orphanage, unaware of his parentage
or of his magical abilities (*Half-Blood Prince* 214).

When Tom is of age to attend Hogwarts, Professor Albus
Dumbledore goes to the orphanage to explain his wizarding
heritage. Mrs. Cole, the head of the orphanage, describes Tom's
character to Dumbledore when he arrives. She says that he scares
the other children:

> on the summer outing—we take them out, you know,
> once a year, to the countryside or the seaside—well,

Amy Benson and Dennis Bishop were never quite right afterwards, and all we ever got out of them was that they'd gone into a cave with Tom Riddle. He swore they'd just gone exploring, but something happened in there, I'm sure of it. And, well there have been a lot of things, funny things . . . (*Half-Blood Prince* 268)

It is clear that, even as a young boy, Tom isolates himself from the other orphans and knowingly harms animals and children.

When Dumbledore meets Tom, the boy tells Dumbledore about his ability to do magic. He says, "I can make things move without touching them. I can make animals do what I want them to do, without training them. I can make bad things happen to people who annoy me. I can make them hurt if I want to" (*Half-Blood Prince* 271). Tom also takes a lot of pleasure in finding out he is different: "I knew I was different . . . I knew I was special. Always, I knew there was something," he says (*Half-Blood Prince* 271). This demonstrates his desire to be different and isolated from everyone else.

c. Values/Beliefs:

Voldemort values life and power and greatly fears death. When Dumbledore and Voldemort are battling at the Ministry of Magic, Voldemort reveals this fear:

"You do not seek to kill me, Dumbledore? . . . Above such brutality are you?"

"We both know that there are other ways of destroying a man, Tom," Dumbledore said calmly. . . .

"There is nothing worse than death, Dumbledore!" snarled Voldemort. (*Order of the Phoenix* 814)

Voldemort doesn't believe anything is worse than death, and he tells his Death Eaters, "I, who have gone further than anybody along the path that leads to immortality. You know my goal—to conquer death" (*Goblet of Fire* 653). There are other examples of Voldemort trying to conquer death, such as when he tries to steal the Sorcerer's Stone, which would give him immortality. It is clear that life and immortality are strong values for Voldemort.

Another value Voldemort expresses is power. Voldemort wants to rule over all wizards and Muggles and create a hierarchical society where pure-blood wizards are at the top and Muggles are at the bottom. He almost succeeds until Harry survives the killing curse. Unfortunately, Voldemort does not stop trying to rule over all creatures. He continues to try to regain his power and eventually returns to his body to prove that he is the most powerful wizard, stronger than the boy who once defeated him. He says, "You see, I think, how foolish it was to suppose that this boy could ever have been stronger than me. . . . But I want there to be no mistake in anybody's mind. Harry Potter escaped me by a lucky chance. And I am going to prove my power by killing him, here and now" (*Goblet of Fire* 658). Nothing is more important to Voldemort than being the most powerful wizard, ruling the wizard and mortal worlds, and escaping death forever.

SECTION III—Major Concerns:

1. Psychological Instability

There are some major concerns with Tom Riddle's psychological stability. As a child, Tom tortures other children and animals, believes himself to be more powerful and more special than others, and actually wants to be different and apart. He is a descendant of Salazar Slytherin and prides himself on his wizarding family's pure-blood status. Even though he is half Muggle, Tom wants to create a hierarchy where pure-bloods are at the top and Muggles serve them.

Tom Riddle may have a personality disorder, which is concerning. Personality disorders, or PD, are described as "an enduring pattern of inner experience and behavior that deviates markedly from the expectation of the individual's culture, is pervasive and inflexible, has an onset in adolescence or early adulthood, is stable over time, and leads to distress or impairment" (Varcarolis, Carson, and Shoemaker 275–276). There are various personality disorders, but Tom shows characteristics common in Narcissistic Personality Disorder. This disorder is described as a pattern of grandiosity, need for admiration, and lack of empathy (Varcarolis, Carson, and Shoemaker 283). Tom believes himself to be special and is very self-important. This is evident in the dialogue cited previously between Dumbledore and Tom Riddle at the orphanage. Another characteristic of Narcissistic Personality Disorder is a preoccupation with fantasies of unlimited success and power (Varcarolis, Carson, and Shoemaker 283). Throughout the Harry Potter series, Tom is obsessed with power and dreams of taking over the Ministry in order to rule over wizards and Muggles alike. His desire to be superior and to be known as the most powerful wizard of all time shows in his desire to be admired by others. The Death Eaters marvel at Voldemort and want to be acknowledged by their powerful leader. Bellatrix Lestrange talks about her master as if he is her lover. When Hermione Granger, Ron Weasley, and Harry are brought to the Malfoys' house in the final novel, Fenrir Greyback states that he desires gold for the three traitor's heads. To this, Bellatrix says, "Gold! . . . Take your gold, filthy scavenger, what do I want with gold? I seek only the honor—of—[Voldemort]" (460–461). To Bellatrix, there is nothing better than to be acknowledged by Lord Voldemort, her master.

The final characteristics Voldemort exemplifies that are consistent with Narcissistic Personality Disorder are exploitation of others and lack of empathy (Varcarolis, Carson, and Shoemaker 283). In order to gain power, Voldemort kills wizards and Muggles, destroys families, and treats everyone with self-important arrogance. Voldemort shows no signs of remorse and does not care whom he hurts. Love is a theme throughout the Harry Potter series, but Voldemort does not have the ability to love, which Dumbledore often explains to Harry, so much so that Harry tires of hearing it:

"You have a power that Voldemort has never had. You can—"

"I know!" said Harry impatiently. "I can love!" It was only with difficulty that he stopped himself adding, "Big deal." (*Half-Blood Prince* 509)

Voldemort lacks empathy for others or the ability to love.

> **Observation:** All of the characteristics of Narcissistic Personality Disorder fit Voldemort, so it is safe to say that Tom Riddle has Narcissistic PD.
> **Thinking Ahead:** Continue observing Tom for other signs of mental illness. Monitor his personality disorder, which could cause more destruction of human life in the wizard and Muggle world.

2. Lack of Support System

Tom Riddle prides himself on being independent. He has followers, the Death Eaters, but they are dispensable to him, as we have noted earlier. When Voldemort comes to Hogwarts requesting a teaching position, Dumbledore discusses Tom's so-called friends, remarking,

> "And what will become of those whom you command? What will happen to those who call themselves—or so rumor has it—the Death Eaters?" . . .
>   "My friends . . . will carry on without me, I am sure."
>   "I am glad to hear that you consider them friends.
> . . . I was under the impression that they are more in the order of servants." (*Half-Blood Prince* 444)

Dumbledore suspects the Death Eaters are actually Voldemort's servants, not friends, and acknowledges that Voldemort does not rely on anyone but himself, stating, "Voldemort likes to operate alone" (*Half-Blood Prince* 502). According to Wilkinson, a good support system can help someone adapt to stress, give emotional support, encourage expressing feelings, and help the person solve problems (554). It is very important for people to have friends and a support system, but Voldemort has neither.

   Though Voldemort has no friends, this seems to be purposeful. He keeps everyone in his life at a distance because he doesn't believe anyone is as powerful as he is. For example, Voldemort does not recognize that underage wizards can have power, as seen when Dumbledore and Harry visit the cave that contains one of Voldemort's Horcruxes and Harry questions whether the boat that will carry them across the river can hold more than one person:

> Harry looked down into the boat. It really was very small.
> "It doesn't look like it was built for two people. Will it hold both of us? Will we be too heavy together?"
> Dumbledore chuckled.
> "Voldemort will not have cared about the weight, but about the amount of magical power that crossed his lake. . . . I do not think you will count, Harry. You are underage and un-qualified. Voldemort would never have expected a sixteen-year-old to reach this place; I think it unlikely that your powers will register compared to mine." (*Half-Blood Prince* 564)

Power, once again, is Voldemort's strongest value. Since he doesn't believe anyone is as powerful as he is, he doesn't understand the need for friends or how anyone could be worthy of his friendship.

> **Observation:** Tom has no support system and no friends. This is clearly important for people to help reduce stress, give emotional support, and help with problem-solving (Wilkinson 554).
> **Thinking Ahead:** Monitor Tom's support system and find ways to help him understand why friends are important.

SECTION IV—Nursing Diagnoses:

Moral distress related to acts of murder and lack of remorse as manifested by Voldemort's continuous acts of murder, numerous attempts at killing Harry Potter, and his fear of death (Carpenito-Moyet 289).

Stress overload related to Voldemort's inability to accept death and continuous failure to kill Harry Potter as manifested by Voldemort creating Horcruxes to escape death and his frustration in never killing Harry Potter (Carpenito-Moyet 444).

SECTION V—Intervention Plan:

Nursing Dx Category: Moral distress
Related To (R/T:) acts of murder and lack of remorse
AMB (as manifested by): Voldemort's continuous acts of murder, numerous attempts at killing Harry Potter, and his fear of death (Carpenito-Moyet 289).

OUTCOMES	INTERVENTIONS	EVALUATION
Tom Riddle will state two moral values by the end of the day.	Explain core Christian values to encourage moral behaviors. Some values to include, based on Catholic social teaching, are: respect, human dignity, community, equality, peace, and care for the earth (Connors 127).	Tom Riddle needs interventions in order to improve his moral distress. If these interventions are implemented, Tom will probably be unresponsive and uninterested in participating. Honestly, he will most likely perform the *Avada Kedavra* curse and kill me if he were forced to do any of these interventions.
Tom Riddle will confess to all of his murders and experience signs of remorse by the end of the day.		
Tom Riddle will create a diagram that shows all of his support systems by the end of the day.	Create a therapeutic environment in which Tom can discuss his past unjust acts.	
	Create an eco-map of social support systems to help Tom identify people he can trust to help him in times of distress.	

SECTION V—Intervention Plan:

Nursing Dx Category: Stress overload
Related To (R/T): Voldemort's inability to accept death and continuous failure to kill Harry Potter.
AMB (as manifested by): Voldemort creating Horcruxes to escape death and his frustration in never killing Harry Potter (Carpenito-Moyet 444).

OUTCOMES	INTERVENTIONS	EVALUATION
Tom Riddle will state three ways to reduce stress by the end of the day.	Discuss ways to reduce stress with Tom. These may include: deep breathing, visualization, relaxation techniques, listening to music, reading a book, journaling, and getting a massage (Wilkinson 553).	If these interventions are implemented, Tom Riddle will most likely be resistant to the teaching. I do not think he will be excited to try positive coping skills. He will probably, once again, try to kill me with the *Avada Kedavra* curse. This being a stressful situation for me, I would probably try some of these stress reduction interventions, but I doubt they would reduce my anxiety as I am about to be killed.
Tom Riddle will discuss two acts that are not beneficial when exposed to a stressful situation.		
Tom Riddle will state two reasons why anger and killing are not appropriate responses to stress.	Discuss negative behaviors when exposed to stress. These may include: overeating, working too much, substance abuse, anger, and violence (Wilkinson 553). This will also help Tom understand that killing and anger are maladaptive coping mechanisms.	

Works Cited

Carpenito-Moyet, Lynda. *Handbook of Nursing Diagnosis.* Philadelphia, PA: J. B. Lippincott Company, 2008. Print.

Connors, Russell B., Jr. *Catholic Social Teaching: Convictions and Connections, Global Search for Justice.* Minneapolis, MN: St. Catherine University, 2009. 123–153. Print.

Varcarolis, Elizabeth M., Verna Carson, and Nancy C. Shoemaker. *Foundations of Psychiatric Mental Health Nursing: A Clinical Approach.* St. Louis, MO: Saunders Elsevier, 2006. Print.

Wilkinson, Judith M., and Karen Van Leuven. *Fundamentals of Nursing: Theory, Concepts and Applications.* Philadelphia, PA: F. A. Davis Company, 2007. Print.

Fourteen

Literary Arithmancy

An Analysis of Number Symbolism in Harry Potter

EVAN GAYDOS

Across cultures, religions, and continents, though our languages, customs, and beliefs differ, the similar use of numbers often connects us. Different groups may focus on various significances of the numbers, but even the basic idea of the number seems to span differences and create a common denominator. As any good writer would, J. K. Rowling uses this cross-cultural language of numbers and their meanings as subtle signals. In this chapter, I examine the numbers three, four, and seven and their significance in the Harry Potter series.

Of course, I could easily look at numbers other than three, four, and seven and come to various conclusions. One easy example is the number two and the concept of duality. This duality can be used to analyze Harry Potter and Lord Voldemort (Harry and Professor Albus Dumbledore or Dumbledore and Voldemort) and to delve into the similarities and differences between the characters (see chapter 12 in this volume). But the number two creates the most basic conflict, and it can be found in nearly any story. Many would also cite the number five, because it is often tied to magic through the pentagram and pentacle; however, this is not a number Rowling emphasizes, so it doesn't offer much insight into her books.

Three: The Number of the Divine and Magical World

Three, "a number of perfection and completion," is often associated with deities, mythology, and the spiritual, as noted religion scholar Annemarie Schimmel asserts in her influential study *The Mystery of Numbers* (69). Three is a number of religious significance, used to discuss the divine and holy. This is true throughout many religions and various belief systems, as Schimmel points out. Sumerians, Babylonians, and Egyptians group their deities in threes, following their structure of the heavens. Sumerians have Anu, the god of heaven; Enli, the god of air; and Ea, the god of the earth. Babylonians worshiped Sin, the moon; Shameash, the sun; and Ishtr, Venus (Schimmel 60). The ancient Egyptians had various sets of three in their mythology. Following the movement of the sun, Horus was the morning, Ra was noon, and Atun was the setting sun (Hopper 7). Greek mythology also separates the realms of the world into three— the heavens, the earth, and the underworld—and it has perhaps the best-known triad of such deities in Western culture—Zeus, Poseidon, and Hades. The Greeks continue the theme with three major goddesses—Hera, Athena, and Aphrodite. Hinduism also includes a "great triad . . . Brahma the creator, Shiva the destroyer, and Vishnu the sustainer" (Schimmel 61). Buddhism has three sources of salvation: Buddha, dharma, and samgha (Schimmel 68).

Among the world's three most prominent monotheistic religions, Judaism, Islam, and Christianity, three also predominates. In Judaism and the Old Testament there are three patriarchs— Abraham, Isaac, and Jacob; sacrifices often required three animals or animals of three years; and both Adam and Noah had three sons. Even though Islam is strict with regard to worship of only Allah, it is not without at least one group of three. Among the Shiites there are Allah, Muhammad, and Ali. As Schimmel explains, "There is no deity save God; Muhammad is the messenger of God; Ali is the friend of God," though the use of the number three varies from group to group within Islam (67). Christianity's most basic belief is in the Trinity, the combination of God (Father), Jesus (Son), and the Holy Spirit as one.

According to literary scholar Vincent Foster Hopper in his book *Medieval Number Symbolism*, many numbers can be used to express the divine or the attributes of the gods, "but either because of its antiquity or because of its numerous simple analogies in the physical and social world, the all-embracing three becomes the most universal number of the deity" (6). The idea of three in Christianity goes even further, to the three theological virtues: faith, hope, and charity (love). In Paul's letter to the Corinthians, he explains, "And now faith, hope, and love abide, these three; and the greatest of these is love" (1 Cor. 13:13). This ties love to divinity and, for our purposes, to Rowling's predominant theme—the overarching power of love, the most potent form of magic in her story.

The number three is found throughout literature, beginning with children's literature in the Western culture's fairy tales, such as the "Three Little Pigs," "Goldilocks and the Three Bears," and nursery rhymes such as "Three Blind Mice" or the three bags of wool in "Baa Baa Black Sheep." As Hopper reminds us, "Legends, myths, folk tales of all nations are abound in three wishes, three tries, three suitors—there is no necessity of prolonging the story when three is all" (5). However, the use of three in literature is by no means limited to stories for children. From *Macbeth*'s witches and the original Musketeers to the number of mates aboard Melville's *Pequod* or Dickens's ghosts of Christmas past, present, and future, three predominates. As the triangle is a three-sided geometric shape (and three is an odd number), authors have for years enjoyed using this structure for more complex conflict (see chapter 15 in this volume). It is the smallest number in which a disagreement can occur between multiple characters. One side of the conflict may have more support, or support can shift. It takes only two to have a conflict, but add a third and you have complexity. Alliances and deception can occur. There can be a majority and a minority.

Rowling uses this structure of three most notably in "the Golden Trio" of main characters—Hermione Granger, Ron Weasley, and Harry. It also extends to the outer circle of friends, including Ginny Weasley, Neville Longbottom, and Luna Lovegood, or the tarnished trio of Draco Malfoy, Vincent

Crabbe, and Gregory Goyle. It repeats in the complex relations of Voldemort, Harry, and Professor Severus Snape, and in the tale of the three brothers and the number of Deathly Hallows.

Rowling also makes use of what Hopper calls the "triad of the family" (6). This is a common social structure of three, made up of the mother, father, and child. While the family unit can, of course, be larger, there are a plethora of family triads in the series. The most obvious is Harry and his parents, but we also have Draco and his parents and Hermione and her parents. Other familial threes include these only children and their parents: James Potter, Neville, Tom Riddle Sr., Tom Riddle Jr., Teddy Lupin, Nymphadora Tonks, Dudley Dursley, and Snape. We could also include the father, son, and daughter triad of the Gaunt family. Along with the use of the familial triad, Rowling also makes (nontraditional) use of the traditional romantic triangle (see chapter 15 in this volume). In *Goblet of Fire*, we have Harry, Cho Chang, and Cedric Diggory; and Ron, Hermione, and Viktor Krum. A few other such romantic conflicts include Ron, Lavender Brown, and Hermione; Harry, Ginny, and Dean Thomas; James, Lily Evans, and Snape; Merope Gaunt, Tom Riddle Sr., and Cecilia (the other woman Riddle was seeing). Romantic triangles continue throughout the series, adding dimension and perpetuating conflict.

Often Rowling's use of three seems to spring naturally from storytelling tradition, such as having three main protagonists or constructing a complex conflict at the tale's center. Sometimes there is no apparent reason for such triads, as with The Leaky Cauldron, The Three Broomsticks, and The Hog's Head taverns. Yet, some sets of three take on a more divine or magical tone, such as the number of times the Potters and the Longbottoms defy Voldemort (*Order of the Phoenix* 842), the number of hours Harry and Hermione go back in time to save Sirius Black and Buckbeak in *Prisoner of Azkaban* (395), and the number of ingredients Voldemort requires to regain his "human" body (bone of the father, flesh of the servant, and blood of the enemy) (*Goblet of Fire* 641–642). Perhaps because these instances are connected with powerful spells or curses, they suggest something more mystical in Rowling's use of threes.

Four: The Number of Humanity and Nature

The number four, according to Schimmel, is the number associated with human ordering of the world (86). For centuries, civilizations have used the number four to organize time. Nature has four seasons; there are four cardinal directions; and we speak of four winds. The ancient idea that the world was shaped as a square or a rectangle gave the world four sides. Followers of Pythagoras saw four as "the ideal number" because of the solidity of the cube (Schimmel 90). Hopper, too, notes the earthly significance of four in his text, stating:

> Thus the fourness of the earth, evidenced by the cardinal points, is repeated in the temporal sphere by the 4 seasons, the 4 phases of the moon, named for the cardinal points, the 4 intercalary days. . . . Four might be said to represent an archetypal pattern for the macrocosm which the microcosm naturally reproduces. . . . Four is also the number of the square, and is represented in the elements, the seasons, the 4 ages of man, the 4 principles of a reasonable animal, the lunar phases, and the 4 virtues. (31, 42–43)

In Christianity this number appears most significantly in four gospels and in the points of the cross.

In Harry Potter, the number four is tied to humanity (and in a sense, the nonmagical) through the home of the Dursleys, on Number Four Privet Drive. This is in direct contrast to the magical Diagon Alley, where a wizard must tap three times on a point three bricks up from the trash cans to gain entrance. The Hogwarts Express leaves from Platform 9¾, combining the mystical and the earthly while setting the location of the platform apart from the rest of the station. At Hogwarts there were four original founders and, thus, four Houses (only *three* of these founders truly agreed on who deserved to be educated at the school, causing the original schism) and four ghosts, one for each House. Likewise, there are four members of the Marauders: Remus Lupin, Sirius Black, James Potter, and Peter Pettigrew.

Note, however, that only three of them were animagis and only three of them were truly loyal friends. These examples all seem to tie to the world, earth, and humanity.

The number four is also connected with the concept of the crossroads. Indeed, *Goblet of Fire*, the fourth book in the series, can be read as the crossroads novel. At the end, Voldemort has returned, even though only our hero and those loyal to Voldemort know of it. The people in the wizarding world must decide which reality to believe—what Harry tells them (which isn't pleasant) or what the Ministry of Magic claims (the pleasing lie that Voldemort has not returned). These choices influence the outcome of events throughout the remaining novels.

The crossroads in the fifth and sixth novels are less dramatic and more focused on Harry and Voldemort than the crossroads of book 4. But, significantly, crossroads abound in the seventh book, in Ron leaving and returning, Harry choosing to destroy Horcruxes instead of looking for Hallows, Harry going to his death in the Forbidden Forest, and his decision to return to the land of the living after his discussion with Dumbledore. Any deviation in these choices would have set the characters upon paths to different conclusions.

Seven: The Number of Perfection and Combination

The significance of the number seven has drawn us at least since the medieval era. Schimmel explains that seven, divided into "constituent principles, the spiritual three and the material four, was used time and again in medieval hermeneutics and is also at the division of the seven liberal arts into the *trivium* and the *quadrivium*" (127). Hopper, too, notes how a concept of seven steps was significant to medieval thinking, as in "7 steps to perfection . . . whether by the 7 arts or the 7 virtues or, more specifically, the 7 steps or stages of contemplation" (18). Seven was viewed as a desired goal, often linked to paradise, and to get there often involved a journey where growth took place.

Seven is probably the most obvious number to perceive in Harry Potter, because there are seven years at Hogwarts and seven books in the series. In *Sorcerer's Stone*, Harry, Ron, and

Hermione face seven challenges to reach and obtain the Sorcerer's Stone. Readers learn in *Order of the Phoenix* that Harry (and Neville) are both born in July, the seventh month of the year, and that James and Lily are killed at age twenty-one, the product of three and seven. The Weasley family has seven children; there are seven Potter decoys in the final novel; and the Room of Requirement is on the seventh floor of Hogwarts. Rowling places emphasis on the number seven in *Half-Blood Prince* when she has Riddle state, "I mean, for instance, isn't seven the most powerfully magical number, wouldn't seven . . ." when he asks Professor Horace Slughorn about Horcruxes (498). There are, then, seven Horcruxes. It should be noted that *three* of these seven belonged to founders of Hogwarts (the possession belonging to the fourth founder being one of the objects that can destroy Horcruxes—the sword of Godric Gryffindor), and there are four instruments that destroy the Horcruxes (the sword, basilisk fangs, Fiendfyre, and the Elder Wand). These examples of seven from the text play a role in Harry's journey toward growth and self-knowledge.

Examples in Harry Potter

One example that ties all three of these numbers together throughout this series is Quidditch. The game that connects the wizarding world is the perfect culmination of Rowling's focus on three, four, and seven. Each team has seven members in four different positions (three chasers, two beaters, one keeper, and one seeker); the game is played with four balls of three different types, and there are three hoops in which to score.

Another key example of the centrality of these three numbers is in the less-examined triad of Harry, Snape, and Tom. These three generational half-bloods are more alike than they are different, from similar childhood experiences to final fates. All three of them have unhappy childhoods, but love saves Harry and Snape from the final outcome Voldemort faces. When Harry and Voldemort die, they both die with a seven in their age (and they are the reciprocal of the other): Harry is seventeen and Voldemort is seventy-one. Snape dies with a three in his age;

depending on when he was born, he may also have been thirty-seven, giving him a seven in his age as well. It should also be noted that Harry and Tom are both born on the same day, which is also the same day Tom encounters his downfall at the Potters' cottage (July 31).

The metafictional literary trio of "The Tale of the Three Brothers" is tied to this triad of Tom, Snape, and Harry. Tom is compared to Antioch Peverell, the owner of the Elder Wand; Snape is paired with Cadmus Peverell, the owner of the Resurrection Stone; and Harry is associated with Ignotus Peverell, the owner of the Cloak of Invisibility. The life that each man choses, what befalls him, and the outcome he reaches underlie these pairings. Tom, always the fighter and braggart, is killed as he tries to prove to the world that he is invincible. One can see the parallel when Beedle the Bard writes, "the oldest brother was a combative man," so "naturally, with the Elder Wand as his weapon, he could not fail to win the duel . . . the oldest brother proceeded to an inn, where he boasted loudly of the powerful wand he had snatched from Death himself, and how it made him invincible" (Rowling 88, 91). This last image of the first brother gloating can be seen in the final duel between Lord Voldemort and Harry. His belief that the Elder Wand, the most powerful wand in the world, belongs to him is evident in their confrontation:

> "It matters not whether Snape was mine or Dumbledore's, or what petty obstacles they tried to put in my path! I crushed them . . . Dumbledore was trying to keep the Elder Wand from me! But I got there ahead of you, little boy—I reached the wand before you could get your hands on it, I understood the truth before you caught up. I killed Severus Snape three hours ago, and the Elder Wand, the Deathstick, the Wand of Destiny is truly mine!" (*Deathly Hallows* 741)

Snape, like the second brother, Cadmus, loses the love of his life, and while he is not able to bring her back to the land of the living, everything he does from that point on is for her. Snape, too, upon learning of Lily's death, wishes he were dead so as to join her. He tells Dumbledore: "I wish . . . I wish *I* were dead"

(*Deathly Hallows* 678). There certainly is a part of Snape that dies when he chooses to protect Harry in Lily's memory, but he never stops loving her, trapped, in a way, in his own "hopeless longing" (Rowling 92). He even "brings her back to him" in his own version of the Resurrection Stone, the casting of his Patronus:

> From the tip of his wand burst the silver doe: She landed on the office floor, bounded once across the office, and soared out of the window. Dumbledore watched her fly away, and as her silvery glow faded he turned back to Snape, and his eyes were filled with tears.
> "After all this time?"
> "Always," said Snape. (*Deathly Hallows* 687)

Harry, who has been hiding from death (both literally and figuratively) is the only character of these three to choose to "go with" death, just as Ignotus went with Death "as an equal" (Rowling 93). This becomes apparent in the seventh book, when Harry goes to the forest to face Voldemort. Granted, Harry does not meet death as "an old friend" per se, but he goes with acceptance and understanding, which is certainly more than Voldemort can claim:

> His hands were sweating as he pulled off the Invisibility Cloak and stuffed it beneath his robes with his wand. He did not want to be tempted to fight. . . . At that moment he felt that nobody mattered but Voldemort. It was just the two of them. . . . Harry could feel his wand against his chest, but he made no attempt to draw it. (*Deathly Hallows* 703–704)

This comparison is doubly appropriate for Harry, as he is the owner of the actual Invisibility Cloak the tale references, and because he is a direct descendant of Ignotus. However, Tom is related to Cadmus Peverell, not Antioch, because the Resurrection Stone is set in the ring that Marvolo Gaunt owned, the one that became one of Tom Riddle's first Horcruxes. This makes an appropriate connection, because Tom is related to the son

probably most afraid of death. He uses this particular Hallow
as a way to extend his own life. The description of Cadmus does
seem to fit Tom and his goal to gain immortality through the
use of Horcruxes: "the second brother, who was an arrogant
man, decided that he wanted to humiliate Death still further"
(Rowling 88–89). While there is no evidence that Antioch had
any offspring or that Snape had any ties to the Peverell family, it
is ironic that Voldemort believes that Snape, a fellow half-blood,
was the master of the Elder Wand and thus a threat.

Rowling uses the form of the fairy tale in her final novel to
tell the story of "The Tale of the Three Brothers." Much like
Shakespeare's use of a play within a play to highlight the importance of theater, Rowling's uses the telling of a story within her
story to demonstrate the significance of literature. The central
role the tale plays in the plot of the *Deathly Hallows* also highlights the unexpected depth of children's literature; it has an
obvious purpose, and several noteworthy adults even believe
the story is real. The concept of the fairy tale as a teaching tool
has been seen throughout recorded history. Such stories of three
individuals (often siblings) cross cultures as a cautionary tale.
Many stories involve three siblings and a choice, and the youngest (or the third if the individuals are not related) is usually the
one who chooses wisely and correctly. One common example of
this is the story of Cinderella; another is the "Three Little Pigs."

Overall, the numbers three, four, and seven recur often
throughout Rowling's work, giving another layer of meaning to
her storytelling and accessing both our conscious and subcon-
scious responses. Her use of time-honored motifs allows her to
tell a story that resonates with readers who have grown accustomed to such patterns. This is not to say that Rowling's story
is predictable; it simply notes that there is an unspoken con-
tract between writer and reader that Rowling accesses by way
of these numbers, aiming for deeper understanding and connection. Because Rowling respects her readers, she uses symbols that they can understand but that are not so obvious as to
insult their intelligence. These symbols are seen throughout history, cultures, and time, and Rowling uses them to great effect
throughout the Harry Potter series.

Works Cited

Calter, Paul. "Number Symbolism in the Middle Ages. Unit 8. Math 5, Exploring Mathematics. Geometry in Art and Architecture." *Dartmouth College*. Mathematics Department. 1998. Web. 18 July 2011. http://www.dartmouth.edu/~matc/math5.geometry/unit8/unit8.html.

Hopper, Vincent Foster. *Medieval Number Symbolism: Its Sources, Meaning, and Influence on Thought and Expression.* New York, NY: Dover. 2000. Print.

The New Oxford Annotated Bible, ed. Michael D. Coogan. New York, NY: Oxford UP, 2007. Print.

Rowling, J. K. *The Tales of Beedle the Bard.* New York, NY: Children's High Level Group, 2007. Print.

Schimmel, Annemarie. *The Mystery of Numbers.* New York, NY: Oxford UP. 1993. Print.

Fifteen

Sexual Geometry of the Golden Trio

Hermione's Subversion of
Traditional Female Subject Positions

RACHEL ARMSTRONG

Any reader of Harry Potter is familiar with the Golden Trio: Harry Potter, Ron Weasley, and Hermione Granger. Throughout the series, J. K. Rowling stresses the importance of this unit: from the retrieval of the Sorcerer's Stone in the first book to the group's calculated destruction of Horcruxes in the seventh, Harry, Ron, and Hermione succeed *together*. Ron and Hermione are not only Harry's best friends but also his support system. As a longtime lover of the dynamics between the three best friends, a reader who wanted to slap some sense into Ron, who shouted "Finally!" when Ron and Hermione got together, and who turned into a sniffling, sentimental mess at Harry's noble (albeit stupid) attempt to hunt down Lord Voldemort alone, I was both excited and nervous to submit the Harry Potter series to critical inquiry in a college classroom. While many of my favorite pop culture phenomena captured my imagination as a young adult, the world of Harry Potter will forever hold a special place in my mind. I grew up at Hogwarts. I celebrated my birthdays along with the boy who lived. I went through the awkward years of puberty (with braces and a questionable perm) with Hermione as my guide. And while I've neither defeated a basilisk nor cast a spell, I worried that in writing this chapter, I would somehow lose part of my wide-eyed,

235

childhood love of the series, feared I would discover something that would lead me to question my heretofore unflagging devotion to the Golden Trio in all their bickering, lovable madness. Thankfully, that didn't happen. My study of the trio—and specifically Hermione's role within it—has only solidified what my twelve-year-old self could only define as their *"togetherness."*

The Erotic Triangle

In her influential work *Between Men: English Literature and Male Homosocial Desire*, theorist Eve Kosofsky Sedgwick establishes the structure of the erotic triangle, focusing on relationships between men and how they relate to women and to the gender system as a whole. Women's primary purpose in fiction, according to a classic reading of the erotic triangle, is to solidify bonds between men. It is the oft heard, eye-roll-inducing classic story of men in competition over a woman who has little or no agency of her own. According to Sedgwick, "the bond between rivals in an erotic triangle [is] even stronger, more heavily determinant of actions and choices, than anything in the bond between either of the lovers and the beloved" (21). Sedgwick argues that in competition over (and pursuit of) the female body, homosocial bonds between males are formed, bonds that are even stronger than the heterosexual bonds between the pursuant and the object of his desire. Thus, the relationship formed with another male through rivalry is asserted in the stories we repeatedly tell as more valuable than heterosexual, romantic love. In the pursuit of a female within an erotic triangle, "it is the bond between males that [is] most assiduously uncover[ed]," Sedgwick argues (21). Approaching male-male-female triangulated characters in this way, it is possible to read male homosocial bonds as homosexual. However, Sedgwick makes a careful point to note that homosocial bonds and homosexuality exist on a continuum:

> "Homosocial" is a word occasionally used in history and the social sciences, where it describes social bonds between persons of the same sex; it is a neologism,

obviously formed by analogy with "homosexual," and just as obviously meant to be distinguished from "homosexual." . . .To draw the "homosocial" back into the orbit of "desire," of the potentially erotic, then, is to hypothesize the potential unbrokenness of a continuum between homosocial and homosexual—a continuum whose visibility, for men, in our society, is radically disrupted. (1–2)

Sedgwick attempts to place homosocial bonds between men back into the realm of the erotic. However, she says, "I do not mean to discuss the genital homosexual desire as 'at the root of' other forms of homosociality—but rather a strategy for making generalizations about, or marking historical differences in, the *structure* of men's relationships with other men" (2). Sedgwick hints here at the possibility of reading male pursuants' desire as homosexual; however, she is not solely interested in arguing that latent homosexual desire is "at the root of" all homosocial bonds. She explains that homosociality and homosexuality exist on a continuum that is rarely recognized in a culture so permeated with homophobia. Within this context, it is the introduction of a female, third party into the homosocial/homosexual continuum that creates the traditional erotic triangle.

Placing the female within this sexual drama precludes homosexual tension between male pursuants, allowing it an acceptable heterosexual outlet. The typical role of the female is contradictory: she deflects homosexual tension between her male pursuants while simultaneously strengthening their homosocial bonds as they compete for her love. Hermione's position as a woman within the Golden Trio's erotic triangle diverts much of the sexual tension between Harry and Ron, arguably making a homoerotic reading of the two boys difficult. However, without Hermione to act as an acceptable heterosexual outlet for any sexual tension, the boys' homosocial bonds would have been less likely to flourish, and they could have been mistaken for homosexual. Thus, the politics surrounding male homosociality are entirely dependent upon the female as a heterosexual outlet. As Sedgwick writes, male homosocial desire is only acceptable "within the structural context of triangular, heterosexual desire"

(16). Rowling's introduction of Hermione as a female character is necessary and calculated. With any homoeroticism between Harry and Ron carefully siphoned into competition (or perceived competition) over Hermione, homosocial bonds between the boys flourish.

Within traditional erotic triangles, females are most often portrayed as passive, while two other active members (most often the men) engage in bond-forming rivalry over the inactive female. Within a European tradition, "women appear to be dependent on the power relationships between men and men" (Sedgwick 25). Sedgwick views this canonical portrayal as another form of trafficking women: "the use of women as exchangeable, perhaps symbolic, property for the primary purpose of cementing the bonds of men with men" (25–26). While Hermione's theoretical position within the Golden Trio is apparent, and does allow for strong homosocial bonds to form between Harry and Ron, her actions within this limited context subvert the assumed passivity so often associated with the female body. According to Sedgwick: "the triangles that most shape [this] view tend, in the European tradition, to involve bonds of 'rivalry' between males 'over' a woman. . . . *any* relation of rivalry is structured by the same play of emulation and identification, whether the entities occupying the corners of the triangle be heroes, heroines, gods, books, or whatever" (23).

Although Harry's and Ron's *theoretical* positions within the triangle would traditionally lead them to be in sexual competition over Hermione, in reality, theirs is never a rivalry between males over a woman. From the first novel, Hermione refuses to fit into the traditional position of female within the erotic triangle. Furthermore, Rowling's refusal to acknowledge any romantic or sexual leanings between Harry and Hermione (except, perhaps, in Ron's mind) further deconstructs the erotic triangle and subverts the readers' narrative expectations.

First, it is important to note the way Hermione is introduced to readers on the Hogwarts Express. Here, despite the limiting narrative technique Rowling uses and despite readers' preconceived gender biases, Hermione establishes herself as a competent, intelligent character:

The toadless boy was back, but this time he had a girl with him. She was already wearing her new Hogwarts robes.

"Has anyone seen a toad? Neville's lost one," she said. She had a bossy sort of voice, lots of bushy brown hair, and rather large front teeth.

"We've already told him we haven't seen it," said Ron, but the girl wasn't listening, she was looking at the wand in his hand.

"Oh, are you doing magic? Let's see it, then." (*Sorcerer's Stone* 105)

Given limited descriptions of Hermione's physical appearance, readers rely on Rowling's portrayal of Hermione's conversation with Harry and Ron to draw conclusions about her character:

"Are you sure that's a real spell?" said the girl. "Well, it's not very good, is it? I've tried a few simple spells just for practice and it's all worked for me. . . . I've learned all our course books by heart, of course, I just hope it will be enough—I'm Hermione Granger, by the way, who are you?" (*Sorcerer's Stone* 105–106)

Hermione exits the compartment saying, "You two had better change, you know, I expect we'll be there soon," leaving Harry and Ron speechless (*Sorcerer's Stone* 106). From this first encounter, the boys seem to have made up their minds about the bushy-haired know-it-all. Due to the third-person limited narrative technique that Rowling uses (see chapter 10 in this volume), readers also adopt Harry's primary assumptions about Hermione. Rather than viewing Hermione as an obviously intelligent, assertive female, readers, too, are more prone to think of her as a bossy know-it-all. Since intelligence and assertiveness are traits more positively associated with males, Harry and Ron channel these typically masculine characteristics into a more acceptable form: intelligent becomes know-it-all, assertive becomes bossy, and Hermione, in the readers' eyes, is placed into a more easily understandable position through the feminine descriptors used to introduce her character. This is as much due to the narration as it is to readers' assumed gender biases; however, from this first meeting, Hermione establishes herself as the intellectual superior and social equal of both Harry and Ron.

Readers' assumptions about Hermione change along with Harry's as *Sorcerer's Stone* progresses. After the trio's friendship is cemented following a run-in with a mountain troll, Hermione spends most of her time in the company of Harry and Ron: "from that moment on, Hermione Granger became their friend. There are some things you can't share without ending up liking each other, and knocking out a twelve-foot mountain troll is one of them" (*Sorcerer's Stone* 179). When Hermione is trapped in the girls' bathroom with the troll, Harry and Ron rush to her aid, knocking out the troll and saving her. In this scene, it is important to note that Harry and Ron trapped the troll in the bathroom to begin with. Here, Rowling slyly mocks the erotic triangle narrative, as our bumbling, eleven-year-old princes only attempt to save the princess after first putting her in mortal danger. Through this ordeal, Hermione is aligned with two male characters and her position within the theoretical erotic triangle, as well as within the Golden Trio, is set. However, even in her assumption of this recognizable role, Hermione subverts its passivity. At first glance, she seems rather like a damsel and rather distressed: "Hermione Granger was shrinking against the wall opposite, looking as if she were about to faint. The troll was advancing on her, knocking the sinks off the wall as it went" (*Sorcerer's Stone* 175). As Ron distracts the troll by throwing metal pipes and yelling, "Oy, pea-brain!" Hermione does not move. Harry yells for her to run, "but she couldn't move, she was flat against the wall, her mouth open with terror" (175). Hermione's reaction to the mountain troll is a narrative cue: readers recognize this plot device, as it has been repeated in our stories. We are presented with a terrified woman, immediate danger, and brave rescuers. While it could easily be argued that initially placing Hermione in the subject position of damsel in distress solidifies her role as a passive, stereotypical female for the remainder of the series, I argue that Rowling deliberately gives readers these narrative cues, playing upon their expectations of gendered behavior, so she can then dismantle them.

Harry and Ron, having succeeded in rescuing our bushy-haired princess, will likely tell the story to their friends over butterbeer for years to come.

However, Hermione's conversation with professors Severus Snape and Minerva McGonagall is a perfect example of the way Rowling consistently cues and deconstructs the readers' narrative expectations regarding Hermione. Rather than sitting quietly and letting Harry and Ron explain the troll situation to Snape and McGonagall, embodying the subject position of damsel in distress, Hermione asserts that the mess is her fault: "I went looking for the troll because I—I thought I could deal with it on my own—you know, because I've read all about them" (*Sorcerer's Stone* 177). For Hermione, a character so defined by books, schedules, and rules, this assertion is important. This assertion is *brave*. Harry and Ron are obviously surprised: "Ron dropped his wand. Hermione Granger, telling a downright lie to a teacher? . . . Harry was speechless. Hermione was the last person to do anything against the rules, and here she was, pretending she had, to get them out of trouble" (177–178). Hermione, after being saved by the boys, rejects the damsel in distress stereotype, taking action in the situation and covering for them in turn.

In a traditional erotic triangle narrative, Hermione's sole purpose would be to embody a position of vulnerability, allowing male pursuants to save her as they attempt to prove their love. Hermione's position as a young female in danger from a monster is stereotypical; however, her actions within this context are not. While in a traditional narrative Hermione would have remained inactive, here she tips the triangle, changing the presumed power dynamic and saving Harry and Ron as they saved her.

Most of the subject positions available to women within the Harry Potter series are based in stereotypical, traditional female positions, such as the damsel in distress. While Rowling's characters are by no means one dimensional, the representation of girls and women within the text is limited, in many cases, to traditional roles: McGonagall, the strict schoolmarm; Molly Weasley, the tutting mother; Petunia Dursley, the shrill stepmother; Lavender Brown, the shallow, competing woman; Fleur Delacour,

the tempting seductress; Bellatrix Lestrange, the sexualized villainess. While many of these representations can be traced to the
fairy tale genre Rowling draws from, girls reading Harry Potter
identify with the subject positions made available to them. In
this way, Harry Potter can reinforce traditional views of femi-
ninity. Although fantasy literature has tended to be more accepting of the female presence than science fiction or horror (other
genres containing supernatural forces), fantasy's use of archetypes many times reflects patriarchal gender norms and the limited options available to women. As with her placement in the
erotic triangle, Hermione's position as a female friend in the fantasy genre assumes certain characteristics. In fantasy, a woman is
either the evil villainess or damsel in distress, and both of these
subject positions rely heavily on the male hero: an evil seductress needs prey, a damsel in distress needs a savior. As with the
erotic triangle, Hermione's theoretical position within the series
would have placed her in the damsel-in-distress category—constantly being acted upon, a female character created to cement
male homosocial bonding, without any real agency of her own.
However, because Hermione embodies multiple subject positions throughout the series outside of the damsel in distress,
female best friend, or love interest, she subverts these roles.

Meredith Cherland, author of "Harry's Girls: Harry Potter
and the Discourse of Gender," observes that in *Goblet of Fire*
"we see Hermione the giggler (on page 77), Hermione the helpful and capable (on page 302), Hermione the emotionally expres-
sive (on page 314), and Hermione the clever (on page 631)"
(278). While Cherland asserts that Hermione's embodiment of
multiple subject positions removes her credibility as a character,
I argue that Hermione's flexibility allows a wider array of subject positions for which female readers can identify. Hermione's
ability to move in and out of subject positions—and to subvert
traditional subjectivities she is placed into—allows girls and
women to recognize that they don't need to fit into one stereotypical position, such as the tempting seductress. As Hermione
demonstrates (and as I discuss later), one can be a seductress
for an evening and continue to be intelligent and book-smart as
well. Though this may be perceived as inconsistency in Hermione, I believe it is a statement: worlds do not exist exclusively

from each other. Young girls reading Hermione's character may realize that one can crusade for human (or elf) rights while at the same time being a best friend, a date, a student, and a daughter.

Hermione the Giggler; Hermione the Hero

In *Chamber of Secrets*, Rowling presents readers with the first glimpse of Hermione's sexuality. Outside the context of the Golden Trio's theoretical erotic triangle, Hermione experiences her first crush. Gilderoy Lockhart, the new Defense Against the Dark Arts professor, has a profound effect on Hermione: "'*Why*,' demanded Ron, seizing her schedule, 'have you outlined all Lockhart's lessons in little hearts?' Hermione snatched the schedule back, blushing furiously" (*Chamber of Secrets* 95). Because Hermione is viewed as a nonsexual, bookish know-it-all throughout *Sorcerer's Stone*, Rowling's presentation of Hermione as a schoolgirl with a crush seems ridiculous. Hermione's attempts at feminization—drawing hearts in her notebook for example—seem frivolous and overdone; her attempts at catching Lockhart's attention fumbling. It is interesting to note, however, that unlike some of Hermione's female peers, she doesn't resort to any kind of physical attempt to impress Lockhart, instead relying solely on her intelligence to catch the professor's attention:

> ". . . but Miss Granger knew my secret ambition is to rid the world of evil and market my own range of hair-care potions—good girl! In fact"—[Lockhart] flipped her paper over—"full marks! Where is Miss Hermione Granger?"
> Hermione raised a trembling hand.
> "Excellent!" beamed Lockhart. "Quite excellent! Take ten points for Gryffindor!" (*Chamber of Secrets* 100–101)

Hermione's use of intellect to her advantage is a recurring theme throughout the series and is especially important at the end of *Chamber of Secrets*. Hermione, petrified by the basilisk, lies immobile in the hospital wing. While it seems that, again, the boys must save the day while Hermione remains inactive, Harry and Ron are only able to put the pieces together with Hermione's help. They find in her hand "a page torn from a very old library book . . . 'Ron,' [Harry] breathed, 'This is it. This is the answer. The monster in the Chamber's a *basilisk*—a giant serpent!'" (290). Even in her petrified state—one of complete immobility—Hermione still solves the mystery of the basilisk; she is not acted upon. Effectively moving the plotline forward, Hermione's discovery is a rearticulation of the importance of intellect and the integral role she plays within the trio.

Hermione's Ugly Duckling Narrative

Ron's romantic feelings toward Hermione, hinted at subtly throughout the first three books, are more evident in *Goblet of Fire*. Sedgwick's erotic triangle is most apparent through Ron, as there is a legitimate reading of the text that suggests no romantic feeling whatsoever between Harry and Hermione (this itself is important, as I discuss later). However, because in Ron's mind there is a rivalry over Hermione's affection, an erotic triangle is created. From *Sorcerer's Stone* on, readers are aware of Ron's felt incompetence next to Harry. Ron, overshadowed by his brothers his entire life, feels overshadowed by Harry in their friendship as well. His negative reaction after Harry's name is pulled from the Goblet of Fire is evidence of this:

> "It's okay, you know, you can tell *me* the truth," [Ron] said. "If you don't want everyone else to know, fine, but I don't know why you're bothering to lie, you didn't get into trouble for it, did you?"
> . . . "I didn't put my name in that goblet!" said Harry, starting to feel angry.
> "Yeah, okay," said Ron, in exactly the same sceptical tone as Cedric. "Only you said this morning you'd have done it last night, and no one would've seen you. . . . I'm not stupid you know."

"You're doing a really good impression of it," Harry snapped.

"Yeah?" said Ron, and there was no trace of a grin, forced or otherwise, on his face now.

"You want to go to bed, Harry. I expect you'll need to be up early tomorrow for a photo-call or something."

He wrenched the hangings shut around his four-poster, leaving Harry standing there by the door, staring at the dark red velvet curtains, now hiding one of the few people he had been sure would believe him. (*Goblet of Fire* 287)

Harry, who does not understand that there is a rivalry between Ron and himself over Hermione (however understated at this point), is confused by Ron's reaction. Ron, however, sees Harry's participation in the Triwizard Tournament as another reason why Hermione should choose Harry over himself. For Ron, the difference in power and social clout between himself and Harry is difficult to navigate and results in feelings of inadequacy. These feelings culminate in the grotesque Horcrux kiss between Harry and Hermione in *Deathly Hallows*. However, because Harry refuses to participate in competition over Hermione and the rivalry between Ron and Harry exists largely in Ron's mind, Viktor Krum ultimately competes with Ron for Hermione's affection and allows readers to witness Ron's budding romantic feelings toward Hermione. Ron's rivalry with Krum mirrors Ron's perceived competition with Harry. Not only is Krum a famous Quidditch player, but Ron also grew up admiring him, just as he did with the Boy Who Lived.

The Yule Ball acts as a gathering point for these tensions and is an important example of Hermione's refusal to submit to traditional female subject positions. Hermione arrives as Krum's date, angering Ron and surprising Harry. Presented differently at the Yule Ball than she is throughout the series, Hermione, for the first time in four books, is described as pretty: "Krum was at the front of the party, accompanied by a pretty girl in blue robes Harry didn't know" (*Goblet of Fire* 413). Harry, not accustomed to viewing Hermione as desirable, does not recognize her as she enters the ball. When he finally does, readers, too, are presented with a new view of Hermione:

> [Harry's] eyes fell instead on the girl next to Krum. His jaw dropped.
>
> It was Hermione.
>
> But she didn't look like Hermione at all. She had done something with her hair; it was no longer bushy but sleek and shiny, and twisted up into an elegant knot at the back of her head. She was wearing robes made of a floaty, periwinkle-blue material, and she was holding herself differently, somehow—or maybe it was merely the absence of the twenty or so books she usually had slung over her back. She was also smiling—rather nervously, it was true—but the reduction in the size of her front teeth was more noticeable than ever; Harry couldn't understand how he hadn't spotted it before. (414)

Until Krum legitimizes Hermione's sexuality by escorting her to the Yule Ball, Harry does not acknowledge her erotic power. Unlike her fumbled attempts at feminization with Lockhart in *Chamber of Secrets*, Hermione succeeds at the Yule Ball. This is the culmination of the ugly duckling narrative readers have been waiting for since Hermione is introduced as a bushy-haired girl in *Sorcerer's Stone*. Rowling purposefully takes Hermione out of the context of school and classes in order to make this narrative move. Harry says, "maybe it was merely the absence of the twenty or so books she usually had slung over her back," suggesting that the erotic cannot exist within the framework of school and classes. While readers are familiar with Hermione's presentation at the ball (a scene that conjures images of cotillions), recognizing it as her blossoming into a young woman, Hermione returns immediately to the world of intellect and books on Monday. In doing so, she refuses the subject position of ugly-duckling-turned-swan. The erotic power she discovered at the Yule Ball, while pleasing for the evening, is nothing compared with the power she finds through intellectual means. Rather than transitioning from ugly duckling into beautiful swan and staying that way, as in traditional ugly duckling narratives, Hermione refuses to accept the limited power allotted to her as a "pretty" girl. Instead, she chooses intellect. Besides the cursory vanity of her shrunken front teeth—a situation she took advantage of after Draco Malfoy's attack but didn't plan on her own—Hermione doesn't revel in the boys' recognition of her beauty.

Ron, who views Hermione in a romantic way, reacts with obvious jealousy to Hermione's arrival at the ball with Krum:

> "It's hot isn't it?" said Hermione, fanning herself with her hand. "Viktor's just gone to get some drinks."
>
> Ron gave her a withering look. "*Viktor?*" he said. "Hasn't he asked you to call him *Vicky* yet?"
>
> Hermione looked at him in surprise. "What's up with you?" she said.
>
> "If you don't know," said Ron scathingly, "I'm not going to tell you."
>
> Hermione stared at him, then at Harry, who shrugged.
>
> . . . "He's from Durmstrang!" spat Ron. "He's competing against Harry! Against Hogwarts! You—you're—" Ron was obviously casting around for words strong enough to describe Hermione's crime, "*fraternizing with the enemy*, that's what you're doing!" (*Goblet of Fire* 421)

Ron's reaction is one of belligerent jealousy: he immediately assumes Krum must be using Hermione to get information about Harry. While outwardly refusing to acknowledge that another man could view Hermione in a sexual way, Ron simultaneously feels threatened by Krum's obvious interest in Hermione. For Hermione, however, Ron's suggestion that Krum is only using her to get information about Harry is a rejection of her erotic power.

Hermione seems vastly more comfortable returning to life as it was before the ball. Her relationship with Krum legitimizes the existence of erotic power in conjunction with intellect: "I s'pose he asked you to come with him while you were both in the library?" Ron asks Hermione (*Goblet of Fire* 422). She replies yes, allowing desire and intellect to exist in relationship with each other. While Harry and Ron don't acknowledge that these two can and do exist simultaneously, Hermione does not seem to care what either of them think, returning immediately to her daily routine of classes and books, continually, casually, outsmarting the boys. By doing so, she demonstrates a refusal to bend to what Harry, Ron, and society generally view as desirable. Hermione subverts the passive expectation of "object" within Harry and Ron's (and Ron and Krum's) erotic triangle. Interestingly, Krum's role as rival to Ron in competition over Hermione does not create homosocial bonds between him and Ron but further deepens the homosocial bonds between Harry and Ron.

What is perhaps most intriguing about Rowling's representation of the erotic triangle structure in her text is that it doesn't exist in a traditional sense. Harry, Ron, and Hermione don't form an erotic triangle. While they exist in the tradition of male-male-female triangulated characters, Rowling's characterizations within the structure of the erotic triangle defies it. Although readers are tempted to read the characters in the context of this familiar narrative, in the end, it is Rowling's ability to strategically present and later manipulate this traditional structure that allows for a subversive reading of her text.

Throughout all seven novels, Rowling consciously manipulates Hermione's actions from the expected passive to a subversive active. Hermione is also active in a version of feminist politics, another narrative cue for readers. Hermione's involvement with the house-elves invites a connection between the Society for the Promotion of Elfish Welfare (S.P.E.W.) and the early feminist movement bearing a similar acronym. One of Britain's earliest women's organizations, established in 1859, was called the Society for Promoting the Employment of Women (SPEW). Like these early feminists, Hermione faces opposition:

> "What's in the box?" [Harry] asked, pointing at it.
> "Funny you should ask," said Hermione, with a nasty look at Ron. She took off the lid and showed them the contents.

> Inside were about fifty badges, all of different colors, but all bearing the same letters: S.P.E.W.
>
> "'Spew'?" said Harry, picking up a badge and looking at it. "What's this about?"
>
> "Not *spew*," said Hermione impatiently. "It's S-P-E-W. Stands for the Society for the Promotion of Elfish Welfare." (*Goblet of Fire* 224)

Some scholars believe S.P.E.W.'s name undermines a feminist reading of Hermione's actions because Rowling—even in naming the movement—mocks it. However, I argue that rather than mocking the feminist movement through Hermione's activism with S.P.E.W., Rowling pays homage to it. Hermione's fervor surrounding elfish welfare echoes that of the early feminists fighting for equal employment opportunities. Through her involvement with S.P.E.W., Hermione advocates for a political underclass (or, in her case, political underspecies). Working from this parallel, Hermione's form of activism not only allows for further feminist reading of her actions but raises important questions about today's feminisms, specifically the "white savior" complex. Hermione, unfamiliar with the house-elves' cultural context, runs into trouble while attempting to free them. While Hermione views her actions as righteous and helpful, Winky, for example, views them as an imposition.

Rowling connects Hermione to the abolitionist and feminist movements through her activism with S.P.E.W. and stresses the importance of Hermione's intellect, which, though it is not mutually exclusive from the erotic, is also not dependent on the erotic. Hermione derives her power not by submitting to the role of desirable object but rather by acting on her knowledge and intellect. This intellect is integral to the Golden Trio.

Though she is placed in a position that has historically been characterized passively, Hermione's actions within this context subvert the expectation of the role. Through aligning herself with Harry and Ron, using her intelligence instead of her looks to succeed, and refusing to accept the limited power grudgingly given to a pretty girl, Hermione tips the triangle, making readers question its structure and the female role within it. Her bonds with the two males are also central, because each has a unique relationship with her, as essential as their relationship to one another. The bonds that eventually form between all three members of the Golden Trio are forged through experience, mutual respect, plenty of bickering, and yes—love. Rowling affords Hermione a space not traditionally given to females placed in male-male-female triangulated relationships, building Hermione's character beyond oft-seen female subject positions in the fantasy genre.

My twelve-year-old, naïve love of the Golden Trio—and Hermione especially—survived long hours of critical inquiry and discussion in the classroom. And while I don't argue that the trio is immune to criticism, I pat my young self on the back for having the good judgment to love a character like Hermione Granger: bossy, assertive, emotional, lovable, and magnificently intelligent. She is, truly, the brightest witch of her age.

Works Cited and Consulted

Anatol, Giselle Liza. *Reading Harry Potter Again: New Critical Essays*. Santa Barbara, CA: ABC-CLIO, LLC, 2009. Print.

Cherland, Meredith. "Harry's Girls: Harry Potter and the Discourse of Gender." *Journal of Adolescent and Adult Literacy* 52.4 (2008): 273–282. Print.

Hopkins, Lisa. "Harry Potter and the Acquisition of Knowledge." In *Reading Harry Potter: Critical Essays*, ed. Giselle Liza Anatol. Westport, CT: Greenwood Publishing Group, 2003. 25–34. Print.

Sedgwick, Eve Kosofsky. *Between Men: English Literature and Male Homosocial Desire*. New York, NY: Columbia UP, 1985. Print.

Afterword

A Conversation with the Contributing Editors

Once more into the text! On August 19, 2013, in anticipation of sending our final draft of this collection of essays to our publisher, the seven student editors read through the whole manuscript one last time, then sat down for a raucous discussion about it and about the three-year process of making a book. The conversation was recorded, after which Professor Cecilia Konchar Farr (CKF) transcribed and edited it.

Kate Glassman (KG): Reading through the whole book this time, it struck me that everybody in this collection really cares about the Harry Potter books; that was really evident. It's also clear that these are real Harry Potter experts—people who know the books really well and won't make dumb mistakes like confusing Snape and Voldemort.

Tréza Rosado (TR): I know I checked out of this project once I started grad school this year, because I was dealing with the horrors that are graduate school. So reading through it was profoundly satisfying—just feeling the weight of it and seeing it all come together. I'm so impressed with the work that went into it, because I remember the first drafts. Oh my god, the drafts! Especially after not seeing them for a while, I could really see the progress in the essays, the work that went into the writing, the interchange between the writers and the editors.

Evan Gaydos (EG): It reminded me just how much of a process writing actually is. It makes such a difference that we each rewrote these at least five or six times with different feedback from several editors.

Rachel Armstrong (RA): And even after ten iterations of my essay, it's still not good enough. I still want to rewrite; I still want to reread the books to make it better.

[A brief—and familiar—argument then ensued, one that we're calling "The Battle of the Oxford Comma." Take my word for it—it was fierce. Oh, and I lost. CKF.]

Cecilia Konchar Farr (CKF): Has your relationship with the books changed through this process?

RA: I feel really terrible about this, but I haven't read the Harry Potter books since the last class we taught [February–May 2012]. I used to read them every year, but I haven't been able to do that since our class. I love Harry Potter, but I think I need a five-year break from this book. I've put so much of my mind and heart into it!

Jenny McDougal (JM): Rachel, you said it really well in your essay—studying the novels made you realize your instincts had been right all along. It puts you in touch with the novels on several levels when you analyze them like this. And you end up still loving the things that you loved in the first place.

Kalie Caetano (KC): When I first read the books I identified very deeply with Harry, because of the way he idealized his deceased parents, fantasizing about them when he was discontented with his upbringing with the Dursleys—which was often. But eventually, he learns incriminating details about his father, and James comes off the pedestal. It reminded me of my relationship with my father, and I think that's a moment every child has growing up—realizing that their parents are human and imperfect. And that moment is really painful. My appreciation now is much more academic and artistic. How really subversive the books actually are in their depiction of the authority, in the Ministry of Magic, for example. There is something deeply subversive about them.

Sarah Wente (SW): I'll admit, I can't read the books simply anymore, because I have studied them so much academically.

RA: And there's a loss in that. It's about not being able to read the books for fun anymore, because there are echoes of all the discussions we had in class, the essays that didn't make it into the collection, the secondary texts we've read. It has, in a really deep way, taken away that childhood, wide-eyed love—that "I love Hermione because she's just like me" approach.

KG: There is something to that loss, but I also became aware of a different loss—concerning representation. It's like you say, Tréza—"Why do I have to be Cho Chang just because I'm a person of color?" Where are the central characters of color? Where are my queer characters? Why can't Dumbledore be openly gay in the books, instead of that aspect being revealed after the books were done? It was so easy for me to slip into the books before and not notice that lack of representation. I can't not see that anymore.

KC: You remember Rachel Rostad, the Macalester student whose slam poem about Cho Chang went viral on YouTube and Jezebel last spring? ["To J. K. Rowling, from Cho Chang" on YouTube, posted April 13, 2013]. She zeroed in on that lack of diversity and how she felt so let down by how stereotypical a character Cho Chang ended up being.

TR: Sometimes I think the only thing keeping me alive and functioning in grad school is remembering my childhood love of the things that I'm submitting to rigorous critique. If I can't sleep, I still pick up Harry Potter. I still love it just as much. But as a person of color who was raised white, it has been hard to look back on the Harry Potter books and on the films and see where there could have been more diversity and there wasn't. I do feel a profound sense of loss around that. And that anecdote about Cho Chang—when my high school friends were dressing up as Harry Potter characters and they just expected me to be Cho Chang—it's a sad anecdote because these kids are not going to notice what's missing maybe for a really long time, because it's missing from every other book they're reading. It fails in a lot of the same places. So for me, Harry Potter changed a lot, but not everything. Not enough.

KC: On that note, I want to ask everyone now that we're at the end of this project: How would you categorize Harry Potter? Is it children's literature?

Everyone: NO!

KC: Is it Young Adult literature [YA]? Can you categorize it?

KG: You shouldn't try to, because the categories are so arbitrary. The *New York Times* invented new categories for Harry Potter!

KC: Is it commercial? Should it be Literature? Does it deserve a capital L?

TR: What I argue in my essay (and with people in my life) is that the books may start out as children's novels, then they might mature into YA, and I think they mature into capital-L Literature. Once you're in the sixth and seventh books, you're dealing with the scope of human tragedy, and you're definitely not dealing with kids anymore. To a certain extent you're not dealing with YA themes either. The designation of YA is not just a disservice to the books that fall under that umbrella, but it's a disservice to the psychology of the people who are included. It's like saying they're not quite human yet. I get that there are children's books and there are adult books, but the YA category feels somewhat demeaning to me. I felt that way when I was a teenager, and I feel that way now. I thought maybe when I became a "real adult" the designation would make sense to me, but it doesn't. I think it takes away from the depth of what people in their late teens are feeling and going through, and the way those things are magnified by the biological and hormonal things that are happening to them. Talking about that is radical! We remember what that was like!

JM: Oh Jesus!

TR: It's intense. It's fully human.

RA: I want to come back to this idea of categories—adult literature, capital-L Literature, women's literature. Do you think that it's helpful for young adults to read books that have mature themes and deal with elements of death and loss and despair so that they can confront and recognize those things in their own lives? That's how I learned to deal with death first, through Harry Potter. I was given that literature, and if it weren't geared toward YA, I never would have had that opportunity. So while I agree that it is slightly messed up that we have created this subcategory, this lesser-than-literature, I do think that as a child growing up reading Harry Potter I was confronted with themes that I wouldn't have been confronted with otherwise—if Harry Potter didn't exist in that category.

TR: That's what these books do; they create a safe space for children, young adults, and real adults, whatever they are, to work through issues of mortality, and first love, and adult love—near the end of the series with Tonks and Lupin—you're dealing with some pretty heavy stuff there. I think that's the nature of any good book, especially any good fantasy or sci-fi book. That's the point: you're taking us outside our world so we can look back with some perspective that maybe we couldn't get by ourselves. But I also think that what is somewhat damning about looking back at Harry Potter is that, as beneficial as it might be to young people and to adults, we have to ask: to which young people and to which adults? Look at our classes and look at how white they were, and look at the people who wrote in for our collection and how white they tended to be. And that's the problem—there's a dearth of diversity, of queer characters to connect with. The publishers want books to fall under this homogenous YA or adult category.

JM: The saddest thing is that there are books that embrace diversity. I'm thinking of Octavia Butler, who wrote exclusively women of color and queer characters of color in her YA novels, and she is just, sad to say, not popular. She died a cult hero; she won so many awards, but she was not recognized—not to the level of J. K. Rowling. Not to the level of Harry Potter. And so there are writers like that. But do we make classes around Octavia Butler? Do we make classes around Sherman Alexie? I think that there are people who write these amazing characters who deserve to have classes created for their work. Because it's important. It's so important. I think Sherman Alexie says it rightly when he says that literature offers weapons to these kids who don't know how to live in their lives—who may live in a house where alcoholism is rampant or physical and verbal abuse, and they don't know how to get out of it. And they read *Parable of the Sower* or *The Absolutely True Diary of a Part-Time Indian* and they realize that maybe there is a life beyond their house. Harry Potter does that, too, of course.

KC: We have an essay that addresses that specifically—Tréza's—where there's that quote about how a child's worst nightmare is not seeing the analog of their fears reflected in reality.

TR: Where I wanted that essay to go, and where someday it

might go, is that I think the true magic of Harry Potter is that it didn't just offer kids a space to safely work out their worst nightmares of, say, parents dying or a friend dying. It offered that to our parents, too. Do you remember your parents reading those books to you? The abuse and neglect that Harry went through—I know for a fact that that was a profound way for my mother to reflect on her childhood and what she experienced. Again, that's where the children's or YA labeling does such a disservice, not to the books themselves but to readers. Because adults need those spaces, too. What else are novels if not those spaces? I don't know why we penalize these really good books that started out directed toward children, when, in fact, seven books in they can captivate anyone who's lost a friend or a lover or has experienced abuse or racism or prejudice. There's a lot happening there that I remember my parents being profoundly affected by. My essay was about the younger generation, but I think it's just as profound for our parents' generation.

SW: I agree. I know a scene that's really profound for me in both the book and the movie—and that speaks to what you were talking about with our parents—is the scene where Cedric dies. In the movie, when the actor who plays Cedric's father comes on screen and he's just sobbing, it's one of the most heartbreaking things I've ever seen. So there's that element where Harry's lost his friend, but also this man has lost his son.

KG: I didn't cry when Cedric died, I cried when Amos Diggory cried. I did. And that's why this series is so hard to classify, because Rowling did that rather innovative thing where she starts—book 1, Harry is eleven—and if you picked it up when you were eleven, you grew up with Harry. Every year he gets older, the writing gets older, and you get older.

SW: And the situation gets older, too. It's so nuanced as it progresses.

TR: I don't know how she did it.

KG: And in terms of adults, my mother still has the audiobook files on her iPad, and because she's a crazy person, she puts all her songs on shuffle. So she'll be in the lab at work and she'll be listening to the B-52's and all of a sudden "The Prince's Tale" will come on for a two-minute clip, and my mom will start sobbing in the middle of work. Or she'll call me, and she'll say,

"Dobby just died." And I say, "You have to take those off your iPad!"

TR: My first experience with literary criticism was standing in the kitchen with my mother, who never went to college, who is not anything like me. Rachel knows her, she can tell you. She's my mom. When I tell her about my scholarly work, she says, "That's nice. Did you see the latest episode of *Parenthood*?" But I remember just talking—for I mean hours, guys—not about how we felt about the books but about the construction of the books. A thing I'd never heard my mother do. I didn't know that was a part of me that I got from her. I didn't know that that existed between us. You hear that all the time when we talk about our experience with Harry Potter. It's so often a joint experience between the parent and the kid. There just has to be something to that.

KG: The novels provide a space for us, individually, to work through death and loss, but they also open a dialogue, a shared space—with our parents and with other people. I know there are people I never would have met if I hadn't wandered into the hallway yelling, "Oh my God, I can't believe Cedric Diggory . . ." And someone would peek out and say, "Oh, Harry Potter? What page are you on?" Instant connection.

KC: The other thing that we've already touched on a little bit but deserves more consideration in our conversation is the skillful pacing of the maturity of the novels. As you grow, the books are in pace with your maturity level. When you compare it to its contemporaries in YA fiction, for example Lemony Snicket's *A Series of Unfortunate Events* or *The Hunger Games*—those two texts are static. The way that they are written is static, and that's not to count against them. Lemony Snicket is clever. And he's always clever, always the same level of clever. And the same with *The Hunger Games*, the level of intensity is constant. The thing that is really fascinating about Harry Potter is how it really does mature in the writing level throughout the series. For example, death (which I thought about a lot for my essay, obviously): when you just consider the end of every single book, it deals with death. The first three just come really close to death: the first one references Harry's parents, and then in the second one Ginny is close to death, but not quite, and then Sirius is close, but not. And then you finally get to book 4, and somebody dies. And you get to book 5, and it's an even more poignant death. And you get to book 6 and arguably an even more poignant death than book 5. [*Editors*: More? Wait—] Arguably. And in book 7, there's a whole war and people are dying left and right. And that's just one example of the way the books mature and the themes mature. I wonder if it was organic growth for her as a writer.

EG: I think it was absolutely intentional.

CKF: That actually really touches me. Going back to what you were saying about parenting, I feel like Rowling was often writing to her daughter, since she just had her when she began writing about Harry Potter. As parents, when your kids are growing up, you go through the stages of life with them again. So as she was writing these books and her daughter was going from this age to this age to this age, she was relating to her at every one of those different places in her life—and revisiting herself at that age. So I feel the need to assert that she was a better writer because she was a mother, because our literary tradition generally asserts the opposite.

JM: And that's what I love about J. K. Rowling is that you sense that connection. She is so honest and respectful of the questions children ask, which you really don't see in a lot of children's novels. The adults in children's books are often absent or untrustworthy; they can't be counted on. And there are so many adults in Harry Potter who can be counted on. I mean, arguably, Dumbledore can be counted on. [Laughter.] Coming to these novels a little later than most of you—as a sixteen-year-old instead of an eleven-year-old or younger—I always found it so amazing just how generous Rowling was with her audience. She never deferred or toed the line on what real young adult or children's literature should be. She reflected the world we live in, one where children experience things at probably a greater level emotionally or psychologically than adults do. I loved that.

TR: She trusted her readers, implicitly. Even when you were twelve years old and didn't know what you were doing! One of my favorite quotes (and I wish I could remember who said this) but it was talking about Harry Potter and *The Chronicles of Narnia*. C. S. Lewis—those are great books—but he didn't really trust his audience. Susan gets kicked out of Narnia because she starts to wear lipstick and get crushes on boys. But look at Ginny Weasley, I mean, she is like the hottest thing going at Hogwarts. There's no judgment there! I mean, Hermione has boyfriends. All of the characters grow up. She lets them grow up. That's not to say that they are experimenting with drugs . . .

KC: What about Felix Felicis? That was some pretty trippy [redacted].

TR: She trusts that the readers are going to grow up with these characters, and it's going to be okay if we see what their actual teenage lives might be like. And that's just missing in other series. It's endlessly frustrating for me now to read *The Chronicles of Narnia*, because there's just no trust there. It's really unfortunate.

RA: And that's one of the reasons that I'm so invested in this kind of critical inquiry of the series, because Rowling did trust her readers so much that I feel like in order to fully return that trust, to fully be a reader and lover of the Harry Potter books, I need to look at them more deeply and not just at the surface level. Not, "They're so great! The plot moves forward so well! They are real page-turners!" There's so much more going on in these books. When I do sit back and think that maybe I miss when I was young and I could read these books and not really think about all this, I realize that there has to be more to it than that. J. K Rowling really trusted us to read the books and read them well, and that's what we're doing here.

JM: And the level of inquiry that you can bring to this series just speaks to how well it is written, how amazing a series it is, because we can sit here and talk about how Grindelwald has Nazi tendencies—that it allows for that kind of analysis. [My husband] Evan [who is also a writer] and I have spoken about how something isn't really good unless you can really interrogate it. And I love when you can bring critical inquiry to something you love so much and it holds up!

SW: It's nice that you can appreciate it on that many levels, too. That it holds up to both ends of that—the story and the characters that I can relate to and that I'm critically analyzing for X, Y, and Z.

KG: And that's what I was thinking about when I was

reflecting on what we as an editorial board drew out in this collection, what we were zeroing in on as we discussed the essays,
and there seems to be an understanding that there's very much
a swinging-door policy between us and Harry Potter. It's really
easy to overlay world events with Harry Potter. We can say the
wizards are like hippies or this is very much like Nazi Germany.
It allows us to come in and make those parallels, to put it into
our world, give it a context, then give it back. To come in, the
way Kate McManus says, without harming the text, without
disrupting the native environment. We're allowed to fill in the
gaps with our imaginations; we're allowed to make a space for
ourselves in it, using things like fanfiction or subtext readings.
As we were just saying, there aren't a lot of queer characters.
There's one relationship [Dumbledore and Grindelwald], which
doesn't even get any major airtime. But we can still go in and
say, okay, Remus Lupin, werewolf: he goes through all these
pressures; he's been ostracized with this thing he has to hide.
There are plenty of essays that relate his lycanthropy to homosexuality and how it's treated by the world. And the beauty of
the series is that it allows you to go in and do that. You're not
doing a disservice to the books, to the stories, to the character of
Remus Lupin, by going in there and trying to work out things in
the space Rowling's provided for you.

JM: And the fact that she supports that kind of participation—

EG: That she encourages it. The trust that Rowling has with
her readers is so present in her writing. We were saying how different it is from Lemony Snicket—he's so clever, and that's it.
There are maniacal bad guys. And then you back to Harry Potter, and there are well-rounded characters, children and adults.
We know now that she can write both—and for both.

JM: And each character changes. You don't see that so often
in children's literature. Each main character undergoes a change,
and it's often a profound, radical change.

EG: I don't feel like you see that kind of change in any literature to this magnitude, across seven novels.

KG: Like the text we used in class, Joseph Campbell on the
hero's journey, where there are these archetypes—the wise old
man, the crazy hermit who lives behind a rock . . . and they
don't change.

[To get the full effect of this discussion, pause here for a moment of revelry, singing of random songs, references to "Rosemerta, the prostitute with the heart of gold," the filling of wine glasses, and the passing of the chocolate.]

KC: Can I tell you? I wrote so much fanfiction! I was in middle school, and I was writing fanfiction, so I had a beta reader, which is an editor. You have an editor! For me, it was a very official process, the first time I engaged with writing in this really adult way. I had very tiny handwriting, and I wrote on notebook paper, two lines of writing for every one line on the paper, sheets upon sheets in graphite.

TR: What was your screen name?

KC: No one will ever know what my screen name was! But I still appreciate the way I learned to engage the writing process so seriously in this imaginative playground that J. K. Rowling provided for us.

KG: It was our only way to get our Harry Potter hit at that age. Because the next book wasn't coming for three years!

TR: Those were long, long years! I scoured those rec lists of fanfiction. Some people were really good at it. It helped fill the void.

EG: I think it was somewhere during that void, when we were reading and rereading the texts, I finally decided my dad was going to have pop culture if it killed me. He worked weird hours and always wanted to read more but didn't have the time. So during that lull, I took it upon myself to read the Harry Potter books to him. It sort of became our thing, and it's something we've shared ever since, the way we talked about sharing these books with our parents. It became something we could talk about and analyze. My dad understands story structure, and it would be so infuriating when he would make a prediction about a character early on (usually Snape) and he'd be right, but I'd have to just shrug it off so I wouldn't give anything away.

JM: Can I bring it down to a somber note? Since I was sixteen, Harry Potter has reminded me why I love to read, why I love thinking about novels. Before that, in high school, I wasn't challenged; I lost the desire to keep reading. I even sort of hated reading. After watching a *Rosie O'Donnell* show where she talked about Harry Potter, I asked my mom to get it for me.

She said, "You know it's a children's book?" But I immediately loved it. It really reminded me how much I had loved reading.

KG: I started with it at eleven. In theory, if she'd been on her game, I would have always been the same age as Harry Potter. But I remember reading *Order of the Phoenix* when I was a bit older and thinking Harry was so irritating. He was just yelling all the time. No wonder no one wants to make you a prefect! But when I went back and read it again, it forced me to confront what I had been at fifteen. I probably yelled a lot of the time. I was not pleasant. Rowling is so on point. As Rachel was saying, when I want to go back and see the world as I did when I was eleven, I go back to *Sorcerer's Stone*. All they want to do is get to the trap door and save the world. That's it. It's not complicated. Complicated comes later. She's so good at getting it right for every age.

EG: So, if Kate was eleven, then I would have been around nine when the first book came out. I was in fourth grade and my teacher—Mrs. Hansen—read us a chapter or two of *Sorcerer's Stone*. As an avid reader, I couldn't believe there was a fantasy book out there that I hadn't heard about. Sometime that week, my family went to the library, and I started looking for this book, but *Prisoner of Azkaban* was the only one available. I was so desperate to find out what was going on in this world that I was willing to skip the first two books just to get my hands on a copy. [Editors: Gasp!] When my mom saw me with it, she told me to put it back; she had a copy of the first book at home. So for me, Harry lived in my parent's bedroom closet, not the cupboard under the stairs, where he waited for my mom to read his story and decide if he was suitable for me, the kid with the overactive imagination. That evening, my mom gave me the book with the gentle reminder—"Evan, remember it's not real." I can't completely say I blame my parents for being a little overprotective of my runaway imagination, because I still remember to this day staying up way too late and scaring myself silly as I raced to the end of that book and not being able to look over the edge of my bed once Quirrell unwrapped that turban. Looking back on it now, coming from a family heavily into science fiction and fantasy—*Stargate*, *Star Wars*, *Star Trek*, *The Lord of the Rings*, need I go on?—and given my experiences with this set of texts, I know what my parents meant when they said "real," but for this age group and the impact this series had, I now think "real" is one of the best ways to describe these books.

TR: I always loved to read. My nose was always in a book, so Harry Potter didn't change me as a reader, necessarily. It just made me read in more awkward places—like brushing my teeth. I was always trying to find a waterproof way to read my books in the shower. The key to my relationship with Harry Potter is that it enabled my hidden feelings of superiority. Whenever I need a boost in life, when I think my life is too ordinary in comparison to what it was supposed to be, I pick up Harry Potter and it makes me hopeful. I could still totally change the world! It takes me back to being twelve, trying to figure out why I didn't get my Hogwarts letter yet. Because I was supposed to get it. That doesn't mean that my Hogwarts letter is not still on its way, in a bigger sense. So maybe it enabled an incredible narcissism. But it also keeps the fire alive in me that the world and my neurosis would have stifled and smothered.

SW: For me, it was such an affirmation of imagination and creative thinking. Not just the books, but what Rowling has done with her life. I love that she made it okay to be thirty and have daydreams about wizards, to have a vibrant imagination and have that be so valuable.

TR: I still feel like I'm a better, more interesting person because I don't wholly disbelieve in magic. Because I maybe still kind of believe in wizards.

JM: We want to believe. I'm still waiting for my Hogwarts letter, too.

KC: One thing I want to add to what Tréza said is that I really believe these books made me a better person—at least for a week when I was thirteen. I did a very explicit psychological evaluation with myself and committed to a practice of WWDD—What Would Dumbledore Do? And I really did enact this. I walked around channeling a wise, old man. Literally, my mother and I never had a better relationship than we did for that week.

RA: I want to go back to this idea of being a better person—

TR: Or more of a narcissist.

RA: —because another way these books make us better

people is in that speculative way that science fiction and fantasy push us. The book we read in class, Kaku's *Physics of the Impossible*, made us think about what could happen—an invisibility cloak? Maybe. How can we have levitation, phasers, invisibility cloaks in the next thirty to forty years if we don't imagine them first?

SW: This kind of writing keeps us believing in something more.

KG: And we get there. On the old Star Trek episodes of the sixties they had communicators, and now we have cell phones. They had phasers; we have tasers.

JM: Yes! Fantasy and science fiction tell us that we are limitless. It's a nice reminder for adults that what we see now is not always going to be the case. And I just want to add that I appreciate this community where we talk passionately about these things that we love and where we all take this work seriously. These kinds of communities don't exist everywhere.

KC: I know it. I tried proposing a senior project based on Harry Potter, and my advisor, who I really admire and respect, could barely even let me finish saying "Harry Potter" without rolling her eyes. She told me, "That's not going to fly in this department."

JM: As I pursue this teaching career that I'm committed to, I hope I remember this and listen to my students and really hear what they love. Because what they love matters.

Appendix 1

Harry Potter Course Syllabus

English 2230: The Novel

Six Degrees of Harry Potter

Course Description:

"The Novel" is a topics course, allowing the professors who teach it to be flexible and responsive to current topics in the field. It can be about Oprah Books one semester, Jane Austen novels the next, and the Harlem Renaissance after that. In fact, the Harry Potter phenomenon is exactly the sort of opportunity we invented the course to accommodate.

"Six Degrees of Harry Potter" was generated by the St. Kate's English Club and their enthusiastic course suggestions, and the former co-chairs of the English Club are now the teaching assistants. Course development began almost three years ago and has continued in nerdy excess among the three of us ever since. We hope the course will reflect both our passionate affection for the novels and our careful analysis of their contexts and complexities.

Together over the course of the semester, we will read, write about, and theoretically explore all seven novels. Each student will be sorted into a small group of six, and each of these groups will be responsible for the "six degrees," that is, the six critical approaches or modes of analysis we will be taking to the novels.

Through small and large group work, paper writing, creative and research projects we will address some key Potter questions such as: What makes these books so successful? In what ways are they traditionally literary and imaginative? Why do they resonate so deeply for this generation of students? How do they change over the course of the series? What are the major issues and ideas they address? How are these issues and ideas relevant to our complex twenty-first-century world?

Texts: Required

Rowling, J. K.   *Harry Potter and the Sorcerer's Stone* (Year One)
Harry Potter and the Chamber of Secrets (Year Two)
Harry Potter and the Prisoner of Azkaban (Year Three)
Harry Potter and the Goblet of Fire (Year Four)
Harry Potter and the Order of the Phoenix (Year Five)
Harry Potter and Half-Blood Prince (Year Six)
Harry Potter and the Deathly Hallows (Year Seven)

We will also read selected scholarly essays (in a course pack) from *Reading Harry Potter* and *Reading Harry Potter Again*, both edited by Giselle Liza Anatol. We will assign essays from "A Wizard of Their Age," in a course pack, including essays by students in previous sections of this class.

Required for individual groups (as sorted):

Ravenclaw   *Harry Potter's Bookshelf: The Great Books* (Granger)
Slytherin   *Physics of the Impossible* (Kaku)
Hufflepuff   *A Charmed Life: The Spirituality of Potterworld* (Bridger)

Gryffindor   *The Power of Myth* (Campbell)
Beauxbatons *The Hidden Adult: Defining Children's Literature* (Nodelman)
Durmstrang   *How to Write Science Fiction and Fantasy* (Card)

Course Requirements:

This is not a lecture course but a participatory seminar-style course. Because of this, your involvement is essential, so attendance is mandatory. Even one unexcused absence will affect your grade, and repeated excused absences have consequences. Students with (rare and) reasonable excuses for absences should contact Cecilia *before class.*

Because your participation is central to the course, it is important that you complete reading and writing assignments by the date assigned in the course outline below and come to class prepared to discuss them.

This is still a new course, and we will be flexible in how it plays out to meet the needs of this particular group. In return, we ask you to be engaged and open, ready to try new approaches and ideas and to shift gears when the situation demands it.

Each student will be sorted into a group for the semester. Each small group (House/School) will be responsible for reading their assigned course text then presenting its ideas to the class in a meaningful and accessible way. This thirty-minute presentation will be the major graded group project (worth 50 points on a 300-point scale). In addition to the theoretical presentation, each group will complete several informal critical essay presentations on material from the course packs.

Other graded group assignments include one fifteen-minute PowerPoint presentation, one ten-minute oral presentation, and one creative interaction of your choice (up to thirty minutes) as assigned in the course outline below and describe on the group work handout (attached).

Each student individually will write three short response papers on three of the novels, as delineated in the course outline below.

☙❧

Response papers are one-page, single-spaced examinations of a text, in analytical college-student style (not a review), with a focus on the novel's values, main ideas, issues, image patterns, structure or language, preferably from the perspective of your theoretical approach. A narrow focus is the key to doing these short papers well, homing in on a single quote or aspect of the novel that caught your attention, so you can spend your space analyzing rather than summarizing the text. Remember that your audience is the class, and they have all just read it, too. So, while there is no need to summarize, there is every reason to speak in your own voice, integrating your ideas and experience with your analysis. *Papers must be typed, titled, and submitted on time with your name and the date in the upper-left corner.* Papers not formatted as assigned will be returned for revision and marked late. Late papers lose much of their relevance as discussion generators, so please avoid as much as possible turning papers in late. Assignments will not be accepted after one week past the due date.

The final project can be either individual- or group-generated; creative or research-based; visual, oral, or written—details to be invented as we go. It will be worth 75 points on a 300-point scale and should be considered the culmination of your thinking in the course.

Grading:

Grading will add up (approximately) as follows:

Group Theory Presentation	50 points
Short Group Presentations	75 points (25/each)
Response Papers	75 points (25/each)
Final Project	75 points
Informal Presentations/Participation	25 points
TOTAL	**300 points**

The scale for final grades is:

276	A (92%)	225	C+ (75%)
264	A- (88%)	216	C (72%)

255	B+ (85%)	204	C- (68%)
246	B (82%)	195	D+ (65%)
234	B- (78%)	180	D (60%)
		Below 180	F

Notes:

Please feel free to share with us any special considerations you might have regarding your performance in the class—time constraints, learning disabilities, pregnancy, whatever. We are willing to negotiate requirements to suit your needs. If you want to request academic accommodations, please contact Disability Services, then bring their letter to Cecilia.

All members of this class are bound by the college's policy on Academic Dishonesty, which can be found on the St. Kate's website. If you violate this policy, you will fail the course.

This class is, for most of you, taken as part of your liberal arts core. The liberal arts goals emphasized here will be mainly "Critical and Creative Inquiry," "Purposeful Lifelong Learning," and "Effective Communication in a Variety of Modes." Most specifically, under this final value, we will aim to:

a) read, view, and listen with understanding and critical discernment;
b) organize, evaluate, and communicate ideas effectively through writing and public speaking;
c) prepare and present information visually and through the use of technology;
d) find expression in fine, literary, and performing arts;
e) develop and put into practice interpersonal, group, and cross-cultural communication skills and listening skills.

This course, like every course, is political—it is as much about us and the culture(s) we're located in as it is about thinking and writing. Because of our differences, our passions, our various opinions, and our often-challenging questions, discussions can sometimes get uncomfortable. In this course, we won't avoid controversy; in fact, one of our purposes is to learn from differences, opening new areas of thinking about these novels that many of us have loved for years. Please be prepared to listen as well as talk; in good class discussions, these skills are equally valuable. Finally, be assured that your views (however different they may be from others' in the class) will not affect your grade, except when they are poorly articulated. Feel free to enter the intellectual fray with the joyful abandon of a serious, educated reader.

Course Outline

January 31	Introduction to the course and each other
	The Sorting
	Review Syllabus
	Generate Norms
	Assign Anatol essay reports
	Assign Group Contracts
February 7	Group Meetings (until 7:30)
	Discussion of readings in Anatol Packet as assigned
	Group Contracts Due
February 14	Group Presentations: Hufflepuff, Durmstrang, Slytherin
February 21	Group Presentations: Beauxbatons, Ravenclaw, Gryffindor
February 28	*Harry Potter and the Sorcerer's Stone*
	Paper #1 Due: Gryffindor, Ravenclaw, Hufflepuff
	PowerPoint: Slytherin
	Oral Presentation: Durmstrang
	Creative Presentation: Beauxbatons
March 6	*Harry Potter and the Chamber of Secrets*
	Paper #1 Due: Slytherin, Durmstrang, Beauxbatons
	PowerPoint: Gryffindor
	Oral Presentation: Ravenclaw
	Creative Presentation: Hufflepuff

March 13	Discussion of "A Wizard of Their Age"
	Readings as Assigned
Spring Break	
March 27	*Harry Potter and the Prisoner of Azkaban*
	Paper #2 Due: Hufflepuff, Ravenclaw,
	Gryffindor
	PowerPoint: Durmstrang
	Oral Presentation: Beauxbatons
	Creative Presentation: Slytherin
April 3	*Harry Potter and the Goblet of Fire*
	Paper #2 Due: Durmstrang, Beauxbatons,
	Slytherin
	PowerPoint: Ravenclaw
	Oral Presentation: Hufflepuff
	Creative Presentation: Gryffindor
April 10	*Harry Potter and the Order of the Phoenix*
	Paper #3 Due: Ravenclaw, Hufflepuff,
	Gryffindor
	PowerPoint: Beauxbatons
	Oral Presentation: Slytherin
	Creative Presentation: Durmstrang
April 17	*Harry Potter and the Half-Blood Prince*
	Paper #3 Due: Beauxbatons, Slytherin,
	Durmstrang
	PowerPoint: Hufflepuff
	Oral Presentation: Gryffindor
	Creative Presentation: Ravenclaw
	Distribute: Deathly Hallows Lectures
	excerpt
April 24	*Harry Potter and the Deathly Hallows*
	Discussion free-for-all
	Final Project Check-in
May 1	*Draft of Final Project Due*
	Conferences/Group Writing Workshops
	Sign up for presentation times
May 8	Class Conference in Jeanne d'Arc
	Auditorium
Final Exam:	Class Celebration (and Nerdfest)

GROUP PROJECTS: Six Degrees of Harry Potter

Group Contracts

Should include:
>   The name of your group
>   Three promises you make to one another (your norms)
>   Your signatures and preferred contact information

Theoretical Presentations

TEXT ASSIGNMENTS:
Hufflepuff   *A Charmed Life*
Your focus will be theological analysis, on Harry as a Christ figure and on the many challenges to Harry Potter as anti-Chris-
tian/Wiccan. You will also be responsible for contemporary
critical approaches based on race and class.

Slytherin   *Physics of the Impossible*
The course science geeks, you will examine the scientific and
technological aspects of Harry Potter, including reports on
online communities and interactions.

Ravenclaw   *Harry Potter's Bookshelf: The Great Books*
Carrying the banner for humanities majors, your job will be
to focus on traditional and contemporary theoretical textual
analysis. You will also be responsible for presenting feminist
approaches.

Gryffindor   *The Power of Myth*
You will address The Big Mythological Questions about how
Harry fits in with "the Hero Cycle" and Western models of
quest and identity development.

Beauxbatons   *The Hidden Adult: Defining Children's
                Literature*
You will keep us centered on the psychological complexities of
the Harry Potter books, including their place as children's or
young adult literature.

Durmstrang   *How to Write Science Fiction and Fantasy*
For everything else the Harry Potter novels are, they are also
prime examples of successful fantasy literature. You will keep
us centered on what this means and how it plays out over the
series. Also, sports fans, you will be the experts on Quidditch.

IMPORTANT NOTE:

Theoretical Presentations should include:

- A PowerPoint (or some other visual) and oral sum-
  mary of your text, carefully outlining its central
  arguments
- *A brief, focused handout* for your classmates to keep,
  including:
     Your theoretical text's main concepts and
     The related questions you will be asking of each
     of the HP novels
- Attention to presentation—make your approach
  accessible, useful, and interesting for your fellow students. Be sure that every group member participates.
- A brief class discussion/Q&A, which you will lead.

Critical Essay Assignments:

Each group will report on an essay from *Reading Harry Potter* or *Reading Harry Potter Again*, and, later, several from "A
Wizard of Their Age." For these presentations your job is to 1)
familiarize yourself with the style and content of scholarly writing about HP; and 2)summarize for the class what the scholars in
your essays are saying. Follow up with some good critical questions, based on your essays and/or your theoretical approach,
for the class to consider.

Group PowerPoint, Oral, and Creative Presentations:

PowerPoint and oral presentations aim to take the main ideas
of your theory and deploy them on the assigned novel (with

reference to other novels, if relevant—but the focus should be the novel at hand). They should add insight and depth to our analysis of the novel being discussed that week.

Time limits will be strictly enforced to preserve time for the discussion free-for-all. PowerPoints—fifteen minutes; Oral Presentations—ten minutes.

Creative presentations were reinvented and expanded by the HP students from spring semester 2010 and fall 2011. They are now their own genre, unrelated to the other two types of presentations and not necessarily connected to the theoretical texts. Let your imaginations roam freely as you examine ways that the HP phenomenon lives among us. Ideas from previous semesters include an HP Trivia, a Quidditch match, an HP banquet, a Divinations class, and a scavenger hunt through the Chamber of Secrets. You will have up to half an hour for creative presentations (please discuss with Cecilia, Evan, or Rachel ahead of time).

On weeks when you have individual papers due, groups will work together briefly, reading and commenting on each other's papers, then presenting ideas from the individual papers to the class in an informal discussion. The better you get to know one another's writing, the more you will be able to help one another write better papers. You are also a Writing Group.

Appendix 2

Annotated Harry Potter Timeline

EVAN GAYDOS

Items in roman are directly from the novels or extrapolated from details in them. Items in *italics* are confirmed in *The Harry Potter Lexicon* (J. K. Rowling lists birthdates on her official site). Interpolations from the appendix's author are enclosed in square brackets. Also consulted: *Harry Potter Wiki.*

c. Tenth Century

The four founders of Hogwarts are born (Godric Gryffindor, Salazar Slytherin, Rowena Ravenclaw, and Helga Hufflepuff).

Hogwarts is founded.

Helena Ravenclaw is probably among the first students to attend Hogwarts.

1881

Summer:

Albus Dumbledore is born.

1882

Gellert Grindelwald is born (or in 1883).

1883

Aberforth Dumbledore is born (or in 1884).

1884

Ariana Dumbledore is born (or in 1885).

1899

June:

Albus Dumbledore graduates from Hogwarts (age seventeen).

Kendra Dumbledore dies (in an accident involving Ariana Dumbledore).

Albus Dumbledore meets Gellert Grindelwald.

Over the next couple of months, Dumbledore and Grindelwald begin to form their plans for wizard supremacy, but their planning ends when Aberforth, Albus, and Gellert get into a violent quarrel that results in Ariana's death.

Ariana Dumbledore dies (age fourteen).

c. 1907

Merope Gaunt is born.

1917

Frank Bryce is born.

1925

Late August–early September:

Bob Ogden, head of the Magical Law Enforcement Squad, goes to the Gaunts' house to tell Morfin Gaunt he must attend a hearing on September 14 for using magic in front of a Muggle (Tom Riddle Sr.). A fight breaks out, the Ministry of Magic sends reinforcements, and Marvolo and Morfin Gaunt are taken to Azkaban. Marvolo serves a six-month sentence, while Morfin serves three years. Merope Gaunt is on her own for the first time in her life; she is eighteen years old.

A few months later (approximately late December):

Tom Riddle Sr. and Merope Gaunt marry and run away together.

1926

c. March:

Marvolo Gaunt returns home from Azkaban to find Merope Gaunt gone.

(Sometime after March):

Tom Riddle Sr. returns home to Little Hangleton.

December:

23–24—Merope Gaunt sells Salazar Slytherin's locket to Borgin and Burkes.

31—Tom Riddle is born; Merope Gaunt dies (approximately age nineteen).

Tom remains in an orphanage from birth until September 1, 1938.

1928

c. September:

Morfin Gaunt returns home from Azkaban.

December 6—Rubeus Hagrid is born.

1935

October 4—Minerva McGonagall is born.

1938–1939

September–June:

Tom Riddle's first year at Hogwarts.

1938–1939

September–June:

Rubeus Hagrid's first year at Hogwarts.

1942–1943

September–June:

Tom Riddle's fifth year at Hogwarts.

Is made a prefect and opens the Chamber of Secrets.

Spring:

Moaning Myrtle dies; Rubeus Hagrid is expelled; Tom Riddle is awarded special services to the school for "catching" the individual who opened the Chamber of Secrets.

Tom Riddle sits his O.W.L.s.

Summer:

Tom Riddle goes looking for the Gaunt family; finds out about paternal family from Morfin Gaunt; kills

Tom Riddle Sr. and paternal grandparents (Avada Kedavra), and frames Morfin Gaunt for the crime. Tom Riddle takes the Peverell ring from the Gaunt house (future Horcrux).

1943–1944

September–June:

Tom Riddle's sixth year at Hogwarts.

Asks Horace Slughorn about Horcruxes.

Creates first Horcrux: a diary preserving his sixteen-year-old self so he can reopen the Chamber of Secrets at a future date.

1944–1945

September–June:

Tom Riddle's seventh year at Hogwarts.

Is made Head Boy.

Discovers the location of Rowena Ravenclaw's diadem from the Gray Lady (Helena Ravenclaw).

Sits his N.E.W.T.s and graduates from Hogwarts.

Upon graduation, asks headmaster Armando Dippet for the Defense Against the Dark Arts teaching position and is denied the post.

Late 1945

Tom Riddle goes to work for Borgin and Burkes.

Albus Dumbledore defeats Gellert Grindelwald and becomes the master of the Elder Wand.

Gellert Grindelwald is imprisoned in Nurmengard.

c. 1947

Tom Riddle kills Hepzibah Smith to gain possession of Slytherin's locket and Hufflepuff's cup.

He resigns from Borgin and Burkes and disappears for ten years (it is speculated that he goes to Albania).

During those ten years:

Riddle collects Ravenclaw's diadem; creates Horcruxes out of diadem, cup, and locket.

He pushes the boundaries of magic, gains follow-ers, and becomes more widely known as Lord Voldemort.

Early Death Eaters included: Nott, Rosier, Mul-ciber, and Dolohov.

1950

February

Arthur Weasley is born

October 30—Molly Prewett (Weasley) is born around this time (if she was twenty when Bill was born).

1951

Bellatrix Black (Lestrange) is born (according to the Black Family Tree)

1954

Lucius Malfoy is born

There seems to be a discrepancy with this date. Lucius Malfoy is a prefect in the fall of 1971 when Severus Snape starts his first year at Hogwarts, mean-ing he is most likely in his fifth or sixth year. If born in 1954, Lucius's years at Hogwarts would be either 1965–1971 (if his birthday is before September 1) or 1966–1972 (if his birthday is after Sept. 1). If Lucius were in his fifth or sixth year in 1971, he would have been born between the years of 1955–1956.

1956

December

Minerva McGonagall begins teaching at Hogwarts (she has been teaching for thirty-nine years in *Order of the Phoenix*)

c. 1957

(1955/1956 at the earliest, but more likely a little later)

Tom Riddle returns to Hogwarts where Albus Dumbledore in now headmaster.

Has begun going by the name Lord Voldemort

Again requests the Defense Against the Dark Arts teaching position and is denied.

Hides Rowena Ravenclaw's diadem Horcrux in the
Room of Requirement.

Leaves Hogwarts and not much is heard of him until
he comes to power as Lord Voldemort.

1959

Fall (post September 1)
  Sirius Black is born.

1960

Peter Pettigrew is born (or in late 1959).
January 9—Severus Snape is born.
January 30—Lily Evans (Potter) is born.
March 10—Remus Lupin is born.
March 27—James Potter is born.

1961

Regulus Arcturus Black is born (according to the Black
Family Tree).

1964

Britain hosts the Quidditch World Cup.

1970

*Voldemort rises to power for the first time sometime
during this year.*
November 29—Bill Weasley is born.

1971

September

The Marauders and their peers start their first year at
Hogwarts.

The term "Snivellus" in reference to Severus Snape
is coined on the Hogwarts Express.

Lucius Malfoy is a prefect at this time, so he is at
least in his fifth year at Hogwarts, if not older.

1972

September

The Marauders start their second year at Hogwarts.

Sometime during this year, the Marauders discover
Lupin is a werewolf.

December 12—Charlie Weasley is born.

c. 1973

Nymphadora Tonks is born.

1975

September

The Marauders start their fifth year at Hogwarts.

Remus Lupin is made a prefect.

During this school year James Potter, Sirius Black, and Peter Pettigrew manage to become Animagi.

1976

Oliver Wood is born.

June

The Marauders sit their O.W.L.s.

After the Defense Against the Dark Arts O.W.L., the Marauders humiliate Severus; Lily defends Severus by yelling at James. The whole confrontation ends with Severus calling Lily a "Mudblood."

Later that evening, Lily goes to talk to Severus outside of the Gryffindor Common Room door. Lily states directly that the two of them have chosen different paths and ends their friendship.

August 22—Percy Weasley is born.

1977

Fleur Delacour, Cedric Diggory, and Viktor Krum are born (could also be born September 2–December 31, 1976)

October

Angelina Johnson is born (somewhere between the 17th–24th).

1978

April 1—Fred and George Weasley are born.

June

The Marauders sit their N.E.W.T.s and graduate from Hogwarts.

Between June of 1978 and sometime in 1979, James Potter marries Lily Evans.

1979

Cho Chang is born (or in late 1978).

Sometime between July 31, 1979, and July of 1980 (mostly likely in winter, possibly early spring), Sibyll Trelawney makes her first real prediction while interviewing with Dumbledore for a position at Hogwarts.

Regulus Black dies (age eighteen, according to the Black Family Tree).

Voldemort uses the house-elf Kreacher (belonging to the Black family) to plant his locket Horcrux in a cave. This leads Regulus Black to discover Voldemort's plans. He swaps out the Horcrux for a locket from the Black family, after which he is killed by the Inferi in the cave's underground lake.

Post-September 1—members of Harry's graduating class are born, until September 1, 1980.

September 19—Hermione Granger is born.

1980

March 1—Ron Weasley is born.

June 5—Draco Malfoy is born.

July 30—Neville Longbottom is born.

July 31—Harry Potter is born.

1981

Colin Creevey is born.

Severus Snape is hired to teach Potions at Hogwarts (it is unknown if this occurs before or after the fall of Voldemort (he has been teaching for fourteen years in *Order of the Phoenix*).

August 11—Ginny Weasley is born.

October 31—James and Lily Potter (aged twenty-one) are killed by Lord Voldemort, who is diminished after trying to kill Harry Potter.

November:

Harry Potter is left on the Dursley family's doorstep.

Harry remains at the Dursleys' until September 1, 1991.

Sirius Black is captured and sent to Azkaban for the deaths of James and Lily

Potter (accused by Peter Pettigrew) as well as the "murder" of Peter Pettigrew, who goes into hiding.

1984

September

Nymphadora Tonks, Charlie Weasley, and their peers start their first year at Hogwarts.

1991

June

Nymphadora Tonks, Charlie Weasley, and their peers graduate from Hogwarts.

September 1—Harry leaves on the Hogwarts Express (*Sorcerer's Stone*).

1992

September 1—Harry and Ron Weasley fly the Ford Anglia to Hogwarts (*Chamber of Secrets*).

1993

Summer

Sirius Black escapes Azkaban.

September 1—Harry leaves on the Hogwarts Express (*Prisoner of Azkaban*).

1994

Nymphadora Tonks qualifies to become an Auror (sometime during the year, probably in the summer according to *Order of the Phoenix*).

June

Sibyll Trelawney makes her second accurate prediction.

July

Frank Bryce is murdered by Voldemort in the Riddle House (age seventy-six).

August

422nd Quidditch World Cup held in Britain.

September 1—Harry leaves on the Hogwarts Express (*Goblet of Fire*).

October 30—Beauxbatons and Durmstrang delegations arrive at Hogwarts for the Triwizard Tournament.

1995

June

Voldemort returns to full human form in the grave-yard; Cedric Diggory dies (age seventeen).

September 1—Harry leaves on the Hogwarts Express (*Order of the Phoenix*).

1996

June 18—Sirius Black dies (age thirty-six).

September 1—Harry leaves on the Hogwarts Express (*Half-Blood Prince*).

1997

June

Albus Dumbledore is killed by Severus Snape (age 115).

Early summer

Remus Lupin marries Nymphadora Tonks (after Dumbledore dies, but before the Weasley/Delacour wedding).

July

Bill Weasley marries Fleur Delacour.

1998

Voldemort kills Gellert Grindelwald (age 115 or 116) and obtains the Elder Wand.

March

Peter Pettigrew is killed by his substitute hand created by Voldemort (age thirty-seven or thirty-eight).

May 1–2—The Battle of Hogwarts.

Severus Snape (age thirty-eight), Remus Lupin (age thirty-eight), Nymphadora Tonks (age twenty-four or twenty-five), Colin Creevy (age sixteen), Vincent Crabbe (age seventeen), and Fred Weasley (age twenty) die.

Tom Riddle/Lord Voldemort dies (age seventy-one).

About the Contributors

Courtney Agar: Courtney holds a BA in biology from St. Catherine University. Though she is in sales now, she may go back and get her PhD in order to continue research (there just may be more to discover around the genetics of Harry Potter . . .). When she isn't rereading Harry Potter for the sixteenth time or one of her other favorite authors, Dan Brown, she loves traveling the world and enjoying the outdoors in every possible way. She is also thrilled to continue reading new works by J. K. Rowling.

Giselle Liza Anatol: Giselle Liza Anatol is Associate Professor of English at the University of Kansas, Lawrence, where she teaches classes on Caribbean and African American literature and literature for young people. She is editor of *Reading Harry Potter: Critical Essays* and *Reading Harry Potter Again: New Critical Essays* (which the students who study Harry Potter at St. Catherine University find invaluable to their work). Her most recent publication, *Bringing Light to "Twilight": Perspectives on the Pop Culture Phenomenon*, is an edited collection with an international array of scholars. The vampire theme crosses over from Anatol's study of children's and young adult literature to her work in Caribbean and African diasporic literature; her current book project, tentatively titled *The Things That Fly in the Night: Images of Female Vampirism in Literature of the African Diaspora*, is forthcoming from Rutgers University Press.

Rachel Armstrong: Rachel graduated from St. Catherine University in 2012 with a BA in English and Spanish. She currently works in independent publishing at Amazon, helping fanfiction authors publish their stories. When she's not marathoning *Star Trek*, Rachel channels her curiosity into cooking. If her Hogwarts letter does arrive, she'll have plenty of failed kitchen experiments to convince Professor Snape that she's definitely up to something. Rachel currently lives in Seattle, Washington.

Kiah Bizal: Kiah has always had a passion for combining creativity and academics, which is one reason for jumping at the chance to take a course about Harry Potter. The other reason, of course, is her enduring love of the books. They have been a source of inspiration and comfort over the years, and they have certainly helped her on the way to greatness. She is currently pursuing a Doctor of Psychology at Argosy University, Twin Cities. She hopes to work with children and families affected by mental illness while always keeping in mind her favorite quote from the series: "Of course it is happening inside your head, Harry, but why on earth should that mean that it is not real?"

Kyle Bubb: Kyle graduated from Morningside College in Iowa, where he majored in English and theater. He is now working toward his master's degree in English and creative writing at the University of South Dakota. When not rereading the Harry Potter series, Kyle spends his time watching and collecting movies, as well as practicing apparating without splinching.

Kalie Caetano: Kalie holds a B.A. in English literature from Macalester College. She has interned with Minneapolis's Loft Literary Center and the independent nonprofit publisher Milkweed Editions and now works at Stanford University Press. Before all of that she could be found voraciously rereading the Harry Potter series and secretly writing Lupin-centric fanfiction that still lurks around on the internet today. She currently lives in San Jose, California.

Evan Gaydos: Evan is a graduate of St. Catherine University. Since leaving the formal realm of academia, Evan now looks for the academic in the everyday while working on various freelance creative writing projects and continues to wish time-turners

existed in the Muggle world. In addition to working and studying wizarding history, Evan enjoys sewing, crafting, and watching British dramas and sci-fi television. To all who have read this
far, she says thank you and remember, for the many of us who
considered Hogwarts a second home on paper, "help will always
be given at Hogwarts to those who ask for it."

Kate Glassman: Kate attributes her love of things-at-midnight
to Harry Potter, and nothing can dissuade her of the belief that
the right book can move worlds. She is the editor and cofounder
of *Versus Literary Journal* and delights in encouraging people
to unabashedly own what they're passionate about. She insists
there is no limit to human beings' capacity for liking things to
excess. She is currently completing her MFA at Hamline University in St. Paul, Minnesota, where she resides with her cat,
Tony Stark, and more books than she has bookshelves.

Cecilia Konchar Farr: Cecilia is Sr. Mona Riley Endowed Chair
in the Humanities and Professor of English and Women's Studies at St. Catherine University in St. Paul, Minnesota, where she
teaches, studies, and writes about modernism, American literature, feminist theory, reception theory, and the novel in contemporary US culture. Her study of Oprah's Book Club, *Reading
Oprah: How Oprah's Book Club Changed the Way America
Reads* (State University of New York Press 2004), was followed
by a collection, *The Oprah Affect: Critical Essays on Oprah's
Book Club*, with coeditor Jaime Harker (State University of
New York Press 2008). Her current project, "We Have Your
Novel: Ransoming a Reading Nation," is a rethinking of how
Americans value and evaluate novels. A Gryffindor, she com-
petes with the Minnesota Roller Girls Debu-Taunts as Professor
Hardcastle, but her favorite sport is Quidditch, particularly on
the St. Kate's quad in October.

Daley Konchar Farr: Since Daley played Fred Weasley onstage
in the fourth grade, her academic and magical experiences have
been tangled up together. She graduated from Augsburg College in Minneapolis with a degree in English literature after

spending her junior year at the University of Oxford's Hertford College. Daley looks forward to returning to school for a graduate degree, but currently she is enjoying time out of the scholarly world to read for pleasure, practice her latté art, indulge in Tonks-esque hair changes, and plan travels and adventures with her partner, Max, and beloved fellow nerd, Tréza Rosado.

Callie Knudslien: Callie, a graduate of the University of St. Thomas in St. Paul, Minnesota, has been part of the Harry Potter fandom since she started reading the books at age eleven, and has done everything thing from writing fanfiction to cosplaying for book and movie premieres. Her favorite character is Luna Lovegood, a fellow Ravenclaw. Despite being quirky (a "loony"), Luna is also very wise and very spiritual, something Callie thinks the books needed as the plot and characters matured.

Hannah Lamb: Hannah holds a BA in English literature from Macalester College. She channels her love of books into teaching preschool students how to read in a bilingual public school. She continues to hope that one day she and her students can enjoy Harry Potter in Spanish translation together. She listens to country music, quotes *Wizard People, Dear Reader* frequently, and lives in Minneapolis, Minnesota.

Jenny McDougal: Jenny currently teaches literature in the English department at St. Catherine University. She received her MFA from Hamline University and is a cofounder and editor of *Versus Literary Journal*. She is a semifinalist for the Pablo Neruda Prize in Poetry, and her creative work has been nominated for a Pushcart and published in *Water~Stone Review*, *Nimrod Journal of Poetry*, *Prose—Paper Darts*, and elsewhere. Her love of Harry Potter stems from a profound wish to produce a Patronus charm. She lives in St. Paul, Minnesota, with her husband, the novelist Evan Kingston.

Kate McManus: Kate is a recent graduate of St. Catherine University where she was sorted into Gryffindor and earned a degree in history. She is now pursuing a degree in library science and archives. Kate has been reading and writing fanfiction for longer than she would care to admit. While she normally writes Robin Hood stories, she's no stranger to Harry Potter, and spends quite a lot of time searching for Marauder tales and stories about the founding of Hogwarts.

Kari Schwab (Newell): Kari is currently a registered nurse in a gastroenterology lab at Columbia St. Mary's Ozaukee outside of Milwaukee, Wisconsin. She took the Harry Potter course in her senior year at St. Catherine University in order to fulfill a requirement, but it became her favorite course. She picked up the Harry Potter books at the age of eleven when her mom forced her to read them. She fell in love with Harry Potter and his friends from day one and still rereads the series almost every year. Since she had to write a lot of nursing care plans on her way to becoming a registered nurse, it only seemed natural to write one for Tom Riddle.

Tréza Rosado: Tréza is a predoctoral student currently working toward her MA in cinema and media studies through the department of Comparative Literature at the University of Washington. She spends her time studying, teaching, and pretending she's only a "casual gamer" when everyone knows that's a lie. Because she hasn't reread the Harry Potter series enough in the past fifteen years, she is now reading them in French and telling herself the practice will help her to meet her program's secondary language requirement.

Sarah Sutor: Sarah, a proud member of Ravenclaw, graduated from Denison University in 2009 with a BA in English literature and a minor in history, and, in 2012, with an MA in English literature from Georgetown University. Currently, she is pursuing a PhD in English specializing in medieval literature at the University of Illinois Urbana–Champaign. Sarah's pursuit of an academic career can be traced directly back to her early love of literature, including Harry Potter, and she has found that remembering Ginny Weasley's words in *Order of the Phoenix* is important when facing the challenges of graduate school: "You sort of start thinking anything's possible if you've got enough nerve."

Julia Terk: Julia was born in Moscow, Russia, where she lived for eight years with her mom, dad, and twin sister before moving to St. Paul, Minnesota. She studied biology and Spanish at St. Catherine University and ran cross-country. Her favorite quote is by Ron Weasley in *Chamber of Secrets*: "Why does it have to be follow the spiders? Why can't it be follow the butterflies!" and she couldn't agree more with him. Currently, Julia lives in New York and is completing a master's in physician assistant studies.

Sarah Wente: Sarah is a graduate of St. Catherine University with degrees in English and theology. Still waiting for her Hogwarts letter, she spends most of her time reading fantasy novels, playing adventure video games, and eating chocolate. Even having not attended Hogwarts, Sarah is a proud Ravenclaw, excelling in dry wit, academia, and a fondness for the color blue. She has a particular affection for Fred Weasley, her counterpart in the wizarding world, and would love (more than anything) to have her very own flying broomstick. Her favorite Harry Potter book is *Half-Blood Prince*, for its intricate exploration of memories and character, and she will be forever grateful to J. K. Rowling and the series for creating such an exceptional dwelling place for her imagination.

Index

death (*continued*)
  assisted suicide, 124–125, 127
  of Cedric Diggory, 79–80
  children's literature and, 79–80
  dementors as symbols of, 118–119
  fear of, 132–133
  government-sanctioned, 116–121
    (*See also* Capital punishment)
  mastery of, as theme of Harry Pot-
    ter series, 113–114, 126–127
  maternal instinct and, 125–126
  Ministry of Magic and, 116, 117–
    118, 125–126
  of Rowling's mother, 113
  self-sacrifice, 147, 154–156
  of Sirius Black, 120–121
Death Eaters
  first, 203
  at Hogwarts, 110
  loyalty to Voldemort, 103
  as terrorists, 77–78
Deathly Hallows, 230–232
Deathly Hallows (book)
  Christian symbolism in, 150,
    153–156
  copies sold, 19, 30
  death of Harry Potter, 154–156
dementors
  Dementor's Kiss, 117, 119
  description of, 118–119
  Ministry of Magic and, 116, 117,
    118–120
Dementor's Kiss, 117, 119
Department for the Regulation and
  Control of Magical Creatures,
  67, 68
Diggory, Cedric, 79–80
Dobby (house-elf), 67–69, 151
"Dragon Challenge" (theme park
  ride), 50
Dumbledore, Albus
  bequests to Harry, Ron, and

  Hermione, 150
  death of, 122–125
  fanfiction about, 41
  Gellert Grindelwald and, 38, 41,
    100, 177–178
  Harry Potter and, 162–177
  as homosexual, 41
  Horace Slughorn and, 174, 176
  moral complexity of, 80, 159–179
  Severus Snape and, 123–125, 173
  Sirius Black and, 117, 118
Durmstrang, 59, 99

E
erotic triangle, 236–238, 241–244. *See
  also* Golden Trio
eugenics, 94, 106
execution. *See* Capital punishment

F
"fair use" laws, 37
family
  blood purity and, 59, 62, 91
  pure-blood breeding, 191
  "triad of the family," 226
fanfiction, 35–46
  Aeneid (Virgil), 35–46
  Alternate Universe (AU), 44
  copyright law and, 37–39
  "fair use" law, 37–38
  Fifty Shades of Grey (James), 37
  historical roots, 36–37
  original characters (OCs), 41–42
  as parody, 38
  participatory, 38
  Pride and Prejudice and Zombies
    (Grahame-Smith), 37
  Rebecca (du Maurier), 37
  relationship pairings and, 44
  Rowling's views on, 39–40
  slash, 44–45
  Wide Sargasso Sea (Rhys), 37

Made in the USA
Columbia, SC
24 January 2018